MAURITIUS
ISLE de la RÉUNION
RODRIGUEZ I.
NOVÉ-TO
ROGUE WAVE
P.E.
P. LONDON

COCOS I.
CHRISTMAS I.
TIMORE
MOA WIN

PENAPE
KUSAIE
MAJURO
NOKUORO
KAPINGAMARANGI

ÆTAT
SVÆ
42

IN THE WAKE OF DRAKE

Fair Winds

Pat Patters

IN THE WAKE OF DRAKE

Pat Patterson

UNITED WRITERS
Cornwall

UNITED WRITERS PUBLICATIONS LTD
Trevail Mill, Zennor, St. Ives, Cornwall.

ISBN 901976 74 1

Printed in Great Britain by
United Writers Publications Ltd
Cornwall

In admiration, I dedicate this journal to the memory
of one of the greatest seamen of all time

SIR FRANCIS DRAKE

long may he continue to be an inspiration to sailors
the world over.

My thanks to:

Gail for some of the typing.

Tom R. for correcting the punctuation and some of the excesses of
English.

Jackie for the maps and sketches.

Gordon for developing the photos.

Alan I, Mike, Scarlett, Alan II, Carl, Denis, Pip, Sue, Henri, Brenda,
Tom, Tim and Allan III for putting up with me for as long as they did
(could) and helping crew the boat around.

Ethel, my wife, for keeping the home fire burning and cooking a super
meal on my return.

To all, of so many different countries, who gave help and showed such
kindness whenever we lowered our anchor.

INTRODUCTION

In 1577, Drake, probably in collusion with Queen Elizabeth I, planned to raid the west coast of South America. His orders were purposely vague; his men thought they were bound for Egypt to engage in the Turkish trade. He left Plymouth in November, 1577, took shelter in Falmouth but then had to return to Plymouth to repair gale damage. He left again on December 13th, 1577.

With a small flotilla, he sailed to Mogador, NW Africa; Cape Verde Islands, across the South Atlantic to the Brazilian Coast and down to the River Plate. 200 miles north of the Straits of Magellan he wintered in Port St. Julian where he beheaded Doughty, a revolting gentleman of his party. (Magellan had, 50 years earlier, hanged two of his Captains here; the skeletons Drake found dangling.)

While the Straits of Magellan were known, they were considered too dangerous for ordinary use. Drake was not an ordinary seaman. He revictualled his ships with 2,000 penguins. They sailed through these uncharted straits in 16 days. Before a terrible gale they were blown south; one vessel sank, the other two lost contact. Drake was blown south of Cape Horn, discovering the passage around South America which now bears his name.

Drake's ship, the *Golden Hind*, now unaccompanied, sailed north to raid the Coast of Chile. The Spaniards thought this coast quite safe and were, so to speak, caught napping. Indeed, at one place they found a Spaniard sleeping by a llama loaded with silver bars. They re-directed him to their ship.

At Callao, the port of Lima, Peru, he heard of a treasure ship ahead. Giving chase, he overtook her, and pirated 26 tons of silver, 80 pounds of gold, 13 chests of plate and several more crammed with jewels. He then sailed on to Guatulco, in Mexico to take on water and provisions.

He was half way around the world and had the difficult task of returning to England with a ship ballasted with loot — a prime prize for every other ship on the high seas. There was thought to be a north-west passage and Drake knew if he could find it, as it was unknown, he would not be molested by other ships. He sailed out into the Pacific and north further than anyone before him, possibly as far as 48° north. But with no sign of a passage and evil weather, he turned south to California. He spent some time here, taking possession in the name of Queen Elizabeth, naming the country Nova Albion. This is often thought to be Drake's Bay, north-west of San Francisco.

After re-furbishing his vessel, he sailed west across the Pacific perhaps via Hawaii and the Philippines to Moluccas, where he took on six tons of cloves. In the Celebes Sea he ran aground in strong winds and came very near to losing all. He jettisoned most of the cloves, and with a shift of wind, managed to free the vessel.

He left Java in March, 1580, and after 118 days, reached Sierra Leone; the longest unbroken sea passage to that date. From there, taking a wide sweep out into the Atlantic to avoid the Spanish Fleet looking for him, he sailed cautiously into Plymouth to enquire who was on the throne. He arrived back on September 26th, 1580.

I tried to follow his route in a 33 foot catamaran, *Ocean Winds*. I set off 400 years and 5 months after him. The following is my personal journal, written on passage. I had the great advantages of knowing, from charts, where islands and continents were. I had good navigation equipment, nautical almanacs, tide tables, lists of lights (which were frequently correct) and other aids which were unknown in Drake's day. My problems were obviously insignificant compared with Drake's, and my achievement minor.

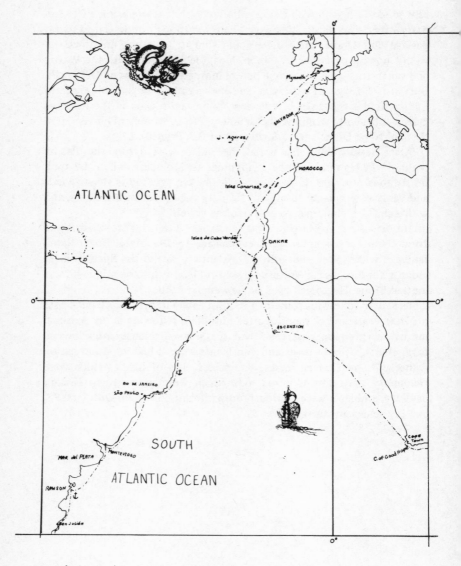

ATLANTIC OCEAN

Plymouth

SALVADOR

Açores

MOROCCO

Islas Canarias

Islas de Cabo Verde

DAKAR

ASCENSION

RIO DE JANEIRO

SÃO PAULO

SOUTH

MAR del PLATA

MONTEVIDEO

ATLANTIC OCEAN

RAWSON

San Julián

Cape Town

C. of Good Hope

Outward bound :-
Plymouth to Port St. Julian

Homeward bound :-
Cape Town to Plymouth

Journal of a voyage around the World by Pat Patterson,
celebrating the quatercentenary of Sir Francis Drake's
epic voyage. (13.12.1577 − 26.9.1580)

5th July 1978

After months of graft, finally decided we were near enough ready so dropped the mooring lines in our quiet West Country backwater of Millbrook, and motored across to Plymouth to ship our duty free stores (H.M. Custom's language for booze). There we tied up alongside the yachts amassing for the Round Britain Race. Sherpa Bill, with whom I sailed in close company on the last race, came and had a yarn and asked if I was not sorry to be missing this one. But with cold NW winds forecast I am glad to be heading south towards the sun.

First day was a short sail to Looe to have the engines finally checked out by the Volvo agents there and a chance for the crew to have a farewell booze-up in the Jolly Sailor. The crew; myself as skipper, Michael Golding, an 18 year old expert at duff pudding, Alan Sargent who makes auto-pilots and was with us only as far as North Africa, and Scarlett Grey whose husband was to join us in the Canaries.

6th July.

Thursday morning and a quay full of holiday makers watch us load 10 new loaves, 5 pints of milk and a little more fresh stores and sail out of Looe at 9.30 a.m. Phew! What a relief to be away at last. Once past the Rennies reef it was a reach for Ushant with a bitterly cold but favourable NW wind. Ted, Scarlett's bro-in-law, was 4 miles out with a fishing party and he crossed our bows to give us a farewell wave. The sea off the land was fairly quiet, but having drunk a quantity the previous night, all except Mike who has a very solid stomach, were a touch fragile, so ate but little.

7th July.

Saw Ushant blinking at full range so cleared this awkward corner comfortably. A great day of WNW winds force 3. The first 24 hours sailed 130 miles and now pleasantly jogging along at 4—5 knots. A large gaff cutter very slowly overhauled us and passed us at 20.00 while we were having the evening meal. It is on a virtually parallel course. While it has been very cold for mid-summer in the wind, the saloon temperature reached 20°C (Yesterday it only made 16°). It is good to have the first few days with quiet weather as it gives time for the crew to get settled into a routine. Somewhere on board a dozen new teaspoons have hidden themselves – we are down to using one metal and two tatty plastic ones. Now Scarlett is busy drawing out a ship's stowage plan – then perhaps at least she will know where most things are.

8th July.   The wind has fallen light and the sun is shining, so it is much warmer – up to 22° in the saloon. It is still like a cold autumn in England; even here in the middle of Biscay cold air is coming in from the north west.

Our track is right in the middle of the shipping lane. Ideally I like to be a few miles west so that you just see the lights distant on the horizon but travelling down the lane makes for much more interest and keeps us on our toes. We are purposely on the west side of the lane so the ships are mostly going the same way. In the night Alan called me as one had been showing red and green for a long while and was now quite close. A flash with the Aldis lamp at his bridge and then at our sails showed him we were close and he altered to overtake us. We have an 'Aqua Signal' mast head tri-colour light which gives a 2 mile stern light and on such a clear night there is no reason for him not spotting us. Also there is a clean radar reflector at the mast head and a calm sea so he could not have been using his radar as well as keeping a poor look out.

The interference on the direction finding radio can be quite painful to the ear, so for position fixing I have gone on to astro nav., which anyway, is more interesting. I have the whole crew practising noon sights – we are all to within five miles of each other.

Several times today dolphins have played around the boat. It is particularly interesting lying on the forward bridge-deck watching them scull just ahead of our bows, then, when they need to breathe, give a quick flip, and shoot ahead and surface. I even saw two come up between the hulls joined together; presumably mating. They shot ahead at about 7 knots – we were doing 4. Later in the day a school of pilot whales went by. They took no notice of us even though they passed very close.

The day has been calm. We have had to motor to make progress. One engine pushes us along nicely, not straining at 4—4½ knots. The port engine was used for 4 hours and then the starboard one all through the night, as this charges the service batteries which run the navigation lights. After lunch I sewed up the head of a new ghoster made from spinnaker nylon. When set it gave an extra knot. The crew handed it when I was below, as the wind, for a short while, increased to force 3 — exactly as per instructions. But on resetting it, they managed to tear it on a split pin. So we mended it with contact adhesive.

9th July.   A quiet morning, however, at 10.00 a.m. a gentle breeze came from astern. Off with the engines at last and up with the twin headsails. A lovely rig in this weather, but our speed was only 2½—3 knots. Like drifting gently across a park lake.

Not very satisfied with the way the autohelm is working, so have transferred it on a peg to the wheel. It works continuously; the compass is affected by the slightest rock of the boat and this sets it off even when on course. Fortunately when the wind picks up to force 3 and above we can use Quantock Pete — our QME wind steering vane.

10th July.   I was not called all night, and I had expected quite a lively one, so I did the morning watch from 6.00 to midday. The dawn sky was ominously red — due, it later transpired, to a small low forming off West Finisterre. This also made us tight on the starboard tack all day and ever since noon have not quite been able to lay Cabo Villano. A sunny day though, despite the evil dawn. A fair swell coming from the W N W made the starboard tack quite comfortable. We tacked at 6.00 p.m. straight into it — and it was abominable; so re-tacked and on with the port motor with just the main set. That way we can just about lay Villano sailing about 30° off the wind.

Earlier, I gave the crew a nav. lesson on working out the local hour angle (L.H.A.). Once that is mastered, sun sights are a doddle using sight reduction tables.

The idea of beating all night around Cape Finisterre through a very busy shipping lane did not appeal so, remembering gentlemen do not beat to windward, put on both motors and hammered into Ria de Camarinas. The water was incredibly phosphorescent and the ria was strung with sardine nets, lit each end with a red and green light. We motored into the port and tied up alongside one of the fish quays.

11

11th July.   Refuelled. As far as I can tell we use about one third gal. (imp. or half gal. U.S.) an hour at 4 knots on one engine. Carry 40 galls. Also topped up with water and all had a shower. Got some fault on the valve though, as I pumped sea water into the boat instead of shower water out.

At the bodegas the local Galician wine, a light white, is dispensed from barrels and is as cheap as beer in Britain. It is a mistake to drink it in similar quantity.

12th July.   Bright but bloody morning. Light head wind and strong headache so motored to well past Cape Finisterre after which a light S W wind set in. Despite getting well south now, the wind is still distinctly chilly. I am sitting in the sunshine writing this wearing a padded deck coat. There is a lazy 8 ft swell; a slight mist on the sea's face and the crew all abed.

Very light wind off starboard quarter so the main blanketing the headsail. Handed the main and jogged along with the ghoster set at 3–3½ knots. Very easy and comfortable sailing. A number of birds had found a shoal of fish. Then came a huge school of dolphins to join the feast, darting and leaping into the shoal. A huge evening dinner of thick gammon steaks grilled with 'taties and onions done in the pressure cooker. The gammon is carved off a bacon roll hanging in the galley. These have to be well salted and smoked; unfortunately they are getting difficult to obtain.

13th July.   Just before dawn Scarlett called me. The ghoster had blown its clew out. Handed it and sailed on with the genoa only, still a very broad reach, in fact almost a run. Left instructions that I was to be called at 6.00 a.m. at the watch change to consider setting the twins. Evidently I did not wake at the first call and so was left. Told Scarlett off, for I woke at 6.30 and then Michael and I set them, but it was more difficult with just the two of us. But just as Scarlett did not like waking me, nor do I like waking the off-watch for anything but emergency.

Running due south, but the dawn wind, which reached probably force 4, soon moderated and by midday was a gentle 3. The air still cool but of course the sun has plenty of power. Scarlett is playing with her sextant, checking the errors. She is dressed in thick ex-postman's trousers and a heavy sweater and we are down to latitude 41° south. (As Oporto, Portugal.)

Some excitement when the curving dorsals of a school of killer whales are spotted, knifing through the water. They move with great speed, up to 30 knots, and the spray arcs off their dorsals making miniature rainbows.

This evening took a moon shot crossed with Venus. The result was poor. However, a latitude by Polaris tallied with the afternoon longitude shot of the sun gave us a believable position.

14th July. During the night I leapt out on hearing the thud of engines. Michael was steering us to port as this nasty big steel ship ploughed through the bit of ocean we would have been in. He should have called me even though he coped adequately, as ultimately it is my responsibility even if it is him that lets us get run down.

The wind fell light in the morning and we were barely doing 2 knots. So the day's run was disappointing. Where, oh where are the Portuguese Trades? The wind is in the right direction but so very light which means that Spain is not heating up as it should at this time of year. In fact the whole of Europe is much colder — Rome is complaining of temperatures around 14°C. Our cabin temperature is now up to 24°C.

After lunch I ordered the decks to be scrubbed, and not before time either. While doing this, Alan noticed a large object awash ahead. This blew at an angle of 45°, so it had to be a cachalot or sperm whale. It was big, at least 40 ft long and took no notice of us as we altered course to pass to one side of it. Not the sort of thing to run into.

On finishing the decks, Alan threw buckets of cold water over me as I soaped down. Then Scarlett cut my hair on the foredeck. Alan slipped down coming forward to take a photograph of the beautification of the Captain, and badly gashed his heel pouring blood all over our lovely clean deck.

15th July. Wind freshened a little giving us a day's run of 107 miles. A lot of shipping have altered course to pass us close and give us a wave. It would be nice to have VHF radio so we could exchange pleasantries.

16th July. This is more like it. A lovely force 4 from dead astern. The twins pulling like real 'uns and we chuntering along between 5 and 6½ knots. By midday we had a 24 hour run of 128 miles. This morning's longitude sight showed we were almost in 11° W so have altered course to due south by compass (170° true). It is only about 270 miles to Mogador which was Drake's first stop. Earlier this morning saw a yacht to starboard while yarning with Alan about the characteristics that cause catamarans to capsize and how you try to design to prevent this ever happening. The yacht was a big one on the port tack and looking as if she was reaching in for the Straits of Gibraltar. We soon passed and she crossed our stern 2 miles away. She was the only boat seen for the last 24 hours.

Each evening I read a chapter or two of John Masefield's poem, 'Dauber'. This is an epic about a ship's painter, on a clipper sailing south to double the Horn. A tale of a weak but determined man, picked on because he is different from the rest of the rough, hairy crew. In places it is quite tear jerking. I am glad to say the crew too recognised it as such. But our progress is now so good I will be hard pressed to finish it before Mogador.

17th July.　　　Noon to noon run of 139 miles, the best so far. Alan has been sick in the guts all day so I have been doing his watch. Not that that has proved arduous. Perhaps it was the cheesey gammon and pineapple of last night that did for him. He is now living on Complan and kaolin.

We have handed the twins and are now reaching in towards Morocco. The wind is force 5/6 and we are under deep reefed main and reefed jib. The speed is around 5 knots and it is pretty comfortable with little spray coming aboard. Scarlett looked anxious at first as it is rougher than she is used to — a contrast from running before a gentle sea, but now, as the wind has moderated a little with the dusk, she is happily out there on watch. Soon we should sight Vega, from which I will get an approximate longitude and with luck, follow it with a sight of Polaris for latitude. . . Alas, Polaris was too faint to show against the horizon.

18th July.　　　This proved a pity as next morning we could have done with a more accurate fix as we closed the Moroccan Coast. The wind freshened to such an extent we reached in towards the Coast under very reduced canvas. Even so we were doing 5/6 knots and could easily have gone faster with the wind broad on the port beam. In the pre-dawn I took in virtually all the jib, leaving only enough to 'blow your nose on' to slow her further. She still insisted on doing 4 knots. With instructions to the watch keeper to call me as soon as the echo sounder showed we were in soundings (in our case 60 fathoms) I went below for another hour's doze.

Then as the day lightened, we let out more jib. First we found soundings, which were logged every mile then the mountains vaguely showed. Two sun sights Michael shot and I worked out gave us some idea of our distance off but really we needed a latitude as it was some 18 hours since our last one. The soundings line made some sense, with the odd anomaly, but finally the mountain cleared sufficiently for us to pick out the tomb of Sidi Yakoub. I pity the poor buggers who had to build it on top of that 2,200 ft bare mountain but it was a boon to us. We were indeed where out plot showed we should have been, having made little drift to the south. From there it was an easy run down the coast for 15 miles to Essouira or Mogador as it was known in Drake's day.

Into the harbour, starting the motors just outside and furling the genoa, the only sail up, we motored into the fresh wind gusting down between the quay walls. Shouts of *'pas de mouillage ici'* made it fairly plain we were no more welcome than Drake 400 years earlier, but after circling the port, ignored the shouts and tied up between two 50 ft fishing boats.

Up went my yellow T-shirt as a 'Q' flag. We were soon visited by the port officer and his cronies with their forms and demands for fags and whisky. They got no fags, but drowned a third of a bottle of White Horse — a going away present from Kevin Cooney along with the reefing jib spar. They left, finally, a lot happier than when they arrived. Then a policeman arrived and carted me off to the Hotel de Sûreté for a couple of hours. No one really knew why but it transpired tomorrow would do to get an entry stamped in our passports. This took all the following morning and in the end they capitulated and let me fill in an entry card which took 5 minutes. My shot-gun the Customs officer impounded until we leave and then asked for a bottle of whisky. What a place, everyone demanding cigarettes and liquor (a good moslem country too). Mind you the women look gorgeous and as their looks fade they can hide behind a yashmak and all you see are their dark and flashing eyes.

Alan was due to leave us here and he was lucky as we were casually visited by an English couple driving around Morocco. They offered him a lift to Marrakesh so now we are down to a crew of three.

The market, in the old quarter, is a bustling thriving place. A kilo of tomatoes cost 14p. In fact that seemed to be the general price for a kilo of anything. Also some super doughnuts were being deftly twiddled around the cook's fingers and then deep fried and cost pennies.

15

A spice stall sold us paprika and curry and kohl for Scarlett's eyes and henna for her hair. She is going to 'kill 'em' in the Canaries.

20th July. Spent the last few dirhams on fruit; collected the shot gun and cartridges and made sail just before 2.00 p.m. It was blowing force 7 so we were soon out, passing inside Ile Mogador and then shaped a course for the north of the Canaries. Under just half unrolled jib, maybe 200 square feet, we zoomed along, occasionally thumping and crashing if we got knocked off by a sea. As we left the land shelter the seas were about 16 ft and if they broke at the wrong moment, slewed the boat off course. 20 miles from the shore the wind moderated to 5–6. It would seem Mogador in the summer has this strong local wind. This makes it nice and cool for holidays and yet it is not very touristy — in fact it is still backward, old Morocco.

21 July. As the day progressed, and we left the African shore astern, so the wind moderated, and we gradually increased sail. By 2 p.m. today we had sailed over 150 miles, and that was less than 24 hours since leaving Mogador. I have slept a lot of the day, not yet properly back into the sea going routine. Scarlett has hardly eaten, until the evening meal which was an excellent stew made with herbs and spices bought in Mogador. This evening we finished the Dauber — but despite his death our eyes were dry. The crew must be getting hard. Actually Masefield's poetry improves towards the end.

22nd July. A few ships in the night and during the day indicate we are on the Canary shipping lane. Our noon latitude showed us 20 miles north of our dead reckoning. This was crossed with a radio fix for a position. The Autohelm has packed in. It goes in alright but will only jerk out neurotically. Fortunately Quantock Pete is managing well, so we do not have the drag of steering, which personally I dread. We had to motor from about midnight to 8.00 a.m. as the wind dropped away, but then a nice little 3–4 nor'-wester has let us reach along. Visibility is down to about 4 miles.

The 1800 hrs log entry reads 'each sight madly different'. I suspect we are getting a false horizon — but it is a bugger when approaching land.

23rd July. By 0225 hrs we sighted town lights. No sign of the 30 mile light on the northernmost hilltop of Gran Canaria (Isletta) have

16

a good radio bearing though.

3.00 a.m. The light was found almost abeam — fleetingly appearing through the low cloud. We reduced to small jib and just jogged slowly towards La Luz where we motored into the inner harbour just as dawn was breaking. Tied up to an outer mooring buoy for a sleep and planned to suss the joint out later. Awoken by a French lady (very comely) leaping on board wanting to know if they could tie up alongside. Turned out to be three of them — two blokes and bird were a good crew — together we later hired motor bikes and did a tour of the island.

La Luz (the port) and Las Palmas are dumps, and not worth visiting. The interior is very mountainous with what looks like some good climbing. Around the villages, the sides are terraced and dew ponds are frequent — but most were bone dry. We only found one spring, and that was descending to Puerto de Mogan. The track over the mountain was rough stones with many hairpins and the view awe-inspiring.

Moored off the yacht club on a very stony bottom, with 6 feet at low water, anchor rope chafed through once, (of course I had two anchors down). Alan Grey — Scarlett's husband — joined us here with a repaired Autohelm. The intention was to leave in the afternoon of the 8th, but we took so long victualling, watering and making the ship ready for sea, it would have been almost dark by the time we were ready, so to the crew's disappointment, I put the departure off until the morning. At least we then all got a good night's sleep.

It was with great pleasure we hauled anchors at 8.30 a.m., motoring out through the moorings — waving to the Swedes in their tiny Golif 5 (which they capsized twice and so were now a bit frightened of it). To a French yacht bound for Dakar — the crewsmen I met first in Belle Ile, and to a luxurious several million dollar U.S. yacht with Skipper David (English) and his wife Joan (West Indian) and crew. They are headed for Cape Verde, so should pass us in the next day or so. They must refuel at Puerto Grande, San Vincente in order to have enough fuel to get across the West Indies.

It was quite breezy running down Grande Canaria — but once clear of the land the wind moderated to the top end of 3. Running under Twins, sun shining — and all very comfortable. We have the fishing line out, with a 30 lb break on a bight to tell us if we catch anything, shark hook on a wire trace, and 4 mm poly line. However, as we have not yet seen any flying fishes, do not expect to catch anything.

17

Every 6 hours we do a casual 2 hour watch, only, owing to an arithmetical error (I added 4 onto 1300) Alan, on his first watch, had a four hour one. Mind you, one could do a 10 hour watch in these conditions with no strain, other than eye from reading. Imagine — you British sailors, a temperature of 26°C (70°F), a force 3 wind with twin headsails set, the self steering keeping you more or less on course. Just the gentle rocking to help you doze at frequent intervals. I have experienced it before, for 20 or 30 miles, but not day after day. This is really sailing.

10th August. (118 miles) Yesterday's conditions did not last. The log for 20.00 hrs reads North East Trades — bliss. 21.30 hrs. — sodding winds headed us. A light head wind, left us slatting around in the swell, so down with the headsails, bowse the main in hard and plod on at 4 knots with the starboard engine (this charges the service batteries). My own pet theory is that the Islands heat up to such an extent they create their own little area of lower pressure, thus creating that calm to the south of the Islands, even as far as 30—40 miles south. The North East Trades gradually get up again from 4 a.m. and by midday were as good as ever, force 3 pushing us along at 4½—5 knots with the occasional flying fish. I was surprised how blue these are, at first mistaken for small birds, but their Tit Willow dive indicated otherwise.

Scarlett and Michael are cooks tonight, Scarlett's part is: corn on the cob with butter, and Hungarian Goulash. Michael's part is Coffee Creme Caramel.

11th August. (125 miles) A quiet day, just running SSW. Alan and Michael cooked dinner — Michael the pudding part. I later suffered bad indigestion so slept little.

12th August. One flying fish came aboard overnight into the companionway, others slid off the deck. During the day you can stand in the hatch and see shoals of fish flying out of our way. They look beautiful with the sun glinting on their wings, and they are very fast, gliding considerable distances.

The noon day entry was forgotten.

13th, 14th & 15th August. Very little happened. One morning we had two flying fish; lightly fried they were delicious. They are the size of large sardines but with a delightful delicate flavour.

A huge school of porpoises stretching right across the horizon, had a brief look and frolic around us, calling out with their funny little whistles. Wonder what they were saying: "Piss off, this is our ocean"?

We have had the fishing lines out since the Canaries, but no joy. All last night we had to motor. This morning backup went the twins, as we have managed to sail at three knots. Mind you a quiet sea meant the noon sight should have been pretty accurate — I crossed it with a radio bearing on Ile de Sal — Cape Verde.

Today we rigged awning over the cock-pit, with the very light breeze this made it pleasant out this afternoon. Usually it is far too hot in the afternoon sun. At midday (local) the sun's altitude is over 85°.

The trade winds should, according to the charts, be blowing gaily to south of the Cape Verdes. As it is, like us, they are barely breathing.

Alan daily practises his guitar and I the melodica. By now there ought to be some improvement.

16th August.　　The night was dark and overcast. Poor visibility was to be expected, as we were making a landfall on San Nicholas Isle in the Cape Verdes. I took regular D.F. radio fixes on Ile de sal air beacon then the sun peeped through at 8.30 G.M.T. Not well, so I graphed 3 shots for accuracy and crossed with the D.F. We were too far to the west due, presumably, to the current, so altered to allow for it. At 12.45 land was clearly visible to starboard. A bare mountainous Isle it appeared too. Behind a point we saw two small open fishing boats, their laden sail down, fishing at anchor. Large flying fish zoomed out of our way. One settlement only, on the south coast, and looked like a prison or army camp. Lots of rivers, one shown on the chart, but they are all dry apparently, and this is the rainy season.

From the eastern point I banged on both engines as I want to get to port before nightfall. Well, we made it, and a lot of good it did us. The anchorage was terribly exposed and I had just about made up my mind to push for San Tiago when a boat rowed out. In it was a people's militia gentlemen who more or less said no tourists, push off for either San Vincente or San Tiago for Stampa. Evidently these are the two entry ports. So on towards San Tiago.

17th August.　　A beautiful moonlit tropical night. Just like the romantic novelists rabbit on about. Alan called me at dawn twilight to take a sight of Rigel or Sirius to cross with Sal Radio beacon, but then he

19

realised the low cloud under Rigel and Sirius was forming up into land. Then the land slowly appeared. At 317 feet up it had been hidden in low cloud. Down the precipitous mountainous coast we ran with a force 3 wind astern. Passed many fishing boats, these are open boats about 20 feet long, usually with 3 fishermen — 2 at the oars, one at the stern with lines. Fish eagles zoom out from the coast and circle them.

Anchored on good black sandy bottom (sand from a volcanic rock) in 12 feet of water about 100 yards off the pier. We rowed ashore to clear but a policeman quickly ran up and shooed us back.

Three gentlemen came out — Frontier police, Customs and harbour authority. Each wanted several forms filled in and a total of 4 crew lists, and a declaration that the ship was healthy. They took away the passports and the ship's registry certificate to be returned when we leave.

The people are very friendly, poor and prolific. Mostly of African origin. The republic must be getting a lot of aid, as several ships came in during our stay to unload. Nothing was exported. The Cabo Verde escudo is about the same value as the Portuguese. We were told that it had not rained at Pria (the capital and port) for 10 years. August and September are the wet months, occasional cloud surrounded the mountainous interior, but not much rain fell there either.

We got transport over the mountains to the village of San Tiago on the east of the island, the transport was a 1 ton pick-up (Toyota). It was full when it stopped, so everyone was pushed in tighter. Then it was full! But still more were crowded in. We ended up with a total of 39, rather more than you get in a green line bus, over twice the length. Then the driver has a road race with another 'transport' similarly overcrowded. All very exciting.

The mountains were very dry and dusty, but the soil all planted out, just waiting for rain to make it all blossom. Where there was water in some of the valleys, and the plantation irrigated, it was thick with bananas, coconuts, paw paws, mangoes and tapioca.

The water here is good. The Gran Canaria water has an evil flavour, so we emptied out our tank and all had the luxury of a hair wash and a shower, and filled up with Cape Verde water. I have taken on 80 gallons for drinking water, as we have the doldrums to pass through, I do not know how long it will take us but I reckon on up to 40 days for 2000 miles to Salvador, but hope to do it in 30.

Our departure was delayed a day as the washing was taken ashore to the laundry (it's a launderette — but they do it for you) and took longer than thought. Made me very annoyed at the time when the crew returned — after I had stayed to water the boat — empty handed. I hate getting all ready to sail then anything other than weather delaying me.

22nd August.   Away at last by 13.45. Away under full sail, and cleared the harbour with one tack; as the locals all sail lateen rigged lighters I felt we ought to make an effort. Anyway, the fuel is to be conserved for the calms and the motors only to be used in the flat part of the doldrums.

Five days is long enough in port.

23rd August.   Winds were light northerly for the next two days, allowing us to sail south. First day 80 miles and the next 70. The air is very humid and hot from 11.00 in the morning until 6.00 in the evening, local time. So we are sweating a lot. Considerable discussion has taken place on how to keep up one's salt content. Alan favours a cup of fresh water after half cup of sea water. Scarlett and I prefer a tomato sliced and coated white with salt which is followed by a glass of water.

In the Cape Verdes we took on a yard length stalk of green bananas (est. 30 kg.) much to Michael's disgust who had to carry it part of the way. Three days later, we are still awaiting the ripening. At the moment we are relying on vitamin pills and muesli for breakfast. Rolls (for three days) and cold meat at lunch, with a stew in the evening.

24th August.   Our problem is shortage of gas. We could not get more in Cape Verdes and one bottle ran out shortly after leaving Las Palmas. So I expect to arrive at Brazil cooking on the oil stove which doubles as the cabin heater.

A shoal of tunny — small ones — kept around the boat chasing small fish. Alas they would not take our lures. Six Terns were swooping on the little fish too. This was 100 miles south of Cape Verdes and 300 miles west of Africa.

25th August.   At 3 a.m. with a slight drizzle and slatting sails we started the starboard engine. Guess we must, at last, be entering the doldrums at 11° 30' north. We are in the showers, making an effort to collect rain by topping up the boom and easing the main halliard with a bucket under the goose-neck. The first gallon of water is pretty dirty from the muck off the mainsail.

12.00 noon and with a force 3 southerly the engine was killed after only 40 miles. For the first 3 hours our course was SE magnetic — but then the wind gradually allowed us to head due S magnetic. With the equatorial counter current setting towards Guinea, our leeway and magnetic variations of 16°W, I guess we are tracking about SE true. This will be about right for the next 5° of latitude, from whence the sailing instructions advise changing tacks and heading SW using the south east trades. It is no good aiming SW too early, for then the wind and current may set you to the NW of Caba Roca the NE corner of Brazil and for sailing boats to try and fight wind and current there, is, I understand, almost doomed to failure. This present hard on the wind thudding to windward is not my idea of sailing, but with any luck, it will not last more than 5 days before we are reaching again.

Gave up trying to get a noon sight. Just could not make up my mind whether to look north or south, the sun being almost dead overhead. There is no land to hit and we are hard on the wind on the starboard tack whatever our position, so navigation is not of much importance for the next day or two. Of course the sun is chasing us south, so when we come to sail west for South America, will be catching us up. Despite the fact the sun is overhead, the wind and the occasional rain is keeping the temperature pleasantly cool.

26th August. Michael shot the sun looking S and I looking N. We determined it was definitely N, in fact by some 42 miles. The day has been exceedingly boring; nothing even slightly amusing has happened. We are not very good conversationalists on board this boat. Mike and I usually manage to have a yarn sometime during the day — mostly about seamanship or navigation otherwise the talk is limited to 'What's for dinner tonight?'.

During dinner, the boat heaved herself to in the light SW wind. I left it until we had finished then started the starboard plonker and motored through the night due S true, at 4½ knots. We are right on the edge of the SE trades, which here, because of the low pressure over hot Africa, are curved in and come as light to moderate S to S Westerlies.

27th August. Michael's 18th birthday. Quite an interesting day all told. It started with the genny halliard chafing through. I called Alan quarter of an hour early at 0045 hrs to help hand and bag the genny and tidy up the foredeck. The deck light makes this sort of thing much easier. This is the first yacht I have had with such sophistication. As it was a virtual calm I plonked on under motor. Dawn broke with Michael manfully setting the No.2 headsail which seems to set better than the genny close-hauled, so despite the smaller area our speed was scarcely any less.

At 12.00 I hoved-to and climbed the mast to reeve a new halliard. Even in this slight sea with the odd white-cap, (wind had increased to the top end of force 3 with about a 5 ft swell), the G. forces at the mast head were strong. I easily resisted the impulse to let go and see how far I would be catapulted. In fact it took only a few minutes and I thankfully regained the deck with muscles aching and nerves atremble. Mike offered to do the job — it is not heroism, just dumb stupidity I suppose, that made me consider the job at sea was so risky that I had to do it myself.

It was pate de campagne and olives for lunch. Scarlett complained about the quality of the pate, however, I pointed out that the campagne, 8°N 20°W was not noted for this delicacy and considering the location this was something of a treat.

In the afternoon it rained. Lord! How it rained. We men all stripped off and soaped down. Scarlett, in her bikini, ignored our nakedness. We collected over 5 gallons of fresh water from the sail together with some dirt which will doubtless add flavour. Then we had tea and special treat for Michael's birthday, opened a 2 1b can of Dundee fruit cake.

28th August.   Hard on the wind, force 4/5; bloody uncomfortable. People who have only beaten across the Channel or North Sea have no conception of what it is like hammering to windward in the open ocean. You would think the boat would open up under some of the spine juddering thumps, as you leap off a big wave and seemingly fall into the following trough.

30th August.   5°N 20°W. 30 hours ago we hove-to for dinner, as it was too uncomfortable to eat at table under way. Then we got going again on the opposite tack, actually heading towards America. Since then the wind has been up and down. Now we have just the mainsail pulled hard in and the starboard engine on. Yesterday, Alan noticed that the torque tube to the alloy luff spar of the jib reefing gear had sheered. We spent 1½ hours making a temporary repair, using bits of plastic and lots of string.

31st August.   Two days ago when setting the genoa, I got a small rope burn on my left hand between two fingers. I ignored it. Jesus! Has it given me jip. The fluid expanded the skin and the bubble ended up larger than a 2p piece. In desperation, I burst it with a sterilized needle. The relief was considerable.

During the night it got a little frisky, so I leapt out. Scarlett was on watch and I asked if we needed a reef. "No" she says. However, after poking my nose over the cabin roof, I decided we would be better with one in, so reduced the main. I told her, that if it got any fresher we would roll up some of the genoa too. "How will I know?" she asks. Well, some things you just cannot tell or teach people, they just have to feel them.

As it turned out, we did not roll the genny until 4.00 in the afternoon. The wind was a good 5. We are hard on it, on a true course of SW — the wind being S x E. Damned uncomfortable it is, too. Bashing to windward for 1000 miles certainly gives the boat, and incidentally, the crew, considerable punishment.

As I have twice come up and got the boat sailing 20° nearer the wind. To encourage the crew to take more interest in the course and watching windshifts, I have promised them that the tin of biscuits, (cream filled!) can be opened if we cross the Equator no further west than 25° longitude. This is very important, for if you cross the Equator too far west you get pushed with the winds and currents to the wrong side of the bulge of Brazil (Cabo San Roque) and end up being swept into the Carribean. If this happened to the old sailing ships, they would have to sail right across the Atlantic and have another go.

3rd Sept.   The last few days have been uneventful. Scarlett has baked some bread. Michael and I have worked out evening star sights. We have all read a number of books. We have run out of fresh water for washing (this is a 7 gal. tank in the loo), after only 9 days out. Earlier, I stressed the importance of only using the minimum. On an ocean voyage, no one should use more than a pint a day for tooth cleaning and washing. From now on we use salt water, or go dirty, unless we can catch some rainwater. We find we have not victualled very well, to give good variety at lunch-time. Today's was an average one — corned beef, tin of peas (cold) and a hunk of bread and pickled onion. Dead reckoning, advanced from this evening's star sight, suggests that we are just over the Equator in longitude 24° 34' W. So we have beaten the magical 25°W. We will celebrate with a champagne breakfast tomorrow morning.

5th Sept.   And very nice it was too. I crisped up some fat port, scrambled some dried eggs and plonked it on fried bread. What a treat, when muesli had been all for brekka, for a week. Especially since we washed it down with two bottles of sea water cooled champers.

It got much easier after crossing the line. The wind has backed south easterly, so we have been reaching, instead of close-hauled. Even so, our speed is well down — on our bottom are growing a crop of goose barnacles. They are still small, but even so, must be causing a lot of drag.

All we men have gone on the foredeck, stripped and de-odorised with buckets of sea-water, more for the feeling of freshness than the lust after cleanliness. Despite the sun being only 6½° to the N of us, it is not oppressively hot. The wind blowing over the cooler sea, keeps the temperature to a comfortable level. Saloon temp. 29°C.

6th Sept.   At 0130 hrs I was woken by a shout from Scarlett — "Come quickly". I leapt out from my berth, groped blindly for my specs and staggered out expecting a ship to be running us down. But nothing. No one out on watch, sails drawing well, on course and a blank horizon. Then I heard Alan say something down in their berth. Looking in, there was Alan, spraying it with the B.C.F. fire extinguisher. An electric wire had chafed through and ignited the plastic and wood of the berth. Scarlett woke up toasting, which caused her panicking cry. The extinguisher worked excellently and being gas, left no mess.

This afternoon Michael baked buns, including banana ones. He ate most of them too.

7th Sept.   I got an extremely satisfying star fix this morning using Cassiopea, Sirius and Achanar. All 3 meeting in a dot, with Capella's position line 3 miles to the north — so I threw that one away, as not accurate enough. Three of them had to be worked out with the old Marc Hilaire method, instead of the R.A.F. sight reduction tables, as their declinations were over 29° which is all the pre-computed tables go up to. (For the Pacific I must get vol. 1 which has all the necessary stars as well). For the star bearings I used Weir's azimuth diagram, on which you can plot the star's bearing instead of working it out using A.B.C. tables. I took a hand bearing reading on each one too. The worst was 2½° in error and the best 1°, so using these bearings would have given a satisfactory position.

After lunch, we handed all the sails and let the boat drift broadside to wind and sea. Scarlett stood on the cabin top, with orders to scream at the first sight of a shark's fin, while the rest of us went over the side to try and scrape off the goose barnacles. This proved a hell of a job; we soon gave it up. The boat would be picked up on a swell and bashed down on you and you would swallow a dose of sea water. Then you would swim in, to scrape away again, but it was difficult to get enough pressure to force them off. A few were got rid of but more, I fear, are firmly glued and enjoying our hard racing anti-fouling.

In order to make up speed, we have put up the ghoster and crammed on all possible sail. But we cannot get her up to 5 knots despite the wind being broad on the beam. Our last midnight to midnight run was only 78 miles and given this lovely force 3, we should have covered well over the 100.

12th Sept.   Our goose barnacles are pretty big now. With both engines going full chat, we can scarcely make 4 knots (should be over 6 knots). There is a light trade wind which should give us a comfortable 4 knots, but with our dirty bottom we are lolloping along at 2–2½. As I would like to make Salvador tomorrow in daylight, I have decided to motor sail.

We bought a whole stalk of bananas in the Cape Verdes. Now they are all ripening fast. Some we are drying on the deck, but mostly we are eating them, or rather, gorging on them. When I remember, (every 2 or 3 days) I take a vitamin C tablet. Not all the crew bother, but no vitamin deficiency shows, so I guess we get an adequate amount from the food.

For 2 days now we have been seeing 3 or 4 ships a day. For the first 12 days we did not see any.

13th Sept.   Midday. We are about 8 miles from Salvador, coasting a mile offshore. We made good landfall, fixing our position using the moon, Venus and Arcturus. However, the pilot warns of the current of uncertain strength but up to 2 knots setting onshore. I went to bed at 0100 hrs leaving what I considered a very safe course, with just the possibility of picking up a shore light if the current was running strongly. The light characteristics I carefully put on the chart. Coming on watch at 7.00 a.m. there was a light dipping astern.

"I can't work out which one it is." says Mike. "It flashes then there is 3 secs., then flash, then 6 secs. before it flashes again." In other words, 2 flashes every 10 secs. I realised the current must have set us in,

26

even more than predicted, or, I had allowed for.

"Why didn't you call me, if you were uncertain which one it was?"

"It was there when I came on watch, so I presumed you knew." was the reply.

No entry of when the light was first seen was made in the log. The fault was, of course, mine. After 2 months the crew had settled in well, but almost all the sailing has been offshore and mostly concerned with the ships' lights and the dangers of being run down. Now the problem was running into a featureless coast, at night, with an onshore setting current, and they just did not have enough experience to appreciate the dangers. I keep telling them to call me if in doubt. As it happened we were still far enough offshore by the arrival of daylight.

We have passed fishermen sitting on stools in the water. As you pass close, you see under the stool is a raft of light timbers, about 9 inches in diameter, lashed together. Without an adequate look-out you could easily run these guys down.

A strong tidal current runs in and out of Salvador bay. By some odd quirk of fate it was with us on arrival, so we made good progress to Salvador harbour where we anchored in 12 ft of water, in front of the Capitanerie. To clear in we had to go ashore and felt very safe where we had left the dinghy as the steps were guarded by a policeman with a tommy gun. This guy had the nasty habit of pointing it at you when he spoke to you.

Salvador was once the capital of Brazil, but is now of far less importance, both as a port and as an administrative centre. It is built in two parts, the lower, or port area and the cooler, better area on the cliff above. In between, on the steep hillside, occupying the middle ground were a number of brothels. They had just had a bad tropical storm with torrential rain which had unfortunately washed away the foundations of some of these houses of pleasure and these slid down onto others below them leaving a big gash on the hillside. This proved a terrible social catastrophe, for if any man died elsewhere the same night it was automatically assumed that he had been visiting the houses.

Salvador is a good victualling port, but no good drinking water. For this you can either go to the naval base at Aratu, or better, cross to the north tip of the island of Itaparika, about 15 miles away. This has beautiful spring water which they gas up and sell in bottles. You can fill by jerry can at the spring, as you have to anchor off. There is also a restaurant there owned by a charming Englishman. Unfortunately, his cook is poor and his prices high.

27

We left Salvador for the yacht club at Aratu, about 20 miles up the bay. This involved some tricky sailing as the winds were fluky. We had air in the fuel line of one engine, so only one was operable. Anyway, I thought it would be a good exercise for the crew to do it all under sail, from start to finish.

The yacht club was very hospitable, even boasting a Port Officer for the Ocean Cruising Club, who sorted out a drying out berth for me alongside a Wharram Tangaroa class cat, the owner of which solved our gas problem by getting our bottles filled for us. I was pleased to be able to give him a 'Polycat Sailorman' magazine — he did not know about the organisation for his class of cats. There are six Polycats at the club and a number of day sailing Hobie cats. The club has showers and of course a bar, at which you can buy a good meal for $5, including a plate overlapping with steak.

One Englishman was in residence, with his boat at the end of the jetty. He had cockroaches on board from Africa, so we were loath to swop paperbacks in case we caught them. He was bumming around with his boat, getting jobs occasionally. A translator in Sweden, English teacher in Dakar and Spain. But now he had a lot of work to do on his boat, before she was fit for sea again.

While anchored there, the mate from an English oil supply ship, loading cement at the works a mile away, came alongside in his rubber 'Z' boat. He was doing a bit of fishing in the bay and saw our flag. He took us back to his boat for a drink and a shower. The skipper was from Plymouth and the engineer also. The engineer offered to look at our diesel, so the mate and I went back for the *'Winds'*, while the others had a shower. Both ships were very pleased to be able to swop paperbacks. Our engine was the smallest the chief had every worked on. He bled it through for me and checked out the fuel line. Somehow, and I can find no leak, the line sucks air in after about 20 hours of running. The fuel line is on a syphon and this only happens after the tank gets part empty. It was great to yarn with the English officers on *Marsk Puncher*. The crew were Brazilians and did not speak English, and undoubtedly, none of us speak Portuguese.

We got a lot of useful jobs done at Aratu. Bottom scrubbed, engine checked, oil changed, roller furling gear stripped and greased and the clothes washing done. Altogether a successful stop, marred only by Michael not getting up, after being called five times, to help get the boat sailing. He is such a heavy sleeper he wakes and then immediately falls back to sleep. Scarlett vanished too, as she wanted a shower. So it

28

ended up just Alan and me getting the boat off.

We sailed down to Itaparika where we had a poor, expensive meal after which we returned on board and had a bit of a yarn which slowly turned political. Alan lost his rag. As he is very left, he called me a fascist and a racialist. As I see it, there is little change between fascism or communism — they both want to kill our freedom and rule by dictate. I told him his intolerance was frighteningly dangerous. All in all I am not happy with my crew; there is too much tension between us. Alan is the most conscientious and the best worker, but humourless. Scarlett has more humour but is slow to learn sailing by feel. Michael is frequently willing with a good sense of humour but stubborn as hell and looks to find excuses for his mistakes instead of saying, 'sorry, made a cock-up'. He also has a tendency to get stroppy and stinks with cigarette smoke. Me, like all captains, I'm perfect. Or, no doubt as the crew would put it, a perfect something or other. This is the big problem, crew compatibility. Wives break with husbands, children with parents, after living together in such frustrating surroundings as a small boat for several months, so it is rather pot luck when four almost strangers like us do it.

25th Sept.   We arrived at Salvador with a favourable wind, but left it close hauled and unable to lay the course. It meant one short tack and one long one. It is a long beat. Quite a few rain squalls, in fact we now have the doldrums, as after the rain it frequently goes calm.

The third day out, I resorted to the engine as I wanted to arrive at the Abrolhos in daylight. We picked the loom of the light up 40 miles away. The shoals extended to some 14 miles to the north of the island, so we had to make a dog's leg to pick our way into the channel and came to an anchorage in the lee of the main island. As we made the approach, a killer whale leapt free of the water, then stood on his tail, we thought he looked at us, then the rain squall hit us with a water spout pointing down from the cloud to the island, just before the land was blotted out by the heavy rain.

We anchored off the main island, on which there are 6 families who maintain the lighthouse and radio. Our first swim was incredible. Along the coral, with its fantastic forms, swarm various fishes, all brilliant colours. It was like looking into a completely new world. The chief of the lighthouse came out and asked for our particulars and told us no spear fishing off the main island, only the smaller ones. On the island were a number of goats left wild and just culled as necessary. Lizards abound, and lots of birds. The longtailed tropic birds gracefully swooped by, and were occasionally mobbed by the redbreasted Frigate birds. As you walked along the cliffs you stumbled over Boobies — which took off with a lot of noise and fuss. At the eastern end of the island there is a solitary coconut palm — the crown has been taken over by an eagle with its mate standing on guard calling from a nearby rock. In the coral pools, a crane stood fishing; these pools were alive with small fish. A number of curlews were also feeding.

We were invited to look over the lighthouse by one of the keepers. Most interesting, built by the French in about 1860, the 20 mile light is lit by a solitary 1000 watt 220v bulb; The fresnel lens system magnify and concentrate the light to a piercing beam.

The next day we took the keeper fishing, off another island. He only caught one small fish, so Michael speared him a gorgeous Clown Butterfly of about 3 lbs, and we gave him some others Alan caught on the line. We kept just a rock cod for our evening meal. Ashore there were some coconut palms. We had one nut that had fallen; in it was just liquid — no kernel. To my suprise, this is evidently the most common type.

Just before we left, Michael had a last swim with the gun and was badly frightened by a curious 6 ft Barracuda — which he claims was all head, and that was mostly teeth. He swam for the shore and yelled for me to come and get him by dinghy.

2nd Oct. Left Abrolhos after spending 2 hours trying to fettle the Autohelm — failed. So, unless the wind frees a little and strengthens, it's hand steering to Rio. We left in a virtual calm, which got calmer and hotter — then hotter. I have, with relief, just finished my two hours at the helm, and am down on my berth penning this. Scarlett is in the galley kneading dough. I am going to ration the bread to a loaf a day. I will make a lardy cake — which will have to be divided up into four.

2 hours after leaving, I had Alan take a back bearing on the light. This showed we had a 10° inset towards the coast. The course was amended.

We had 11 hours of engine before a breeze got up, then on with Quantock Pete. What a relief to be able to escape the tyranny of the helm. All the way down to 'Demaga' oil rig 22° 18'S 40° 58'W we have had gentle reaching winds of force 2/3. Being clean, we have been averaging 5 knots very comfortably. All in all, "le yachting".

4th Oct. I took a sight this dawn, of Sirius and Canopus and amended

30

the course by 3 degrees, for the oil rig (the position of which was given to me by Bill, the navigation officer of *Marsk Puncher*). 9 hours later, passed it 2 cables to starboard.

It was a great sail past Cabo Frio, at times picked up to over 8 knots and then, within 2 hours of dawn, it fell flat calm. It so often happens that when you have been making a notable passage and start to count the hours, it all falls to pieces. So it was on with the motor to get to Rio before nightfall. Rio was shrouded in mist. We first sighted the offshore islands, then the false sugar lump. This, approaching from the east, looks like the real thing and could really throw your navigation out if you were not aware of it. However it is marked 'Falso Pão de Açucar' on the chart.

We tied up to a pier at the Rio Yacht Club, right under the Sugar Lump. A beautiful posh club that charged 500 cruzeires ($25 U.S.) for the privilege with a limit of 30 days. They also did all the fuss of clearing in and out.

As usual, we had plenty of little jobs to get on with — first a shower. That is the great thing about yacht clubs; personally I prefer them not quite so exclusive as this one (we are told it costs in the region of 10,000 pounds to join). Here they have guards and it is safe for us all to leave the boat together. Michael went to the pool for a swim, but was stopped, he had to get medical clearance first. I received a note 'Capt. Patterson please remove your yacht from our pier.' So I moved to the next one!

Fortunately, in Rio, a lot of people speak English, as no one on board can master Portuguese. We are all terrible linguists. However, I do not think English can be well taught in schools, so none of the poorer people speak it. We should have made more of an effort to learn a smattering. It must be one of the loveliest natural harbours in the world. Unfortunately the waters and the beaches are badly polluted and the traffic goes like hell; bus drivers assume that any pedestrian with the temerity to cross the road has a death wish. There are no jay walkers in Rio. Any building, small and beautiful, is pulled down for a towering block of flats. There is bad overcrowding, and the really poor live in slums that cling precariously to the mountain sides. It has to be too steep to be practical for a tower block — not places to go wandering in out of curiosity. There is a lot of crime in S. America — and life is cheap.

On an overcrowded bus someone tried to pick my pocket, so I trod on his toe and loudly declared against him. He slunk down the bus and off at the next stop.

We met an Australian girl who was travelling around S. America on her own, and she was a diabetic. I admired her courage — it seemed to me such a dangerous thing to do. She had had her bag slashed and a 100 cruzeiros taken, but was generally fairly cautious.

I invited Peter Lane from the British Consulate Industrial Office to the boat with his wife. They were not allowed in to the yacht club; I was most embarrassed. However permission was eventually obtained from one of the managers. Security here is tight, but I suspect that rule was more to make sure visiting yachts did not become too comfortable and abuse the privileges of temporary membership.

I was surprised how little interest our cat generated at that club. We had but few visitors. An American, Paul Flynn, came on board for a yarn as he was planning to build a large motor sailor from the board of Hugo Myers. So we had an interesting discussion. He then invited us to his flat for a meal. It was a penthouse flat and the view from the balcony at night was breathtaking. Paul sailed with us for 60 miles to Ilha Grande.

This is a gorgeous sailing area. From Rio there is 60 miles with no harbours and then a bay dotted with superb, well sheltered anchorages; small islands, clean water for swimming and one main town, Angra de Reis. Of course the opportunity is too good for the planners to resist. An oil terminal is now built and a Nuclear generating complex is sprawling over one corner. I sometimes think God dropped an awful clanger inventing human beings, but then we were designed in his image, so since He made the original fuck up, it is no wonder we are busy screwing up our environment so diligently.

We felt our way into the anchorage at the eastern end of Ilha Grande 2 hours after dark. I crept in very carefully under motor, for there were no lights. Next morning it was a beautiful sight. Golden beaches, palm trees on the shore between a few houses and steep, wooded hillsides. I cooked breakfast and we gently sailed out.

Then Scarlett asked, "Where is the promised champagne?" I had clean forgotten it was my 39th birthday, (again). So later that morning Scarlett made some fruit salad, and we had a couple of bottles at 11 a.m. out in the cock-pit. A very pleasant yarn and laugh. Paul is a smiling, round, exuberant person, so helped the party swing.

In Angra we crept into the inner basin, and tied up with an anchor astern, in 5 feet of water (aground at low water), so we could walk ashore. Here Paul introduced us to 'Caper-reina' (not too sure of the spelling). A super local drink of lime, ice, sugar and more than a little hooch. The price is between 12 and 20 cruz, and it is delicious. After 2 of them I celebrated my birthday with a haircut, very short for the hot summer. Michael had one too, he lost all his golden locks which were overhanging his shoulders. Returning happily to the boat, we found Alan and Scarlett showing a German couple, Rolfe & Loi, over the boat. He was a civil engineer at the power station 25 miles away. They invited us for the evening meal, and came to collect us. To my surprise his children sang 'Happy Birthday' in German to me. It was a very pleasant evening with lots of beer, it has turned out to be a gently alcoholic, good day. This 40th year has started well, long may it continue.

A pleasant sail, but beating to windward, so distance covered but 10 miles; all in sheltered waters, and we spent the next night in the SW of Ilha Grande. It was so very beautiful. A long haul of 60 miles to Ilha Bella; as the daylight is only 13 hours it means one cannot quite do it in the light so we left at 9.00 local time. The head wind gradually eased and then fell calm. Then wonders of wonders, a wind from astern giving us a gentle sail at 3/4 knots.

As darkness fell, no sign of the necessary light to starboard. This was needed for a running fix to make sure of clearing the islands ahead, as I was not sure of the current's speed and direction. Always discretion — 'There are old sailors, There are bold sailors, but there are no old, bold sailors', (quote via Rudy Choy). So we hauled off to port, 40° off course, to pick up the only other light, then a dog's leg back. Enough light (moon) filtered through the clouds to allow fixes on the darker island land masses. He must have thought we were making it too easily, so a black thunderstorm arose and smote us. Visibility cut to less than a mile and an entrance which normally easy, turned somewhat risky. I was very careful, stopping and taking bearings of the entrance lights every ¼ hour. Despite the calm of the anchorage, I put down 2 anchors.

The morning dawned bright, clear and beautiful, with a low barometer. (And I never wondered why!) So all ashore to this lush tropic isle, with fruit for the taking, rocks that sound like bells when struck, and reputedly the finest distiller of aguardente (cane liquor) in all Brazil.

3 hours later and 3 miles from the boat, the sky went black. 50 foot palms bent 30° with the wind. Fast pace back to the boat — I was worried. The poor old boat was dancing up and down, exposed to a 5 mile fetch, like a bloody rocking horse. With relief I saw Michael was

on board, he got back just before it started. Rightly, I presumed he would be motoring up in the gusts to relieve the strain. Waves were breaking on the beach so off with trousers and wade out to him when he rowed ashore for me. He backed the dinghy in and I went in over the transom with Michael rowing like mad over a steep sea breaking. The other 2 were fetched off singly a little later in a lull. Then another lull and Michael rowed out our 3rd anchor, a 20 kg Hold Fast or Danforth type. This, with the 35 lb C.Q.R. and 56 lb fisherman in good holding eased my worried mind a little. But still until midnight we kept an anchor watch. The morning showed one local boat up on the nearby rocks, (we had rocks not a cable under our lee) and floor-boards of a sunk boat all around, which we rescued and delivered to the quay in the hope they would find their rightful owner. There are some honest people in Brazil — I think.

So we left Ilha Bella, no ring of the rocks, the fruit unripe mangoes, and the liquor still brewing, with of course a wind less than favourable. We had only the exit chart and the Santos port chart, leaving some 40 miles uncharted. With numerous islands the pilot was carefully read. They do not give the long. and lat. of the islands, only 5' SSW of port X etc. But careful study and reference to the list of lights (which do give exact positions) and ignoring the fact that the one point, 'Ponta Mandula' is shown in the pilot with long. and lat. — a degree too far north — we plotted a course free of danger. The distance was obtained from the 'Departure to d. long tables.'

Both engines used, as with the very light wind we would otherwise do 50 miles in 24 hours instead of in the 12 I was aiming for. The entrance to Santos was reached just before sunset. Santos is the busiest port of Brazil. Personally, I won't feel terribly deprived if I never revisit the place. The yacht club though, made us welcome and served good cheap caiperenas. At night they have an armed guard patrolling, so this is a good reason to always stop at these clubs. Here, unlike Rio, they made no charge, and we were able to fill up with fuel; we were down to our last 10 gallons.

What a pantomime to change travellers' cheques! In the end we used Banco de Brazil and unfortunately it had to be at the official rate, but at least we did not have to pay commission there. The black market rate (which is all open and above board) is 3 or 4 cruzeiros (20%) better, but unlike Rio, not available in Santos.

We made a trip to the orchidarium, but it was early in the season so only a few were out. Even so, a good visit, as there were many exotic birds there. Returned after a stroll along the beach. Under the canvas tents many Samba bands were practising the latest rhythm. It had changed markedly from the earlier one I used to dance to, but that is still played too.

24th Oct.   Lifted dinghy inboard, generally got ready to sail. Michael, with rest of crew, called and answered. He answered grumpily — did not appear. So the three of us did everything. Now we hoist the dinghy in with the boom, it can be done by 2 persons, but it is easier and quicker for the whole crew to get the boat moving. This is the 2nd time he has done this. I told him quietly that he will not do it again.

I can see me ending this trip solo. I am not sure whether it is the fact that I am such an obnoxious character to get along with, or expect too much from my crew. I like to think it is not necessary to run a tight ship with lots of standing and continuing orders. Rather a "would you like to?" or a "we must do so and so" and the job is done. Alan and Scarlett are better, Scarlett doing a lot of things off her own bat.

We needed the motor to get clear of Santos. For the first 12 hours not a breath of wind. Then a glorious run for 12 hours with the wind on the ¼ and just the Genny set.

Again it fell calm for a spell and then the inevitable head wind. I cooked rice, bacon and pineapple with courgettes for dinner, becoming worse and worse tempered with the thumping into the seas trying to spill my fat and goodies. Even this wind did not last. It looked as if we were in for an evil night, black with lightning flashes, but it all came to a calm. So the crew put on the motor and kept her headed SE instead of, now no longer beating, to the SSW. I almost leapt up when the motor went on to make sure they corrected to the original course — but no, I thought, one must have some trust in them, and they knew full well we had to pay off with the head wind.

I fixed our position with a morning sight on Jupiter and a later sun sight, all the heading off shore has not hurt, as we are almost back on our original course line.

After 2 days, most of which has been under engine, and we have used up about 13 gallons of fuel, which is under ½ gals an hour, our speed is around 4 knots — but the log is under-reading; I suspect weed ahead of the impeller — the impeller I've cleaned.

27th Oct.   The day started well, running south under twins: it had to rain at the start of my watch, for 2 hours. Just after lunch saw our first

35

Albatross, gracefully swooping over the seas. Not a flutter of the wings – just gliding on the updraughts from the waves. This one had a wing span of about 6 feet, with white below and black on top.

A funny day with a bit of a gale inland, 25 miles offshore and we were getting insects and birds blown off to us, but the wind was not more than 4, if that. Then towards evening a head wind set in and became quite strong. Michael should have reefed – or called me up for my opinion. Alan thought it a bit strong so had a fierce argument with Mike. I pointed out that we are not racing or hammering her in the shelter of the Solent, but have a long way to go and must nurse her and the gear. Heavily laden she will stand up to being overcanvassed – but the gear will part. Now we are deep reefed, and the jib well reefed and aback, hove-to 20 miles offshore on latitude 29°S. The wind is from dead ahead – force 5/6 so to hell with bashing through it. I hope for a wind shift with the daylight.

29th Oct. I first surfaced an hour before my watch, as the motion was bad. Mike assured me all was OK. He had just operated on a growth on his hand which had relieved the pressure, and the wind was freshening from astern. We just had up the full genny, boomed out to starboard. During my watch I knocked off the Autohelm, it just could not cope. The gusts were up to 7 and the seas were getting up. We had the very occasional sizzler when the boat went through the 8 knot barrier, guess she was screaming at 10 or 11 knots. At such times, because she is going so fast, she is feather light on the helm. In these conditions, she is a little tiring, but not difficult to hold once you have the feel of correcting just as the wave starts to swing your stern, then again when it throws the bows! – On a 30 foot monohull it is another kettle of fish.

Alan was not happy, so we deep reefed the genny, which slowed us only a little, and made her very easy to control! I could not get a fix, there was that much electric interference that the D.F. hurt the eardrums. Things looked a bit black up ahead.

A thunderstorm with winds up to force 8 hit us from astern. I had out a bridle off the backstays, trailing in the water to act as a lightning conductor. We reefed more of the jib, and then took the pole off. In so doing, it clean ripped for 2 feet. So the genny is now out of action for a spell.

The squall passed. We now had up just the storm jib, and needed more, so hoisted a deep reefed main. It was still black and thundery, but generally we were very undercanvassed as the wind was scarcely

36

more than 4, but varying a lot in direction, causing a lot of gybes.

Michael's watch, and I was due on in an hour. It was raining but not strong wind, so I was resting below. I heard a winch go and a sheet blast the deck. Thought I'd better have a looksee, Christ! Why wasn't I called? Mike had just hauled the main and then the wind hit, with rain — or was it spray? — horizontal. "I need a line to tie the main." he cried.

"Steer her off — dead down wind," I shouted "I'll tie the main." I leapt up with a line. I lay astride the boom, tying the gasket. She gybed. The jib aback. "Run before it — dead before it." I screamed to Mike. The boom, with a slack sheet flew across, me with it, smothering the sail. The wind was a full force 10, I got a line 3 times round and just hauled it tight and hitched it, Mike gybed her back, the boom flew back — I hung on, arms around and went with it. The line jammed in the door, then Alan came out freeing the line so I hanging underneath it got 3 more turns around the main. Mike gybed a couple more times. He kept looking astern — or trying to. There was nothing to see, just white blinding spray. "Keep running dead before." I shouted. But the wind was strong, your breath was pressed out of you if you looked to windward, and the spray hurt. The sea, what little you could see beyond the rail, was a mass of white. I was hanging under the boom like a sloth, trying to get turns of line around any loose sail, as it swung 3 times across. Alan had the sense to harden the sheet in. Mike finally got the idea, and kept the storm jib full and the boat running; at I suppose some 8 or more knots. Which must have considerably reduced the wind force on us. The seas were not big, the tops just left their native element. The spray was mixed with very heavy torrents of rain. It lasted somewhere between 10 and 25 minutes (at such times you don't watch the clock) and then passed. The sea was left mostly long white streaks, with green between. The rain rained! We stood all 3 in the cock-pit shaken and breathless. Later, Mike and Scarlett described the onset as a line of black, rolling towards them with electric green lights underneath.

I was very annoyed at not being called. I had told them earlier about the El Pamperos, and that I must be called before one hit. "But, we didn't know." they said. They knew enough to take the main down before it hit us, which was right and wise, but I despair. I keep telling them, 'If you are uncertain give me a shout'. The trouble is they now have experience enough to think they know a lot more. So they know enough to be dangerous.

We struggled on SE by 1600 hrs. there was no wind, so on with the engine for 3½ hours. The barometer had started to rise. It became black ahead. We were off sailing again, with the wind on the beam. Another squall — obviously not as bad but still looking black; had us deep reefing and hauling up the No. 2 jib. Darkness, squally, wind dead ahead, so I hove-to with the storm jib aback and the main deep reefed. Midnight and the wind still dead ahead, but no more than force 4. Still it is a little black ahead, so I am leaving her 'hove-to' rather than try struggling on beating to wind-ward, with the discomfort that entails.

30th & 31st Oct. If it is not a head wind, then there is scarcely any wind. Mind you, if things start looking black and with the odd bit of lightning, we reduce the sail down to about the size of Scarlett's knickers — she wears small ones, just as well judging from the size of her bum. Close hauled since Rio Grande for 100 miles, only just laying the course, with a force 4 wind. With the working jib (number 2) set, she sails well, hard on the wind.

1st Nov. Past the border of Uruguay/Brazil. The wind, with the dawn, fallen away, so on with the starboard engine. Without the plonker, we would only be ½ way by now. Just past a seal colony off Cape Polonio, two came cavorting around the boat — the female a flighty piece, leaping up then standing head first with her tail vertical like a weird top naked pillar buoy. Her mate, a big whiskered character, looked on somewhat reserved, so she sidled up to him, and gave him a kiss. Yes! Twice she went to him and kissed him, they were very close to the boat.

2nd Nov. Entering the River Plate in the early hours, there was quite a lot of shipping, and one tanker messing about with Not Under Command Lights. Of course it was right on our course, so it meant I was up for most of the night. With daylight it became calm so put on both engines and motored the 40 odd miles to Monte Video. Picked up a mooring off the Uruguayan Yacht Club in Puerto Buceo. A lad came out to tell us what to do, he was a sailing instructor, Alexandar, and spoke very good English. He solved all the hassle of the entry with the mooring guard, who totes a gun so was called 'The Sheriff'. As we only had cruzeiros, we were given drinks in the bar by a member. This turned out to be typical Uruguayan hospitality. We found the people here very patient with out very limited Spanish, and almost too helpful. Michael was even taken out one night by two members (one a doctor) and treated to a whore. We had an invite to a British Diplomats' cocktail party. Alan and Scarlett and I went, and while it might not have been quite as exciting as Mike's night out we enjoyed ourselves and, as everyone, got delightfully sloshed. Met some very pleasant teachers from the English school who invited us round for a meal 2 nights later.

One night we went out with Alexandar to a steak-house for a meal. It was a terrific scoff. It is all cooked on an enormous grill – fed with 3 foot logs. The orange sweet black pudding sausage was particularly good, and of course the steaks huge – we had to leave some. Met another local, Jorge, who has the only cat in the club. He joined the ship to sail with us across to Argentina.

13th Nov.   Alan worked out that he and Scarlett were over the top of their budget, so left the ship. He was going to make his way slowly back overland by buses to California. It is costing us about 15 pounds ($30) a week each for food and boat expenses. I suspect there are other considerations for while he is a good crewman, he is not I find, much of a companion and has not gone out of his way to make it a happy ship. He is what you might describe as the strong silent type – but too quiet and solemn for my taste. It does mean that we will have to do 3 hours on rather than 2 to have 6 off. Not that that should prove too much. The voyage has been easy, but I think we are now entering the first difficult part. The weather is incredibly changeable. A Pampero has screamed through on each of the past 2 days. Now there is a bitterly cold light southerly wind.

The filthy wind had caused a short lop in the Plate and poor Jorge was quite ill, but like a good lad he did his watches. Then the wind dropped all away and we just had to motor on the starboard engine. That plonker is getting a lot of use but it charges the domestic battery. Approaching the other side (Argentina) of the Plate Estuary we had a mirage effect. The trees and buildings floated in the air – and appeared and then disappeared. It was a fine sunny day but with cold Antarctic air.

Jorge picked up and was quite chirpy – almost his usual self – but Scarlett started running a temperature with an earache so she went on antibiotics.

Had 12 hours of good wind to make Mar del Plata. Scarlett stayed in bed and we all shared her watches.

As I only had a big passage chart I sketched out a rough chart of Mar Del Plata from the information in the Pilot. This proved quite useful to find the yacht club which was hidden behind a protective mole butting onto the submarine base. On the end of the mole big black lumps moved. We got closer, and they turned into a colony of sea lions. They were diving all around the boat too.

The gap through the mole was 5 metres wide in the deep water. We are 5 metres wide, so it was a bit tight. I was asked to stay outside, but Jorge explained that we needed a quiet beach on which to dry out and to clean the boat. So they let us in, but we were given solemn warnings about rowing across at night. Any cry of *'attention'* or *'basta'* stop immediately − preferably with hands in the air. The BBC Darwin expedition called on their way back last November. Rowing to the club late one night the guard shouted to them to stop in Spanish, but they, not understanding, took no notice. Next thing they knew he was shooting at them. That scared the hell out of them. In minutes the yacht club was surrounded by another trigger happy patrol. No one was actually hurt − but it was a near thing. So we gave the guard a whisky and some fags by way of bribery and corruption. Do anything to remain living.

The boat was badly fouled, took a tide to scrape her clean and another to rub her smooth with wet and dry. Then another to paint her. Jorge helped out and worked really well. He could not return to Monte Video until the Prefectura (Argentina Coastguard) let us enter. Since they did not know how to enter a yacht, this took 1½ days. It was backwards and forwards with various forms and crew lists. Jorge had to be entered as a passenger or he would not be allowed to leave the ship. Finally they fingerprinted us and with a photo gave us an identity form showing us as sailors, so now we can go ashore without the passports.

The club officials and members were all very pleasant and helpful and some took us out to see Mar del Plata. Scarlett and I were vainly trying to buy powdered milk, when a gentleman shyly helped. He took us to the supermarket − then picked us up in his car and took us home. Teresa, his wife, spoke rather more English, and their eldest son George and daughter Maggi more still. Next thing we were sitting down and eating lunch − and what a lunch. I thought, Mother, no wonder you are a bit plump (delightfully so I may add) but then I learnt she was 8 months pregnant. I felt the same after 1½ hours at table and 3 courses later.

They were building their own house — no slates on yet, just roofing felt. Boys on camp beds at the back of the garage, Maggi when home from University (studying medicine) also, but behind the bookcase. Father — Charlie — was foreman mechanic at the fishing boat repair yard. They were a jolly family and so naturally kind. The second son, Alex understood a lot but spoke little English. They had spent a year in Australia. Teresa was of Hungarian parents and Charlie actually came from Budapest some 22 years ago. It was an ideal family with which to get your feet under the table. They drove us round on Sunday afternoon, after visiting the boat.

Mar del Plata has an enormous pitch for football and rugby for the poor, polo for the rich, kite flying for the kids of all ages — and some went up really high, also g.r.p. swans for the 5—8 year olds which were a pretty sight.

20th Nov.   Only 2 hours at the Prefectura to obtain clearance to leave. Soon I am sure it will be easier, as they will have drowned under a sea of paper. The boss Captain drove me back and came out to the boat to check I had a distress radio, life-raft, distress flares and nav. lights. He was very pleasant and polite but what a load of bullshit. I was relieved to get away. The boat went a 1/3 faster with a clean bottom. The sea lions gave us a shout and a splash — and judging by the smell, farted. We were off through the entrance, headed we hoped for Puerto Madryn 450 miles away. A very light wind meant starboard engine and sails, and off south at 5 knots.

For lunch chicken liver pate made by Charlie on light Italian bread; for tea, cake made by Teresa. For tomorrow's breakfast, Seville marmalade made by Teresa's mother.

So, for two days we just motored SW. It is I think, the longest period of uninterrupted motoring we have done. It seemed we were in a high pressure area. Despite the sea cooling the air my face got sunburnt. Then on the third day the barometer started falling a millibar an hour for 10 hours. This gave us a lovely ¼ wind — much of the time jogging along at 6 knots just under genoa, at times it freshened to a full 7 so there was not a lot of genny out. Quantock Pete was doing most of the steering. Scarlett started getting real moody, not answering when spoken to. I made no comment at first hoping she would improve, but then when she was bitchy to Mike too, I jumped on her and told her she could either be pleasant or get off at Puntas Arenas (it was forbidden in Argentina for crew to leave ship). That did the trick, she realised

41

I was not making an idle threat, but I want it clear that they do not have me over a barrel — so no need to get bolshy.

23rd Nov. I got a poor star (Sirius) and Jupiter fix this morning through thin cloud, and later a sun longitude. Then the noon lat. showed we had been pushed too far to the east. As the wind strengthened we were some 15 miles further S and the same E of our D.F. The wind dropped right away to about 2 so I handed the genny and on with the starboard plonker once more. I think we are probably some 20 miles south of Ponta Delgado, but it has clouded over just when we really need a sight. The tides run very fiercely off here and cause bad overfalls off the headlands. I planned to pass 10 miles off the Ponta Delgado. It was a good job I managed a noon lat. Not too happy heading for a shoreline from a position up to 5 miles in error and unknown (but strong) tides. The barometer is now steady, or just rising — and it is generally a weather shore.

Just before dawn Michael got a good fix on the lights, 10 ft apart marking the entrance to Gulfo Nuevo — an inland sea about 30 m wide and 40 m long, at the head of which lies Puerto Madryn, which is where the Welsh settlers of the region first landed more than 100 years ago (1865). Their leader was Parry Madryn. They marched over the bleak windswept scrub to the Chubut River some 40 miles away to settle. Now Madryn has an enormous aluminium plant so in the last 5 years the town has mushroomed — but looks to me very much a frontier town set in bleak country.

As Madryn was so exposed to the east I decided to carry on south to the 'derelict fishing port' of Rawson at the mouth of the Chubut River. There is a shingle bar, so entrance can only be effected near high water. It was a fine 30 mile sail south, much of it under motor as the wind fell away. The land of Patagonia abounded with penguins who always dived on our approach and Albatrosses glided past. But it looked bleak and lonely to starboard. The sun was very hot. As we approached the Chubut the sea became alive with black and white porpoises. At first, because of their colouring, we thought they were killer whales but as they came nearer and played around us we could see they were smaller and different in shape. A fishing boat offered us a tow in, which was declined, but we did follow her in over the bar. We caused quite a stir — only one other yacht (English) having visited the place 2 years ago. We tied up to a fishing boat. The Prefectura wanted to know why we came to Rawson. Fortunately he spoke

English, we explained we were tourists and following Drake's route and had called in for water and fuel.

We drank Mate from the fishing boat next door, and were overwhelmed with gifts of fish. We showed all who wanted over the boat — but on the quay the locals had to ask permission of the prefectura guard so were almost always accompanied onboard by an armed guard.

The local radio announced our visit, so then the press came down and after that the television. Many people with English families or ancestry came to make our acquaintance, and often to take us out to tea. In fact the hospitality was terrific. Even the sea elephants that kept bobbing up alongside us (they were fed the thrown out fish by the boats) seemed friendly.

A deputation from the Yacht Club Nautico de Sud of Madryn drove over to welcome us to Patagonia. They took us back to Madryn for a Paella cooked over a wood fire out in the open, and a meal next day at the Yacht Club. The Captain, Hugo, and committee members, Carlos being the chief spokesman, were designing a small alloy cruising cat, so kept me up talking design points until 3.00 a.m. Next day the wind blew like hell, and I was quite apprehensive for *Ocean Winds*, 50 miles away — but I need not have worried; the 35 lb C.Q.R. held her with no bother despite the force 9 winds.

An English couple, who kept a farm in the Chubut Valley 15 miles from Rawson, took us home to tea. It was a little England; Olive, the lady, had beautiful roses around the house, also nasturtiums, and the veranda was dripping with honeysuckle. Bertie, her husband, saddled their two horses for Mike and me to have a canter up the lane. The dogs startled a hare which startled the horses but we managed to control them. Neither Mike nor I are great hands on horseback though it is great to try. Mind I do wonder that horsemen remain fertile.

Olive and Bertie showed us various gear of the sheep rancher, and gave us each an arrowhead which Bertie had found at various times in the bush whilst out with the sheep. The original Indians had lost them when hunting. They were flint and were, I suppose, anything from 200 to a 1000 years old.

Carlos, from Madryn, joined the ship to sail 100 miles south. Considerable difficulty was made by the Prefectura as a precedent was not written in his book so he would not take the responsibility of giving permission. In the end, Carlos drove back to Madryn and got permission from the head prefectura, (he would not answer the phone from Rawson as he was watching an important football match on TV) after signing a paper to say he could swim. The South American Countries are ludicrous with this sort of thing. You have to have a piece of paper for everything, and no one likes to take the responsibility should something go wrong. No wonder the Falkland Islanders do not want to join the Argentines.

29th Nov.   At 5.00 a.m. we were woken after an hour's sleep by the neighbouring fishing boat. He had cast off and now wanted to be free of us. We landed Hugo, and Maria his wife, to drive back to Madryn and we motored out of the river in the first of the dawn light. All our stay it had been blowing hard. The fishing boats had not been out since Saturday owing to the wind. Now there was virtually no wind so it was on with the motor, south. Carlos, being our guest, and entered on the 'Roll' as a passenger, was given the first 2 hours watch while we, the crew, went back to bed. Actually as I forgot to wake Mike he never surfaced anyway.

Carlos, who is boss of the research dept. at the Aluminium works at Madryn, proved a good lad to have on board. One of his main interests is cooking. He also didn't seem to mind doing extra long watches. He wanted to see how the boat sailed, and all we did was motor through a virtual calm for 80 miles. As evening approached I picked out a sheltered anchorage from the pilot and chart and we headed in. At last the wind increased sufficiently to sail, so the last 3 miles were done with the motor off. Seals watched us sail past the headland, penguins dived on our approach. Low grassy hills swept down to the coast. A big empty land lay beyond.

In the morning a good wind was blowing, but this was straight into the open roadstead where we had planned to land Carlos. I persuaded him to come with us all the way to Deseado 3 degrees or some 200' further south. At last we were sailing with a broad reach until we were into the Gulf of San Jorge where the wind fell right off. So back on with the plonkers to motor for 100 miles to pick up Cabo Blanco right on the nose. I was pleased that the navigation proved so accurate as the tides set strongly along all the coast and anyway it is nice to impress the guests!

We tucked ourselves in behind the Cape in a bay that was sheltered from SSW through to NE. There was a house on the shore but this appeared deserted though I expect the one further up by the lighthouse had a keeper living there. We saw no one. The sky turned evilly black, lightning flashed, clouds rolled by low and threatening. We expected a violent short storm, but we only got a few drops of rain. So we had a damn good meal, and a couple of hours kip. With the dawn came a light south wind. We had 30 miles to go to the south and had to get to Port Deseado by high water at the latest.

We motored out, and then just plugged our way south against a freshening wind. What a sod, the tide was under us a full 2 knots. With the wind getting up to force 6, the lop was quite nasty. Short steep breaking seas. Flat out on both plonkers making about 4 knots + tide. Scarlett let the boat crab away from the land and over the offshore banks where she was quite impressed with the overfalls. The rest of us were fast asleep as with running an anchor watch and a dawn start meant we had all had but little sleep. It was getting nasty, although we had made good progress south. The boat was banging into and off some quite vicious seas, so I decided with the wind now piping up to a full 7 to put up the storm jib and deep reefed the main, and motor sail offshore on one tack. This was much better, taking the wind and sea on one bow. Spray way flying, sun shining and we felt very wind blown. I kept on the leeward motor.

At about 10 miles offshore we tacked and then gradually made out Deseado. I was surprised to find we could lay the entrance. The leading marks were very difficult to pick out. I hung about a ½ mile off the entrance. The church tower was a lattice construction (to let the wind through as it blows so hard here!) and was at first mistaken for one of the entrance marks. Finally picked them up and motored in the channel which is deep but narrow with a slight kink in it. The tide goes in and out at 5 knots so you do not want to stray to one side and clobber a rock. Dolphins (beautiful black and white ones) played around on our approach, but not so many as at Rawson, perhaps because ½ dozen had been netted recently and were in a pool ashore waiting shipment to Japan. Penguins, cormorants and gulls were all disturbed by our arrival. The prefectura boat showed us the way to a good anchorage. However, there was not a lot of space, so we laid all 3 anchors, to keep us off the rocks at low water.

Drake came here 400 years ago, and burnt the *Swan* as he had insufficient crew to go around so many ships. There was also some dissension among the crews and gentlemen but this was resolved at Port St. Julian. Apart from the pier and 2–300 houses and a military barracks on the north shore, nothing much else can have changed here. The south shore is deserted, you can go for miles without seeing a sheep let alone signs of humans. But here at Port Desire soon there will be quite a change as a fish factory is being built and some boats are due from Spain. This should bring more prosperity to the town. The dock is little used now as the meat and wool is all transported by road. The railway has ceased — that station is a grave yard of old British railway engines — that stopped 2 years ago. I just cannot believe that it is cheaper to move such cargo to B.A. by road than by ship, but I suppose it is progress. Not long ago, coasters used to call at entrances along the coast to load — but no more. This means that they are all well documented in the pilot which makes it easy for us.

I feel a bit of a fraud following Drake with good charts, a pilot book, tides tables and radio aids. When he had nothing and a ship with no motor, poorer ground tackle and less ability to beat to windward. Mind you, even with all our aids, I am finding it quite sufficient of an adventure, especially as I expect it to get a lot more difficult once past Puntas Arenas.

Very rarely do we find a conveniently near petrol (gas) station. The one at Puerto Deseado was over a mile away. No taxis were available so each carrying 2 five gallon containers of diesel, Mike and I struggled to the road out of town, then a kindly gent in a pick-up stopped and went out of his way to deliver us and the cans to the boat. This sort of casual kindness is typical of the people here. You ask the way to somewhere and as like as not they will take you there.

5th Dec.   Scarlett woke with the dawn, like a good girl, then woke us with a cup of tea. Michael, who sleeps as sound as a log, was shouted for 3 times. It was very conveniently a flat calm, and top of the tide. We got the C.Q.R. in with the dinghy, by tightening up on the tripping line over the transom, then Michael going forward and bouncing on the bows. This way they usually come out quickly and easily, but she was so well dug in it took us over a ¼ hours hard graft. The three anchors, and stowing the dinghy for sea took 1½ hours. Normally we are away from an anchorage in ½ an hour.

We motored out by 6.30 with the tide now well in our favour — I guess it was running some 4 knots — and with dolphins escorting us out. The barometer was low, but slowly rising; had we picked the only quiet day of the week?

There were masses of Penguins off Isla de los Penguinos. It was here a Welshman in Cavendish's expedition of 1586 gave the name pengwyn (white head) to a certain strange looking bird. Or so the story goes.

There, Megallenin Penguins actually have a black head with a white band from their beak and around their neck and white fronts. In the water they look odd — floating like a bath duck. With no wind, the albatrosses were just sitting in large groups on the water. At our approach they took fright and waddled off running splay footed on the water and flapping madly their huge wings. They look funny and ungainly taking off, in marked contrast to their beautiful ways in flight.

In the afternoon we had that strange phenomenon — a following wind. For 5 hours we sailed south with the main and genoa wing and wing. Then at seven in the evening, the sky went dark and once again a sodding head wind. From then on it was reef in, reef out. Squalls hitting hard. To add to our misery, during Scarlett's watch in the early hours we went through a bad tidal race. There was no rhyme or reason to the seas — we got thrown about something rotten. Books hurled on the floor, wicked thumps under the bridge deck. Oddly the wind had dropped light, and what there was left was being thrown out of the sails by the motion, so on with both engines to get out of it.

We reached the entrance to Port St. Julian at dead low water, on a quiet sunny day. I put Michael on the helm while I worked out the transits over the bar. We crept over with 5 feet to spare. On an island to starboard hundreds of penguins were fussily waddling up and down the beach. Off the port we were first welcomed by the black and white dolphins, then the prefectura. It was a bit of a hassle with this prefectura nonsense, but it keeps them happy, giving them something to do — and after a while you get used to it, so it becomes less of an annoyance. The lieutenant asked us ashore for drinks in the evening at 8 p.m. We waited, and though he did not arrive other locals did. A farmer of Scottish descent paid a short visit, but as he was busy shearing, could not stay. Then from the bank we were asked to come and eat asada. This was in their garage. There in the corner was a charcoal grill with a whole lamb roasting on the grid. Delicious it was too, washed down with good Argentine wine.

As I wanted to check the bottom, and also for convenience of getting ashore, we were up next morning early to put the boat on the beach. An anchor was dropped up tide and moored off the port ¼. A line was ready to row ashore, I spun the boat on the engines when bang — the dinghy painter wrapped around the starboard prop and parted. The dinghy started floating down and would be lost out to sea. The starboard engine was u.s. with the prop fouled. It would

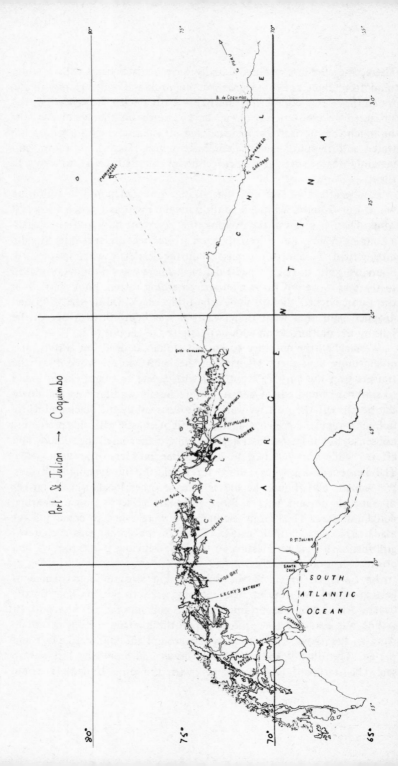

Port St. Julian → Coquimbo

take a while to get the anchor in and perhaps we would not be able to motor back against the ebb. So I grabbed a life-jacket, on with my flippers and swam for the dinghy. As I was in an exposure suit, this acted like a thin wet suit so was not too cold. I eventually caught the dinghy up. Jesus I thought — just before I reached it — I might well drown as I probably will not be able to get into it. The dinghy was well out in the stream. But I thought, I'm not giving up now! As I caught hold of the boat a dolphin surfaced nearby and I thought about all these stories of them helping drowning men. I could not lift myself over the transom with the life jacket and wet clothes. I made 2 attempts, the last pretty desperate, but it was not good. So I hooked the belt of the life-jacket on the rudder pintle, and on my back started swimming across the stream and for the shore. I kept looking upstream and saw I was making across, by two bearings moving. It was a long way and I was beginning to feel very tired — but when I looked over my shoulder the shore was not that far off — so I struggled with renewed effort. Sod I thought, can't do much more — wonder if it is deep, put my feet down and found I was in 3 feet of water.

It was a real job to lift my legs into the dinghy — not only because of the weight of water in my trousers and suit. Suddenly I realised I was almost completely exhausted, and getting very near the end of my reserves. I managed to row back to the boat keeping well inshore out of the current. All were relieved to pull me aboard *Ocean Winds*. Michael started sorting out the lines with the dinghy — Scarlett had a cup of hot alcoholic chocolate ready. I then had to call on her to help get my clothes off (all but my knickers that is) I was completely shattered from head to toe.

Mike and Scarlett had done the right thing. They had put a buoy on the anchor line all ready to slip. Mike then climbed the mast to watch me round the bend of the channel and reach safety. If it had looked like I might be drowning he would have come with just the one engine and then anchored the boat with the C.Q.R. in the channel if the one engine was not strong enough to stem the ebb. As the tides run so strong here this was very likely. Thinking afterwards, this would have been the best thing to have done anyway.

The wind was freshening — but it usually does during the day. At low water we tried the dinghy to the penguins island 2 miles towards the entrance. Almost there when, under each black cloud a hard squall hit us, and the waves were short and steep. The dolphins zoomed so close their spray was also coming aboard. It was getting too hairy, so

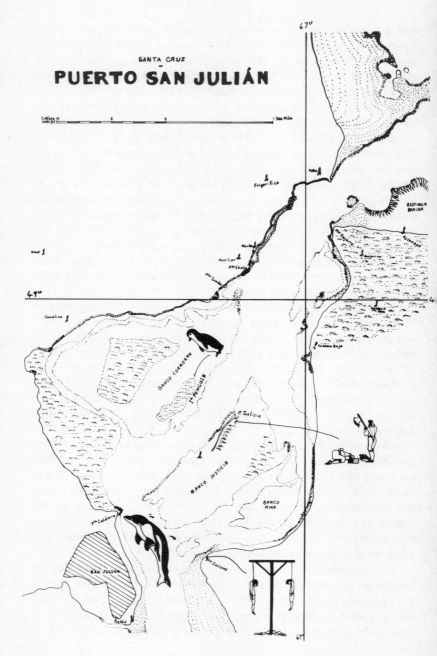

PUERTO SAN JULIÁN
SANTA CRUZ

we turned back. As well we did too, for the wind soon piped up to force 9 and we bounced hard on the beach in *Ocean Winds* when the tide came in.

I had been asked, by letter, to get some photos back for the Christmas Press. So Saturday at 4 hours ebb, we made another attempt at getting to the islands. The wind was about force 4, alright providing it did not freshen much. With the outboard on the dinghy we reached Isla Justicia – Justice Island. So called because this is where Drake meeted out summary justice on Doughty for fomenting discontent; Doughty lost his head. My well behaved crew stood on theirs on the island to have their photos taken.

The wind started to freshen – spray lopped aboard as we attempted to cross the ¼ mile channel to Penguin Isle. The outboard conked out, we rowed like hell but it started getting dangerous with the wind across the current causing a lop. So we turned round and back to Justicia. On there Michael caught a penguin and immortalised it on film. It didn't seem to mind Michael stroking it. Drake victualled on them, but we are not yet that desperate.

At the end of the island were masses of sea-birds and a colony of cormorants nesting. Black backed gulls were gliding overhead waiting to zoom down to feed on the young ones or steal the eggs. Other gulls and sea birds abounded including herons fishing in the gulley behind the isle.

As I feared we might not get back tonight, we rationed out the pint of water and saved the pint of milk for later, ½ of a pint of milk for now and ½ for lunch. The rest we saved for supper. We portaged the dinghy over the island to the gulley behind, then with the tide floating up it, crept 2 miles along it in its lee. It was hot out of the now strong wind.

I guess the wind was up to about 6 or 7 and showing every indication of increasing. With Michael and I taking an oar each, we fought our way out of the lee of the island. The tide carried us up-channel, but we could only make across in the lulls. In the gusts we lost ground. After ½ an hour, perhaps longer, of hard rowing with the sea sometimes dangerous, we turned the boat, and headed down wind, in fact surfed in to Gallows point, so named as it was where Magellan effected the ultimate discipline on two of his revolting captains.

The channel is only about ½ mile wide but for all our chance of crossing it with the dinghy, could have been 50 miles. This side of the estuary was just wind-swept scrub, with a few sheep and several hares

51

and sea birds as the only inhabitants for 20 miles and no water near. So we upturned the dinghy, went over the brow and prepared a night camp in a small dell. With such a wind we would have to control a fire carefully, so we all collected sticks and dried horse dung. Then with two hours of daylight still, decided to try and sleep before the cold of the night set in. Supper was saved until later. As the sun was setting, we were awoken by a shout. There, striding into the dell, was Ruben, an Argentinian friend made here, with a local fisherman who had seen our plight from across the channel and knew we could not get back at least before low water. Then I guess we would have made it for the channel is then but ½ its width.

Ruben had asked us, Michael and me, how we liked the Argentine women? "Don't know," I joked back "No experience." So that afternoon, as a pleasant surprise for us, he had turned up with a couple of professional ladies to make our acquaintance. Very hospitable chap, sat on the boat awaiting our return – alas all were disappointed. When he realised what had happened, he decided to call out the lifeboat in the form of his 1 ton Chevvy pick-up and drive the 40 kilometres over dirt track to our camp. I was not sorry to end our adventure so safely and early, but I do not think we would have had too much difficulty getting back at low water. But we were very tired – and salt caked. He also gave us a shower in his house to wash off the caked salt. Boy! That was really good. Went out like a light and slept very heavily.

10th Dec.   Next day, taken by an English descendant, Alan Walker, out to an estate run by another 2nd generation limey – Lionel Pickering and his wife Mary. He was a volunteer from the Argentine in the last war and was captured at Arnhem. The estancia he manages is larger than the old county of Rutland, and carries one sheep to about every 10 acres. That amounts to an awful lot of sheep. He took us out to an outlying station to see the shearing. This was done by a Chilean team under contract. Each man manages a sheep in about 2 minutes. Sweat pours off them, they are paid about ¼ dollar a sheep, so they have to go some to make money. A high proportion of the labour in Patagonia is Chilean, so if war comes, as seems possible, there will be a tremendous social problem.

For Sunday lunch we had an 'asada'. This was a whole lamb split and barbecued over an open fire. It was stretched out on a 1" X ¼" steel cross with the point impaled in the ground and carcase leaning over the fire at about 30°. This is all done by the men, though there were sons and daughters, their children, grandmothers and one cheerful great granny, Granny McClean — who was born in Yorkshire and came out in 1911 to Puntas Arenas. She moved up, on a long horse back trek, to settle on the sheep farms in Patagonia. Her grandchildren speak Spanish — but she, while fluent, insists on speaking in English. They understand mostly too. A lot of the toddlers are spoken to in words of either Spanish or English — it does not seem to matter.

A lot of the talk over the problem with Chile. Argentine claims 3 islands at the entrance to the Beagle channel. These have been disputed for years, but whenever it goes to arbitration or the Hague, it is found in Chile's favour. Well, Argentine cannot stomach this, what with the oil potential, and the fishing potential and the fact that it would allow Chile jurisdiction over 200 miles of Atlantic following the trend of the Beagle Channel. Argentine insists that the 3 virtually uninhabitable isles belong to her. So the Navy is there and the troops are moving south. A large number parked their lorries away from the boat the night before last — we were challenged going back aboard. At the moment the two states are sometimes talking to each other, but the general feeling is that the pot is coming to the boil. This may well mean that we cannot get to Puntas for Christmas which is our aim. One thing is sure, if there is a war, the border — and that means the Straits — will be closed.

11th Dec.   Been blowing a strong gale from the SW all morning. I planned to leave on the night tide, all very doubtful, and then in the afternoon the wind moderated and went to the East. Got my mail all ready for off. Some problem with changing money, the banks would not. Fortunately Ruben offered to change pounds, so Scarlett went off with him clutching 30 pounds. I go off to the Prefectura to arrange clearance. Back on board, while she and Mike are off to buy the victuals (we were flat before the money exchange) I made the evening stew and generally sorted out on board. A routine check of the bilges — and in the galley, water was almost up to the floorboards. Mike had removed the log impeller to clear the bilge of gas, leaving the floorboard up so the rest of us would see but going away forgetting he had left open a 2 inch hole in the bottom of the boat. Scarlett, seeing the floor-board up thought 'that's dangerous, someone will break their leg falling into the bilge,' so replaced it. I was in the middle of a big bilge pumping session by the time they returned — unfortunately minus a whole cheese which they had somehow lost. There was no time to go back and look for it if we were to catch the tide. So, somewhat shortly, I tell them to get cracking on getting the dinghy aboard and the anchors up and we leave just as dusk is setting in. This was only just in time, as several of the leading lights no longer work and the entrance is a mass of sandbanks and with sluicing tides, so any error in navigation could be disastrous.

It was a headwind thump out of the channel for the wind was actually from the north — a fair wind of force 4, a very rare beast! I kept telling myself this is too good to last, but hour after hour a fair wind. It was a very good night, sailing at 5 or 6 knots. A red dawn and a falling barometer augered ill and through the morning the wind was piping up from the NW. Several times we had her sailing at 7 knots. We were about 5 miles from Santa Cruz bar when the wind increased to a full gale. Scarlett deep reefed the main and we rolled up the jib to handkerchief size. Being only a mile off the shore the seas were short but not big and giving us quite a bouncy ride.

We approached the bar. We had an Admiralty harbour chart from a survey done in 1948. Had the bar changed? We crossed it at a deeper point than on the leading marks as it was only an hour from low water but this meant taking cross bearings and quick plots. We were making progress while the wind was force 7 or less, but the stronger (8—9) gusts stopped us. We had both engines going flat out for it was dead up-wind. The echo sounder showed down to 7 feet and then got deeper. Phew!

Helped by the deep reefed main the engines managed to push us across the channel to the lee of a 500 ft cliff where we dropped the big fisherman anchor in 3 fathoms on what the chart reckons is a stony bottom. At times, in the gusts, the wind indicator shows force 9. We are about a cable (600 ft) from the shore and the waves are almost 2 feet high.

The tide has started to flood and we are beam on to the wind. Not a happy position but the anchor, all 56 lbs, appears to be holding. I had Michael bind the anchor warp where it passes over the bow roller in case of chafe, and we have a 30 lb weight on the warp 30 feet ahead of us; this helps the warp act as a spring. Scarlett has just made a soupy stew. We are hoping the wind will back with the tide. It is now 5.30 p.m. High water is at 10 p.m. and the town anchorage is 14 miles up the estuary, which at the moment, is dead up-wind. The barometer shows 971 mb steady which is very, very low. When it blows a gale here it does so out of a vivid blue sky. The only point in its favour, coming off the land the wind is also usually dry and not too cold.

Well the wind did back, but not moderate. This meant that we were exposed to the seas. It all happened very quickly so just as quickly the decision was made to up anchor. Unfortunately just at that moment Michael was taken short, so to speak, but as the waves were getting decidedly nasty he could not enjoy a leisurely crap. Michael pulled on the anchor line, Scarlett was to clear it and take a turn around the cleat as necessary. I was on the helm with both motors going full blast. Scarlett managed to take a jamming turn. The bows were held down by the anchor warp and the weight of Michael and Scarlett must have made a difference. Even with her high bows and buoyancy forward, waves came sweeping up and Michael and Scarlett were enveloped in clouds of spume. It looked most spectacular and dangerous. It was also touch and go as to whether we could get it in or if we would have to buoy the anchor line and ship the cable — a thing I was loath to do as that fisherman anchor is the most versatile anchor on board.

In the end we managed it thanks to our two little engines and Michael's strength. The cable was brought back to the cockpit to be sorted out ready to let go again and also to make sure it did not go over the side. Then a shackle pin bounced on the deck. The boom had come half loose. Scarlett managed to replace the pin for we might well need a bit of main if the engines failed.

We zoomed up the first bit of channel with the wind and current with us. On the corner was good too with the wind abeam but then in the narrows we could see up ahead, was a wall of white water. It was blowing force 9 against a 6 knot current. The waves were about 6 feet high and seemed vertical. The air was thick with spray. I had to try and keep the bows dead into the wind for when they got off she was immediately blown beam on and then I had to put one engine in reverse and one in ahead and with the helm hard over, fight her back on course. The engines, struggling valiantly, but only 7½ h.p. each, could only just hold us. It was the strong current which carried us through. The waves swept over the top of us — very rare that this happens on *Ocean Winds*. I could see little through my salt encrusted glasses. Michael was the eyes and was trying to identify the leading marks while Scarlett's job was to call out the depths but unfortunately the water was too aerated for the echo sounder to work.

Once through the narrows, I put the wind on the starboard bow and slowly crabbed across and near the shore by a naval base. The wind and seas eased somewhat and we made up to Santa Cruz.

We were tired and thoroughly salted, so did not attempt to land — ignoring the military men shouting from the shore. The wind was too strong to row the 30 yards to shore anyway. It was time for a whisky or two (actually 4).

Even in the morning it was still blowing a gale and to get ashore I decided the safest way was to motor up on the anchor, and then run the boat aground. We now have a line ashore with the dinghy on an endless whip so no one can miss the boat and get blown across the estuary when ferrying to and from the boat.

15th Dec. Santa Cruz has, in normal times, a population of 1,500. It had trebled with an armed soldier on guard at most corners. The atmosphere is getting very tense. Argentine has said Chile can have the three islands but not the sea rights into the Atlantic — that is the trend of the Beagle Channel. Chile does not agree. The vast numbers of lorries armaments and troops that have passed through here over the past week makes me amazed at the size of Argentina's war machine. Quite frightening for us, sailing down to the frontier. The road frontier is closed but the Straits are still open to shipping — at the moment. When getting the departure papers from the Coastguard the Chief first said "Not possible". I have a lot of faith in the semi-military being wrong, so we left in beautiful weather at high water, sailing gently down the estuary to the sound of hoots and waves from the several friends made in Santa Cruz.

It has been jolly interesting visiting Patagonia; the early history is only a generation away. We had tea yesterday with a Miss Halliday and her brother whose parents came from Scotland at the end of the last century as pioneer sheep farmers. On their dining room wall was a sepia photo of 'mama' in Victorian dress and looking frail and lovely. Yet she must have been really tough for it was only a few years prior to her arrival that Darwin had explored up the Santa Cruz river just failing by a day's journey to reach Lake Argentina.

We left with a light favourable wind which outside the bar picked up to a grand force 3/4 easterly for the sail south. A fair wind and a falling barometer probably means a gale by tomorrow. At the moment I am more frightened of the Patagonian gales than the combined navies of Chile and Argentina. When the firing starts I expect to speedily revise that opinion.

16th Dec. Morning dawned overcast with the barometer slowing its fall. The wind was quickly freshening from the west so I set the course for the cliffs due south. The coast trends SSE and for 15 miles NNW of Cabo Virgenes cliffs fall sheer to a steep beach. We reached them during Scarlett's watch, sailing under deep reefed main and very small jib. Again it was blowing a gale. Under the lee of the cliffs we paid off down the coast in 8 fathoms. The shelter reduced the wind to force 5/6 but I kept all the reefs in as we were mostly sailing at 5 knots and the wind really hurt as it came screaming down the valleys between the cliffs.

10 miles from Cape Virgenes we made in to 6 fathoms and dropped the fisherman with the anchor weight. After a lunch of soup and wine, I got my head down while Scarlett kept anchor watch and Michael sorted out the dinghy outboard motor. After little more than 2 hours I leapt out of my berth, awoken by an engine roaring away. Panic stations, I thought, to start an engine. But no, it was Michael testing the outboard.

The weather had changed. The barometer was steady and a gentle wind of force 2 had started from the SE. A front had passed about ¼ hour earlier and all was now different. A good job Michael woke me. So up with the anchor and mainsail and, using the starboard engine, motored along to Cabo Virgenes with the last of the south going tide.

Lady Luck really smiled; we carried the tide to the Cape and with Michael using the sextant to measure the distance off the shore we skirted the shoal and 2 miles off we sailed along the inner channel which is only suitable for small craft. The tide was still fair past Dungeness Light and the weather incredibly fine. We could hardly believe our luck. A fair tide and fair weather — what evil is brewing? We toasted our entry into Chilean waters with good Plymouth Gin and had a busy photographing session. A school of black and white (Commerson's) dolphins welcomed us to Chile. Tierra del Fuego is lit with oil flares but there was no sign of the military. As the BBC news made no mention of the dispute we guess the two countries are not yet at war.

We have 6 hours of fair tide (time 8.00 p.m.). I am desperately hoping that our fine spell lasts. The weather here changes so rapidly, and almost always for the worse. I have the tin can oven on the stove with a leg of lamb inside and onions roasting. Potatoes are boiled and ready for tossing in hot fat. But banks of dark cloud loom ahead.

17th Dec.   We motored through the night — mostly with just the

57

starboard engine. As it was calm at the entrance to the first narrows, and by my calculation, still with two hours of fair tide, I decided to carry on through. With at least 5 knots of current under us it did not take long either. There were big tidal eddies and whirls which threw us about but seemed not to worry our accompanying dolphins one jot. As dawn was breaking we made up into Gregory Bay (which pleased Scarlett as it is her maiden name) and anchored just after the tide turned foul. We dropped two anchors and all went to bed.

At the change of tide morning was well on and the usual gale was setting in. The barometer was very low. I expected it rough as where we were there was a 2½ mile fetch against a 2–3 knot current. So we sweated up the anchors and motored 4 miles to Puerto Sara. I decided against beating through the 2nd narrows as, with the wind blowing between force 5 and 8 and dead against a 5 knot current, my guess is that it would be really nasty.

Two hours before nightfall it had calmed down a lot. We just floated with the rising tide, I having earlier miscalculated the tidal range. Fortunately a cat does not hurt going aground on a smooth bottom – this was hard clayey sand. I was a bit doubtful as to whether or not to try and shoot the narrows as the gusts were still fresh and I did not know if they would increase blowing straight up the narrows. It was half tide which is the turn of the tide here. Funny old business – I guess there must be a strong undercurrent for it does not make sense the tide going out and rising at the same time unless it is something to do with the fact that it can also flood in at a different time from the Pacific and up the channels from the south.

Tides are also peculiar at the opposite end of this great continent. At the Northern tip of Labrador the tide has a rise of 10 feet while through the McClellan Straits in Ungava Bay the range is 18 feet. This means there is a slope with a 14 knot current – slack water is also at about half tide. The major difference between the two Straits is the distance. You crack the McClellan Straits in a day, particularly, if like we had in 1966, you have an Eskimo pilot to take you via the back eddies. The Magellan Straits is over 200 miles long with the town of Puntas Arenas about half way.

We approached the 2nd narrows and oddly, instead of freshening, the wind fell right away. So we just plonked through on both engines. Night had fallen by the time we got through, so with Scarlett on the helm, Mike taking frequent bearings which I plotted, we found our way across to the west and anchored 3 miles SW of Whitsand Bay and Rame

Head. We dropped the anchor on some kelp, but backing off with the engines the anchor held firm so we left it. This kelp is thick and long. Josh Slocum moored to some to wait over a foul tide. He measured some in the Straits at 180 feet long. Capt. Cook found some 360 feet long in the Keguelens.

To the south lay Elizabeth Island and Pelican Passage, named by Drake 400 years earlier. I wonder if he also named Whitsand Bay and Rame Head as they also lay at the entrance to Plymouth Sound.

Because the pilot warns that by mid-morning the wind in this area generally increases to gale force I wished to be up at first light. I decided to doze all standing (fully clothed) in the saloon. Scarlett made a warming drink of hot chocolate liberally laced with vodka (one of her many specialities) which assured us of a sound sleep. I woke at dawn twilight and thought — just another half hour. Luckily Scarlett woke an hour later and called me. Mike was not pleased at being shouted 3 times. The anchor was thick with kelp which had to be cut away before we could move off at 5 a.m. A breeze was already hardening in. We drove south for two miles then turned right into the very sheltered bay of Puerto Zenteno where we anchored in 6 feet of water in front of an estancia.

Through the glasses we could see that the estancia was occupied by an army platoon. The local peons were in a bunk-house 100 yards away. Over the brow of the hill appeared a horseman herding a dozen horses for the day's work. We prepared the dinghy to go ashore to show them our documents. Knowing the military mind this was certain to be necessary. Half way through the preparations they shouted from the shore. Mike gave a wave. But as we did not set off shorewards immediately they borrowed a dinghy and tried rowing out to us. The wind was freshening to force 6. I had to despatch Mike with the outboard to go and rescue them as they were being fast blown out to sea. We took them back ashore with me rowing their boat and Mike towing us.

The Estancia workmen invited us into the bunkhouse for a doughnut and a coffee. Unfortunately our Spanish is so limited the conversation is less than stimulating. The grass here is much greener and thicker (though thin enough) than in Argentine Patagonia. Here they have black and white cows and even a pig grunting merrily away chewing bits of raw sheep thrown it for breakfast.

As we had anchored in 6 feet with the tide not quite full and the pilot suggesting a tidal range of only a metre, I expected to remain just afloat. Actually we dried out by 6 inches, but on mud so it mattered little. It is a lovely anchorage and as the wind howled and the rain, hail and sleet poured upon us I was glad to be here. Almost mid-summer and so cold. I guess we will be here at least a day waiting for the weather to improve. Puntas Arenas is only 25 miles away but I would prefer to sail there with little, or better still, no excitement as befits a gentleman of my advancing years.

While here I have sorted out the next run of charts. I find I am missing the large scale one of the southern part of the Straits. While we can probably manage on the small scale one, it is taking an unnecessary risk so I hope a large scale one will be available in Puntas. (It was.)

Essayed making bread in the frying pan. Forgot to add the salt otherwise I think it would have been alright although not good. Scarlett has been writing out a list of jobs before we tackle the SW strait. So far she has 16 lined up. These include sewing in an extra very very deep reef in the mainsail. The present reef is alright up to force 8 to 9 but then we need something up to 100 knots so it's hey ho, and a deep, deep reef. It is surprising how much a little mainsail helps the engines. It holds the boat up to the wind whereas without sail, in the gusts the bows get blown right off. Considering we have sailed about 9,000 miles our list of jobs is surprisingly short. Even so, we need at least a quiet 4 days to get through them.

19th Dec.   Late afternoon; the wind still gusting strong but periods of almost quiet. The barometer still very low. As the wind here seems to moderate at night, and we were only 25 miles from Puntas, and if we stayed put we would be aground in an hour, I decided we would sail. We bombed out of the harbour with just the reefed main set.

The wind was a good force 6. As soon as we cleared the entrance to Puerto Zeneto it freshened up to 8 which is gale force. Then increased to force 9 (strong gale) and the sea got decidedly popply. To make matters worse, we were entangled with a large bank of kelp which was impossible to dodge, so we just let the wind drive us through at 5 knots. I feared for the propellers, but as they fold like a duck's bill when sailing nothing entangled in them.

Clear of the kelp, I started the port (leeward) motor to keep the leeway at a minimum. Mike wanted to up helm and sail around the eastward side of Elizabeth Island. This meant going back and the water mostly too deep to anchor. The wind was strong from the WSW. So I kept her hard on the wind trying to get across the channel and to weather. If any problem did develop then we would turn tail and run for the other side of Elizabeth Isle. At times that wind was really hard. With virtually no fetch the seas were still a good two feet and very short and as we clobbered them, oh bitterly cold spray slammed my face. It felt as if icicles should be forming on my beard. I was relieved when I could definitely see that the SW end of Elizabeth Isle was moving relative to the land beyond. We were weathering it okay. It was definitely a mistake sailing in such wind. Michael was obviously ticking — criticism oozing from his bearing. I ignored it. When I stop making mistakes I will be in a wheel chair or pushing up daises.

The wind really was piping up and so when I realised I could keep her safely beam on with just the two engines, we handed the main. This was a case of needing that planned deep deep reef. Beam on, a yacht does not blow down wind because of her underwater shape. So with both engines and the wind up to force 10 (storm) we reached boldly down to Pelican Passage at a good 6 knots, then ran off before it around the Cape and into the lee of the cliffs. There all was quiet with a local fishing boat sheltering at anchor. We joined it, dropping just the 35 lb C.Q.R. and a 30 lb weight halfway along the anchor line.

That night, despite being in the lee of the cliffs, the wind really howled. The boat shuddered. I kept leaping up to check from shore lights that we were not dragging. The C.Q.R. held firmly. That is a really good anchor given a bottom into which it can dig. How strong it blew I do not know. Certainly some of the worst we have, so far, been anchored against. A good job there was no sea and we had those 200 foot high cliffs ahead.

It was but a 14 mile sail south to Puntas. I got the crew up at 5 a.m. and within half an hour we were sailing. A good sail too as the wind had moderated to a respectable force 6; it was a close fetch under deep reef and small jib. Even so we made better than 6 knots very comfortably. It is bitterly cold. This is about the same latitude south as London is north and midsummer. It felt like a bitter January day off the North of Scotland.

We looked around the harbour before deciding where to anchor or tie up. It looked quietest to the NW end of the jetty in 10 feet of water alongside a pilot boat. There, waiting on the quay was Alan Grey. He had decided to come south and be with Scarlett for Christmas, which is very nice for her. Since he left us in Montevideo we have been a happier ship, I suspect because we all realise that being down to the minimum of crew we have to rely on each other. With four people on board the frictions are greater.

In the harbour office I have had to spend a day with a Naval lieutenant making a plan of the voyage up through the channels. How in fact it will all work out is in the lap of the Gods for in such an area of strong unpredictable weather one may not make the progress one hopes for or even go where one wishes. So we have planned for 15 miles a day for 1,000 miles. The Navy to some extent appreciates the problem and as we are in a war zone such bureaucratic nonsense has to be tolerated. Also if one does get into trouble, the Chilean Navy has a good reputation for rescuing stranded yachts.

I had a look around the shops today. I wonder how anyone can live. Meat is cheap, but clothes and materials are a frightful price, sometimes as much as double the cost in England. However wine is not only good, it is also cheap. Get pissed in poverty.

21st Dec.   This evening scrounged a shower in a Danish ammunition ship. Glad war was not declared as a bomb on that lot would have had us all playing harps. The Skipper said his Company told him he had permission to sail through Argentine waters to enter the Straits which he found hard to believe as he was carrying ammunition which in case of war would be used against the Argentines. Otherwise he would have had to sail around the Horn and in the western entrance which, in such a small ship (the size of a coaster) could have proved hairy.

A seismic survey vessel, *Western Shoal*, took us under their wing and let us use their showers; gave us Christmas dinners aboard and ashore. They are working between the 1st and 2nd narrows for the Chilean petrol company making a very detailed seismic survey. There are some very pleasant helpful guys on board of many nationalities, mostly English speaking ones, but do they drink! Not on board though, as the Captain runs a dry ship and also bans women other than as guests in the galley/diner. They sink enough liquor in port though. To them I am indebted for the statistic that there are 43 whorehouses in Puntas Arenas.

The British Consul here was very helpful and apart from collecting our mail for us, very kindly entertained us for Christmas tea. The Consul had waiting for us a new motor for the self-steering pilot which Alan soldered in. He and Scarlett also sewed in the new 'Cape Horn' reef in the main so now we can reduce the sail to about 65 sq. ft.

On Boxing day the navy made our bathroom *(Western Shoal)* move to anchor a mile out. Very inconsiderate of them, particularly as they took the berth up with two Navy ships. In fact they took over the whole pier with their fleet. We gather that Argentina has also withdrawn her fleet from the Beagle Channel area.

The Port Captain gave me clearance (first, by mistake, another ship's which caused some red faces) and instructions that I must keep to the stated track. So on the 30th Dec. 1978 I roused the crew at 6 a.m., dumped Alan ashore with his bags and he cast us off. We were away with a force 4 wind towards the snow clad mountains that could be seen to the south. A 10 day stay in port is too long so I am glad to get away.

It was soon necessary to bend in a reef in the mainsail so we tried the new deep one. This proved the right amount, rigging her as a cutter with an inner storm jib and the genny rolled up small which we could let out in the lulls. The wind was varying between force 3 and 7 and so cold. The ship sped along, sometimes up to 8 knots so after Point St. Anna I thought we might as well try for the next anchorage 10 miles south. 5 miles later it was blowing really hard and drawing more ahead. So we gybed around and zoomed back to Puerto de Hambre where we anchored in 6 feet of water. Now it is blowing hard, pouring with rain and a beam swell setting in. I reckon a swell has to be caused by very strong winds and the last one, on Christmas Eve proved all too true a prognostication — it blew force 10 at Puntas on Christmas Day.

This place was first settled by Sarmiento in 1584 to repulse any further English incursions after Drake. Alas the going was hard and when Thomas Cavendish visited here in 1587 it was already ruined with only skeletons left. He renamed it Port Famine. Now, facing us across shallow water, is a deserted settlement of rusting corrugated iron — I guess about 50 years old.

31st Dec.   I got up at 5 a.m. hoping all would be quiet and so beat the strong day wind. It was gusting strong and raining, so I killed the alarm in Scarlett's cabin and went back to mine. 1½ hours later I was awoken by an apologetic Scarlett who thought she had slept through it. As it seemed to be a little quieter, and the sun came out at 8 a.m. I decided on a leisurely breakfast and then sail. The mountains to the south and east looked beautiful in a fresh cloak of snow.

Sailing from our quiet anchorage was a mistake. We were close on the wind and not laying our course with the wind reaching up to gale force in the gusts. The starboard engine was kept going to help us keep tight to the wind. It was hard, but marginally less rough and windy tacking along close to the shore. We had the tide under us which, while helping as it was wind against current, caused an evil head sea. At one stage I was about to give up like yesterday but Michael persuaded me to carry on to the next anchorage. It was particularly nasty rounding Cabo Isidrio where the seas seemed about 10 feet high and about 30 feet apart. I was on tenterhooks in case anything, particularly rigging, should part, as this is no place in which to lose a mast. It was with no small relief we got into the lee in Bay del Aguila. There was deep water right up to the head. Michael was sounding with the hand lead as the echo sounder is no longer working. We were almost ashore before he found the bottom. So we dropped the fisherman near the beach, hoisted the dinghy over and rowed the C.Q.R. out astern in case of a windshift. We also put out a line ashore off the port bow.

This is a gorgeous little anchorage — well worth the pain getting here. Michael saw some hares so we made an expedition ashore with the gun — of course they had vanished. There used to be a small pier here and a saw mill. Traces of the old timber shoot remain down the mountainside. There is still a lot of timber left and the price of wood now what it is one wonders that work is not recommenced. At Port Zenteno, less than a degree (60 nautical miles to each degree of latitude) to the north there are no trees, only grassland. Here there is so much more rain. The change in such a short distance of both terrain and weather is very marked. The weather goes from terrible to sheer terrifying. I dread the turn right around Cabo Froward for by all accounts the weather then really deteriorates.

1st January 1979

The alarm woke me at 5 a.m. It was flat calm, with a slight drizzle. How I wanted to go back to bed but could not miss such an opportunity for making progress, so shouted the crew out, and in Mike's case it has to be loud at that unearthly hour. What with rowing ashore to retrieve the shore line, weigh two anchors and hoist up the dinghy it was 1½ hours before we got sailing. We motored out under just the starboard engine — it was very still so we chuntered south west at 5 knots. Some difference from yesterday. We ran one hour tricks on the helm. I was dozing in the saloon dreaming of tropic isles and hula girls when Scarlett wiggled my left boot.

"Come and see Cabo Froward," she said.

It was black and forbidding; wreathed with mist and rain. So one mad photo and a celebration of hot lemon/rum toddy. Mike refused to interrupt his kip to look at the most southerly tip of the American mainland. 2 hours later a head wind set in but only force 4 so we hoisted sail and keeping on the motor, beat up to Fortescue Bay and into Port Gallant which is wholly protected. The C.Q.R. was dropped in 3 fathoms at high water in gooey black mud. With such holding, am not bothering with a second anchor. We have made good over 40 miles today which has to be exceptional.

Off on two abortive duck shoots. The steamboat duck runs ahead using its wings as paddle wheels. It can go at over 10 knots. There were a lot of ducks and some geese here, but cunningly resting over soggy marsh so out of range. We ate the last of our fresh meat today.

Morning dawned damp and still with a rising barometer. This is not the Straits weather I have read about. We motored out of Port Gallant chasing a steamboat duck with Mike as marksman on the bows. It ran behind an island and so kept out of range.

Past Cape Gallant there was a force 2 headwind so with just the mainsail, which we left reefed to the 2nd points, expecting the wind to blast out at us at any moment, we motor sailed through Paso Ingles. Here the current is strong so you must go with the flood stream. Mussel Bay on Isla Carlos III opened up to port. This was where Drake victualled with mussels which grow to the size of your feet and so are called 'shoe mussels' and are prolific all along the coast. Two ships going east passed us with a wave and a hoot. We carried the tide past this island and at the infamous Cabo Crosstide the steering was thrown a little with the big upwelling bubbles — like sailing through boiling water — but there being no wind it was not too bad. The pilot says 'The weather in this part of the straight is very unstable due to two air masses of different characteristics meeting, one from the main strait and the other coming down Canal Jeronimo. Violent squalls with heavy rain and low cloud may reduce visibility to zero.' Phew!

Paso Tortuosa was no problem either. A few miles to port could be seen the lower slopes of a glacier with its ice fall. The mountain tops were covered by cloud which is usual. On the charts it frequently says 'height approximate' for peaks over 3,000 feet are rarely seen. A beautiful white arch was seen to the NW. Was this the dreaded, to quote Josh Slocum, 'old familiar white arch, the terror of Cape Horn rapidly pushed up by a SW gale.'?

We motored across to the other side of the channel and into Caleta Notch. You thread your way between islands and into a land locked cove. We disturbed some steamer ducks. Mike, with four shots, got one. Big grey plumed birds they are, with a bright orange beak. Hanging about close to the shore while Mike and Scarlett collected it with the dinghy, I scraped the starboard keel on a rock, which heart stopped me, but all was okay.

We dropped an anchor astern and a rope ashore and lay in 3 fathoms. The bird was hung off a tree's branch for us to pluck. It was thick with down. Not many ducks would be required for a superb duvet. But what a job to pluck! And then it was too big for our oven and when cooked, which we did by quartering and frying very slowly, proved more suitable for soleing one's shoes than filling the stomach. We also picked some mussels which were rather easier on the teeth and quite tasty. From its innards apparently the duck also feeds off the abundant mussels.

3rd Jan.   Caleta Notch is a superb anchorage although Slocum did not enthuse over it — I suspect because without an engine it would have been difficult for him to get behind the islands. You line up a stone cairn on the hill with a white stone with rust marks on the shore. This leads you through the islands — then left then right and you are in an enclosed basin surrounded by mountains. This morning, armed with cameras, we struggled to the top of the one to the SW and built a cairn (very small). After so much inactivity the climb made my ticker bang like mad. We were all dressed for the cold with polar suits, sweaters over trousers and waterproofs and climbed in sea boots. We were soaked with sweat. The mountain sides are a botanist's paradise. Very remarkable are the pillars of moss growing on some rocks. These grow vertically for about 18 inches. They could easily be dislodged from the rocks and I am surprised they can stand up to the winds here. Scarlett and I got lost on the way down so Mike was back aboard an hour before us. I was anxious to get sailing as the weather was still so good — and this the third day. The other two complain that I am pushing ahead too fast but I feel we have such an exceptional weather break we must take advantage of it.

It took us only about 20 minutes to get the two anchors up, the shore line in and the dinghy stowed, which we thought good. Motoring out steamboat ducks paddled ahead in a flurry of water. The glaciers here are impressive, particularly the ice falls which almost reach the sea. As we left rather late in the day we only made 15 miles to east. Rocalloso where we dropped our stern anchor in 12 fathoms and motored against it slowly almost to the shore to drop the fisherman

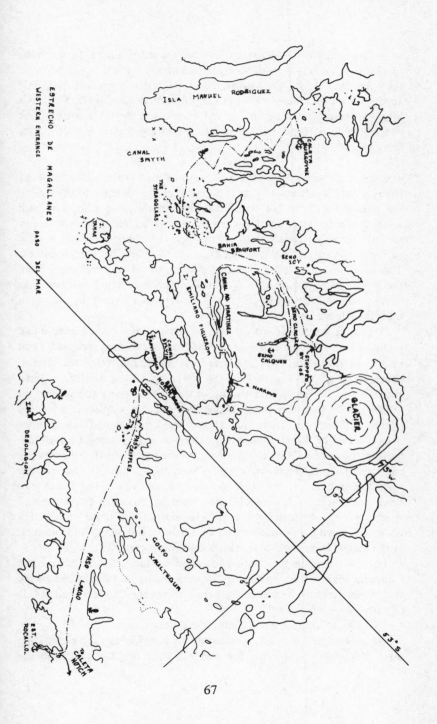

ESTRECHO DE MAGALLANES
WESTERN ENTRANCE

PASO DEL MAR

ISLA MANUEL RODRIGUEZ

CANAL SMYTH

CALETA QUIRAGONNE

THE STRAGGLERS

I. YAMA

BAHIA BEAUFORT

SENO ICY

I. EMILIANO FIGUEROA

CANAL AO. MARTINEZ

SENO CLOQUE

STOPPED BY ICE

CANAL SILVA

ISLA DESOLACION

PASO CRIPPLES

SENO CALQUEN

I NARROWS

GLACIER

PASO LAROO

GOLFO XAULTEGUA

EST. ROCALLO.

CALETA NOTCH

53° S

in 4 fathoms, then middled up and took a warp ashore to the head of the cove which is from where I reckon strong winds will hit us if they decide to blow. On English charts this place is marked on as Isla Jacques but on Chilean ones as Isla Desolacion. An apt name. The isle is long and thin stretching out to the Pacific and for the most part the shore line is hatched on the charts indicating that it is only partly surveyed.

4th Jan.   It was so quiet the boat was reflected in the water. With the trusty diesel we chugged away at 5 knots for the entrance to the straits. We passed inside of Isle Richardson and along canal Cripples where some fur seals were jumping clear of the water. The glass was steady at 1010 mb. so I decided to go up Seno Northbrook which is only partly surveyed and try and get through to Canal Admiral Martinez. The pilot describes it thus: 'Canal contra Ad. Martinez extends from the N side of Seno Northbrook for 10 miles NW to Bahia Beaufort; it is narrow with a least depth of 1.2 m (4½ ft) and can only be used with local knowledge.'

At 4 p.m. we turned up through the first narrows. Michael sounded — down to 2 fathoms where there had been a terminal moraine. Then into a deeper basin. The 2nd narrows, looking through the glasses, appeared to be thick with kelp. So we launched the dinghy for Mike and Scarlett to first sound through before attempting the passage in *Ocean Winds*. Dolphins were playing in the narrows or perhaps feeding if they like mussels. There was, according to my calculations, another 3½–4 hours of flood tide. Fortunately it was flowing through the narrows against us. Mike and Scarlett returned after a difficult sounding exercise. They told me there was 6 foot right through. First on the starboard side and at the other end on the port side — but it was very thick with kelp — too much, they thought, for it to be possible. I was very loath to turn back as drawing only 3 feet there was enough water so, leaving the dinghy tied to the side and with the fisherman at the dangle from the bows, made a cautious approach.

Halfway through the motors laboured terribly. 'Let go Mike,' and I cut the engines back to nuetral. We were anchored to kelp. Mike then rowed out ahead to the end of the narrows with the C.Q.R. It had 300 ft of warp on it, just enough.

"You look fantastic stuck there." he shouted back.

We cleared the props — fortunately an easy job as they are folding ones which close and allow the weed to slide off. We hauled up the

68

fisherman — Mike having to cut the kelp away leaning over from the dinghy before it could be lifted clear of the water, then all hands to haul us forward. She stuck firm — aground on the port hull. Mike sheered her with the anchor, I gunned her on the port engine then Scarlett and I bounced on the starboard quarter. She came free. Quickly back to the helm and straighten up the rudders. Mike and Scarlett were pulling us through nicely when clonk — stopped short. Hard aground on the starboard keel this time. I thought it must be a rock the way she stopped, but no. Through a patch clear of kelp you could see the enormous mussels. Guess we gave one a headache. Slackened the anchor line, the boat hook bent as Mike shoved us aft, then with the engines in reverse, off she came — alas, almost immediately to go back on. We obviously had to get her to sheer right across to port and tight to the shore. Another go — Mike and Scarlett sheering us on the anchor line while I played the engines and the rudders. Then we were through after half an hour of real sweat and graft. The C.Q.R. was brought aboard as we motored out into very deep water once more with the dolphins playing all around us. As this is glaciated fiord country the rocks and shoals rise very steeply from deep water. But it was an interesting exercise though not one I would care to repeat.

It was a 10 mile drive to Bay Beaufort then 5 miles to Seno Icy, 5 miles along Seno Glacier before we could turn into Seno Caiqun for the night. The sun was setting, lighting up snow clad mountains in a rosy glow. We could find no bottom at the recommended anchorage off the waterfall, so went on and tied up between two islands. The aft islet, for want of something better, Mike had to take a turn right around as it was bare of rocks to tie to. Fortunately we carry two 300 ft warps which are proving essential for shore moorings.

5th Jan. We wanted to see the glacier falling into the sea, so were away by 8 a.m. motoring out on another calm morning. The glass has started to fall so this rare calm is not expected to last much longer. We motored as far as some narrows but could get no further as it was blocked with brash ice coming out with the current and light wind. We still could not see around the corner to where the glacier fell into the sea only two miles away so had to be content with collecting some ice for the ice bucket then turned back for Bay Beaufort and Canal Smyth. Surprisingly over the ice came flights of king Cormorants. Steamer ducks were disturbed; seals and dolphins were sporting around so there must be plenty of fish here.

As it was calm, instead of going all round the 'Stragglers' I decided on a tricky piece of navigation through Paso Leucoton, past Isle Mogote and into Paso Labbe. This would save 2 hours and be more interesting to boot. I pre-plotted the courses and looked on the chart for possible transits for it was a narrow but deep pass through many rocks and islands. Almost always the shallow rocks are marked with kelp, so if you avoid that you avoid rocks. Michael had just finished preparing lunch when we entered so I told him it would have to wait three quarters of an hour. He was not pleased. It was not a gourmet's lunch, and when we did eventually have it, not better for being cold.

Once through the pass we at last had a wind — of course straight down Canal Smyth so it was a beat to windward for the next few hours. As we passed Isle Fairway which is in radio contact with Puntas Arenas, we saw three men standing at the base of the lighthouse. Scarlett dipped the ensign — the lighthouse dipped their flag so back up went ours. All very proper.

We reached the first anchorage, Caleta Burgoyne, with a falling barometer and a freshening N wind, and tied up at the head of the lagoon to a big steel mooring buoy — I presume laid by the Chilean Navy for the lighthouse supply ship. Ashore we collected mussels which I plan to fry in batter and have with rice. Then to celebrate the successful navigation of the straits, opened Peter Greenwood's present given me over a year ago and marked: 'Not to be opened until Cape Horn is astern'. Well, as the Horn is now well astern, we found inside a Christmas card and a bottle of champagne, which we drank sitting in the cockpit looking at some wonderful scenery. The empty bottle we re-corked leaving inside a cheerfully asinine note and tied it to the buoy to disappoint the next mariner to pass this way.

6th Jan.   Morning dawned wet and dull. As we all were too, we remained abed for most of the morning. Then Scarlett and Mike went exploring the cove in the dinghy while I read a book. We washed our hair, watered the ship from the brook which fell into the cove. Scarlett cooked a mussel appetizer which, while tasty, was so under-cooked in the middle. What do you say? 'Made a pig's ear of that' when she has spent some considerable time and effort on trying a real special. So we both made a few commiserating grunts. Actually the mussels, even raw, had a lovely flavour. This is a lovely anchorage — easy of entry, attractive with a backdrop of mountains, but then down here they are all exceedingly picturesque. Ever since Bay del Aquila every anchorage has been gorgeous. There is a remote grandeur about them which defies description. This afternoon actually gave a fair wind and we did not take advantage of it.

7th Jan. Up betimes at 6 a.m. After a cup of tea I leisurely got the boat sailing by myself. This is easy when moored to a buoy. Just hoist the main, single up on the mooring line and walk it round to the starboard then slip it through the eye of the buoy. Walk aft and let the genny unroll and you are off at 4 knots for the entrance. Scarlett surfaced and made paranoid superfluous comments about me sailing the boat off without calling for her somewhat excellent assistance at coiling the ropes. Mike made no paranoid comments whatsoever. In fact, 2 hours later when called for his watch said "Are we sailing?"

It was, of course, a beat up the channel. Another sodding head wind. God! How I hate head winds. Scarlett and Mike quite enjoyed the sailing. Tack, head up, tack — all day of beating to windward up channels about a mile wide through mountainous and spectacular scenary.

That evening, Michael asks — "What, Pat, do you like about sailing?"

"Getting pissed in the evening," I replied.

In a tone of utter amazement Scarlett exclaimed "Do you really?" Answer, amid the chuckles, came there none as Scarlett emptied the last of the apricot liqueur into her glass.

In the channels were two groups of fishermen, who, after catching a number of fish, then smoke them ashore. These they trade with passing vessels. The smoked fish were not so good as our kippers or even smoked mackerel but tonight, to the south of us there are some happy fishermen tippling a bottle of Vodka and Cinzano.

For the last hour we gave up sailing and plugged on direct under motor to get into Port Welcome off Smyth Channel. Using the superb chart atlas given to us by the Chilean Navy ship *Aquilas* at Christmas, the harbour plan showed how to enter and we came to anchor in 3½ fathoms. These anchorages are called ports, but not to be confused with our ports, as here there are no people, docks or houses. They are just remote, but usually sheltered anchorages. We let go our trusty C.Q.R. as the lead by its feel suggested it might be mud. With the engine hard in reverse we dragged it back. Hauling it up we found mussel shell and hard clay — too hard for the C.Q.R. to get its point in. So it was down with the fisherman. Full astern — it had bitten well, so we added the 30 lb weight and more warp to make doubly sure. I stipulate that when these boats are supplied, they have as standard a 20 kg fisherman, 3 fathoms of chain and 150 ft of nylon warp. Why not, I am often asked, a high holding power anchor like the C.Q.R? Well the only really versatile anchor is the fisherman (this is the type you will always see on the R.N.L.I. lifeboats), this will hold through rock and weed to mud. Experience has taught me that if not supplied as standard many customers will not bother to get one, preferring the easier to stow and generally lighter high holding power patent types like the C.Q.R. and Danforth/meon types. Of course no boat should do serious cruising without two anchors and my personal preference for *Ocean Winds* is a 35 lb C.Q.R. which we have proved this trip is adequate given reasonable holding.

It rained and blew in the night. I fell asleep in the saloon after dinner and woke about 1 a.m. with my dirty plate and wine glass still before me. So before the tooth cleaning ceremony, I washed up. I put off getting up until 8 a.m. Made tea for the crew. They reluctantly surface to a wet dismal day. We weighed and went out into the channel to the usual bloody head wind — but this time accompanied by very low cloud and a cold driving drizzle. Shit! We should have stayed in bed. But no turning back and we motor sailed the five miles to the next Caleta. Meanwhile two naval vessels slowly overhauled us, the first, a tank landing craft full of officers' cars, replied to our dipped ensign. We turned into Ensenada. The lead showed at the entrance only 2½ fathoms. Mike reckoned he was bottoming on kelp, but we crept dodging the thick weed which is death to the engines. Inside we lost bottom until almost ashore at the head. First we tried the C.Q.R. With both engines hard in reverse it dragged. Then the fisherman — for the first time that did likewise so we gave the C.Q.R. a second try. It held. The fisherman was relaid later as there are some half-tide rocks rather near which we cannot afford to kiss. The sides of the fiord are almost vertical. The winds drop down them from different directions and hit with evil intent in what are called here 'williwaws'. However our anchors are holding well but this is not so good an anchorage as Bahia Welcome.

9th Jan.   It was a cold blustery morning — the wind apparently from the west but there was no telling if that would become N or S as soon as we were back in the channel. So it was heave ho on both anchors and slowly motor out. Of course the wind was from ahead — about force 5. Initially we had too little sail up, but we increased this to only

Ocean Winds II

Autohelm Steering

Alan & Scarlett gluing chafe strip at Camarinas.

Scarlett smartening up the Captain.

Donut maker in the Kasbah — Mogador.

Michael

Sailing Lighter — Cape Verde Is.

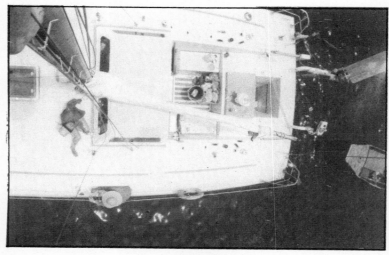

Looking Down

Mid-ocean lash-up.

Trading schooner — Salvador, Brazil.

Frightening work in mid-ocean — reeving new halliard.

Michael

Preparing a running before a light trade — Michael, Scarlett, Alan II.

Michael making a net.

Celebrating crossing the line. Mike, Scarlett, Alan II.

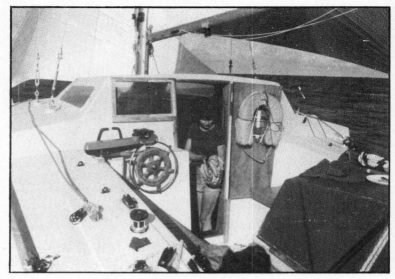

Scarlett going to her hideaway.

Goose Barnacles

Picking up the Maté habit.

Bananas all ripening fast.

Booby Bird — Abrolhos.

King Cormorants — Port St. Julian.

Port Deseado (Port Desire). They have recently closed the British built railway.

A quiet day off Patagonia.

On Justice Isle — Port St. Julian

Mike nearly got his finger bitten off.

Preparing to survive the night — Gallows Point,
Port St. Julian.

Justice Is. Doughty lost his head. My crew stand
on theirs.

With Plymouth Gin — celebrating entering the Straits.

Mike taking a distance off the Cape of a 1000 Virgins.

Anchored in Port Zenteno — Magellan Straits.

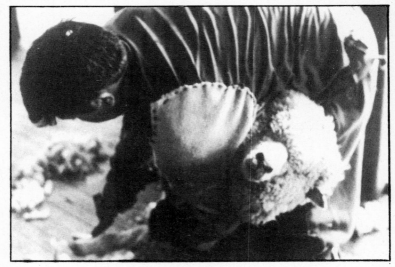

A Patagonian sheep shearer.

Scarlett & Alan caught 2 Centolla (Spider) Crabs
off the Piles at Puntas Arenas.

Cape Farewell — The S. tip of Mainland America.
Named by Francis Drake.

Est. Rocallosa

Moss Pillar

Caleta Notch

Looking down from our Cairn.

one reef in the main and most of the jib out to get her sailing at 4—5 knots. It was 5 minute tacks across the channel which gave us plenty of practise but such progress is frustratingly slow. In Victoria Pass we expected a slant of wind to favour us but instead the wind died away altogether so we motored for a mile and then we got it back stronger than ever down Collingwood Strait. It was more rolls in the jib and a beat against a wind of up to force 7. Not my sort of sailing, and as there was a small caleta, Williams, just inside the two headlands to port which the pilot described as temporary shelter, we made in to have a look.

We anchored in 3½ fathoms on a thin bed of kelp. With both engines going full astern we slowly dragged the fisherman. We then motored up past that anchor and dropped the C.Q.R. The two held us. Michael and Scarlett went ashore with the gun and 2 shells while I had my siesta. What a surprise when they returned with a lovely little duck — silver grey head and back with a bronze collar and black wing tips. Now drawn and plucked and hanging in the galley for tomorrow's dinner. It is now raining and the glass falling, so it is good to be at anchor even though we have only made good 8 miles.

I was unhappy about the conditions as it looked as if a gale was threatening. I rowed a long line astern to some rocks. Then, as we did not have another one long enough to reach the rocks ahead, Mike rowed out the 20 kg Holdfast and dropped it ahead of the kelp onto sand in just a fathom of water. It was about 500 ft, and only just had enough rope to reach back to the *Winds*. Well that lot will surely hold us — williwaws and all.

10th Jan.   After a windy night, through which I slept fitfully, the morning was bright and cold. We could see the channel and it was free of whitecaps so I thought sail on to Columbine 7 miles to the north. Then I looked at the barometer — it was down to 974 mb. As the pilot claims this is a better anchorage than Columbine which is much subject to williwaws, and we are so well trussed, I thought we would stay over a day. Within the hour the wind was once again whining in the rigging and the rain lashing down. Michael went ashore and climbed a nearby hill to the snow line; I did little but read a book and in the evening get an alcoholic glow on three whiskies. It is my last bottle of Glenmorangie. After that it is Plymouth Gin as a luxury and the local rum and cane liquor as regulars. Not that we are great topers, but we usually have a couple of drinks before the evening meal.

Tonight's was the duck. Roasted in the oven with parsley and thyme stuffing and roast taties, it was very good.

Morning dawned after a wet and windy night. The barometer down to 972! This so frightened me I decided on yet another day here. Michael and Scarlett went ashore to climb up to a hanging valley. Then of course the wind dropped and became almost favourable so we could have left by 2 p.m. Such is the law of perversity. That evening, while washing up, Mike shouted "A sailing yacht". We rushed outside to see a Dutch yacht, about 45 ft motoring past with just a reefed main set. We waved but got no response. We were disappointed they did not come in and share our anchorage and a yarn.

12th Jan. Underway at last and it took over an hour to get the shore lines in and the anchors weighed. For almost two hours we had a wind which allowed us to close haul up the Estrecho Collingwood. It was on with the engine to pass through Paso Farquhar and then beating again up Canal Sarmiento. We motored the last 3 miles to Lecky's retreat and into Caleta Occassion. Just off this Caleta is another shallow cove with just 2½ fathoms of water. The anchor would not hold in the soft sludge of rotting kelp which was thick on the bottom so we rowed out three lines and are now triangulated from the shore. Mild williwaws come at us from three directions while outside the wind is freshening. This place, Caleta Balandra, is superbly sheltered and there is fresh water from a brook, although it is quite a small one so takes some time to fill a 5 gall. container.

13th Jan. It was pouring with rain so we postponed leaving. Through the glasses we could see a lot of white water in the channel — of course, blowing from the north. Here we could hardly notice the wind, so good is the shelter. The next desired port is about 23 miles away, which, if you have to beat the whole way means a long sail. The day has not been wholly wasted. Michael and Scarlett, as the commendable crew they are, have been sewing up a small tear in the genoa where it caught on the crosstrees.

14th Jan. After a night of being hit by williwaws, some of which were quite strong, the morning dawned wet and dismal. However it did not appear to be blowing hard outside. So we laboriously untied ourselves and hoisted in the dinghy. Hard on the wind it was wet, cold and miserable. The wind was varying between force 4 and 7. In one really strong squall I decided we had had enough: we turned tail and ran back to Caleta Occassion — 2½ hours out and ¾ hour to get back. As soon as the anchor went down the sun came out and it was a different world. We are all chocker as we are making good no more than a 5 mile a day average.

15th Jan.   What a day. It has been raining solidly since an hour after we anchored. Now the williwaws come screaming down at us. The boat shudders then lurches backwards and the bows lift until the full weight comes on the anchor line. It is very frightening. Some of the winds that hit us must be at least force 10. We have the paraffin (kerosene) stove on in the saloon and Mike has made some shortbread, Scarlett some ordinary bread and I cooked supper of tinned steak and kidney (a super one from Fray Bentos) with potatoes and lovely rich gravy. In the evening the wind moderated somewhat but the rain continued. The dinghy was full of rainwater and a 5 gall. dustbin into which we coil the long warp to stop it tangling was over ½ full. We estimate that something like 10 inches of rain has fallen. As a fitting end to the day, on retiring I found my bedding wet due to a window leak. I turned my bedding over leaving the wet patch to steam in the least uncomfortable way and pretended it was not happening. The Eskimoes have this philosophy. If conditions are terrible, go to bed and when you wake up perhaps it will have gone away.

16th Jan.   Up at 6.30 a.m. — almost calm. Admittedly still heavy rain showers but good enough to move off. We motor-sailed north for 4 miles with some heavy squalls but these gradually backed so then, wonder of wonders, managed to sail north with the engines off and frequently making 5 knots. Occasionally the wind screamed down the valleys at gale force, then, rather than deep reefing the main, for the squalls were short lived, I played the sheet keeping the main on the verge of luffing. When the wind came true (instead of being deflected by the high land to the west) over the lower land on the north end of Isle Piazzi, we were actually able to let out all the genoa and full main. 5 miles later, approaching the south end of Vancouver Isle it fell so light we needed the engine. Then it all fell to pieces. The wind picked up to 7 and 8 in the gusts. It was long and short tacks across the channel for 5 miles of hard sailing. You have to be reefed right down for the squalls and then you do not have enough sail up to sail properly in the lulls. So to overcome this, when the wind eased I helped her on with the motor.

We made Puerto Mayne by about 3 p.m. and a charming spot it is. You fiddle your way up between islands and the shore, the channel being but 300 ft wide. In the inner anchorage there are two brooks gurgling down. We dropped the anchor from the stern 200 ft from the shore, then motoring up against it, held the boat 50 feet from the shore while Mike took two lines to trees ashore. We have watered from the brook up ahead and feel pleased with today's progress. The log shows that to make good 22 miles we have actually had to sail 32.

17th Jan.   It poured with rain all night. We left in calm conditions at 8.30 a.m. which is rather a late start. We motored for 6 hours then just 2 miles from Port Bueno it started blowing really hard again. We had 4 tries at getting the anchor to hold at the head of the bay in 8 fathoms. It must be a bottom of pretty smooth rock for neither the C.Q.R. or fisherman could get a bite. It is no joke hauling up and down a heavy anchor and chain. In the end we used the fisherman and a 30 lb weight on a very long anchor warp. Then Mike rowed ashore 600 ft of warp and moored us round a boulder.

We have about 22 gals. of diesel left and if these head winds continue, as seems virtually certain, we are going to have to try and get some more at Port Eden where there is a small fishing settlement. The alternative is to beat laboriously north and expect to be beaten back sometimes by the weather deteriorating. Hardly a day passes when at one period or the other the wind does not pick up to force 7 or stronger. So it is a question of making as much progress as possible in the calmer spells and so to make the distance to the next adequate anchorage this needs the engine. We notice that the winds usually increase in strength in the early afternoon so it pays to make an early start and get to the next anchorage by 3 p.m.

18th Jan.   Early morning it was raining hard but by 7.30, after we had hauled in the shore line, hoisted the dinghy into its davits and weighed anchor, the sun was shining. Not for long though. Down the channel swept hard squalls which made the watch keeper wet, cold and miserable. The barometer was rising and between the murky squalls the sun shone so there were moments when it was almost pleasant. We managed on just the starboard engine as far as the narrows 'Angostura Guia', when, to make progress through we had to have both engines running hard. In Canal Inocentes it widens out and the wind was increasing. I considered beating the next 20 miles to a decent anchorage but could see us arriving after dark so off the end of Isle Juan I said, 'To hell with it' and made up for the shelter of Bay Wide.

Here was a problem — the anchorages were deeper than 10 fathoms (60 ft), which for a small yacht is really the maximum depth. Seeing an isle encumbered bay to port, we slowly motored in. There was no bottom almost to its head, where there must have been an underwater cliff as suddenly we were in 3 fathoms. We dropped the fisherman after backing off a little and the anchor fell straight down. So it was haul the bugger back up, creep forward very slowly and drop it just before we ran aground, then back off again. A line then had to be taken out to the island off our port quarter and one to the Isle off our starboard, and now feel nice and secure.

The glass has risen to 1008 mb. We have made good some 24 miles while the log shows 32 which indicates a foul tide for much of the time.

19th Jan. A calm morning with no rain. Nor, during the night, were we woken by rain drumming on the deck. So with the barometer high, we collected in the lines and motored out at 7.30 a.m. Soon the sun was shining and even the head wind never increased above force 4 and was mostly 3 or less. We motored down Canal Innocentes and then tacked across Canal Conception for a couple of hours. It was a fine clear evening but with high cirrus cloud and the barometer falling bad weather is presumably on its way. As it is so calm, I decided to keep going through the night. The channel is lit about every 5 miles with a shore light and the half moon should rise shortly after dark. The channel is deep with steep-to sides and no isolated dangers.

In the evening light, the snow capped mountains look magnificent. The starboard side of the channel is littered with brash ice from their glaciers.

The night was bitterly cold. Navigation along the channel proved easy enough. Off Isla Mason where one turns right along Canal Icy (aptly named) we were overtaken by a Chilean gunboat. They lit us up with their searchlight which blinded the helmsman for a spell. We are still doing the 1 hour watch and 2 off which gives very interrupted sleep but it is too cold to be outside longer than an hour. As far as we could tell this would be one of the most awe inspiring parts of the canal — trust us to pass it at night.

Morning dawned sunny and by 10 a.m. we were motoring into Port Eden. How strange to see houses and people after so long. We dropped anchor and started peeling off clothes. Locals came rowing out; we had anchored off the shop, so bought some supplies but they were poorly stocked. A lady with one tooth who was rowed out by two lads sold us 2 centolla (spider crabs) for just under £1. They were delicious and did, not only a super evening meal, but tomorrow's lunch as well.

We then moved across opposite the police post and the main settlement where we had to have three goes before we could get the anchor to hold. We finally managed to find a bit of mud for the C.Q.R. Ashore, we tried for diesel. This was a problem as they were almost out, but a boat was expected within the next day or so. The police launch driver took us round to various fishermen to see if they had any to sell, but no luck. We were giving our launch driver a drink on board when a boat bumped alongside. Our luck was in. It was another fisherman who said he had a 45 gal. drum we could buy. So he came on board and we negotiated a price over a drink. It cost us 2,500 pesos (£36) which, while somewhat more expensive than in Puntas, was a price we were very glad to pay and thus get completely refilled. We can now motor all the way to Castro if the weather is calm or the head winds not too strong.

This is a pretty place; houses mostly on stilts by the water's edge with a snow capped triangular mountain peak behind. We were lucky with the sunshine. The barometer was falling and it rained in the night but by morning the small depression had passed and the weather was good again, so, with 2½ hours to low water we sailed for the English Narrows (Angostura Inglesa). You have to pass here with the current or at slack water as the south going stream runs at up to 7 knots. We had the last of the ebb; there were a few tidal swirls but nothing very bad.

We anchored just to the north of the narrows in Caleta Hoskyn. Unfortunately it is rather deep at 10 fathoms. It is as well we stopped after only 10 easy miles as with the increasing wind and a foul tide progress would not have been good. We have to leave at 7 a.m. tomorrow to carry a fair tide for 6 hours. We have all washed our hair and I have changed the engine oil. It is actually warm enough to be dressed in ordinary trousers, shirt and sweater. No long johns or polar suits. This is a great pleasure after 22 days of being cold while dressed in as many clothes as one could physically get on.

22nd Jan.   A moment of worry this morning; the C.Q.R. would not budge. "It's fouled a rock." cries Mike.

We sweated it rigid up and down and bounced on the stern, but to no avail. Leaving it tight, I tried a blast full ahead on the engines. Suddenly the bows sprung up — we were free. Hauling it in, we found stiff clay adhering to it, so it was just exceptionally good holding.

There was the perpetual head wind — fortunately again quite light, so we just motored north. A ship passed and gave us five toots. The only shoal patch in this part of Canal Messier is well marked — by a ship parked on top of it. Approaching Ile Farquhar a four masted sailing ship hove in sight. This was the *Esmeralda,* the Chilean Navy training ship. We dipped our ensign, they replied and then their band struck up. This gave us a great boost — having a brass band play in our honour.

We anchored in Caleta Connor with our stern pulled into the river mouth with two warps so we lay in little over a fathom. Here the wind had eddied right round so we are looking into it and down the channel. It has started to blow quite hard outside — a pattern for the last few days — a calm morning with a very fresh breeze in the afternoon. We made a dinghy trip up the river for almost ¼ mile, taking the gun, but saw no ducks. On the shore there is what the chart calls, 'a Notable tree'. On this are nailed boards with ship's names. *The Northern Light,* a Swedish yacht called last year. We are leaving our name in a Plymouth Gin bottle.

23rd Jan. 28 miles made good under motor to Puerto Islands. We had to stop to water the vessel and here, at the head of the Caleta, is a lovely waterfall. It has been a quiet day but Scarlett has promised us a noteworthy meal tonight — I suspect of dried beans soaked and boiled. (Right, & did they make us fart!)

24th & 25th Jan. Glad I had two warps out forward as the weather became very bad. After one day, Mike motored ashore in the dinghy to check the shore lines for chafe and put doublers around the trees. Then I had him take forward the big fisherman. That has a good bite so now we have three lines forward. We are periodically hit by williwaws, God knows how strong, but easily force 10. The boat shudders and lurches back on the lines. It has now been raining for 24 hours and shows no signs of stopping. We are only 20 miles from entering the Gulf of Pain — glad I am to be that far from it and so firmly anchored.

It is depressing and boring on the boat. We do not have much literature left unread. Food supplies are now getting low as also are the grog supplies. It has been a fantastic passage inside the archipelego but now is becoming rather a drag. We still have several hundred miles to go to Castro and the next 150 are across the Golfo de Penas, of fearful reputation. I am full of admiration for those early sailors who battled against this lot. Many are remembered by having given their names to the various straits, islands and anchorages, most of which you will notice are British. I shudder to think how long and painful this passage would have been without the diesel engines.

26th Jan.   This evening the torrential rain has ceased, changing to heavy showers. All in all it has rained for 3 days solid and everything on board feels damp. The waterfall ahead now looks magnificent. When we arrived there was no detectable current out of the caleta; now the surface water is running out at 1½ knots and 2 feet down at ¾ knot. We have all read a book and then played cards, blackjack, which was mostly won by Scarlett.

27th Jan.   After a lot of heavy rain in the night the morning was calm with light showers, so we decided to sail at least as far as the entrance to these straits. It took a long while to get the warps in and the dinghy stowed in its ocean stowage, upside down over the aft cock-pit. At first there was little wind, but then a southerly squall came along – this from aft. What a mess the sails got in. However we bent in a reef and all sorted out.

At the San Pedro light which marks the northern entrance to these straits or for us the start of the Gulf of Pain, it was gusting hard, just gale force. We could easily lay across the bay so this was a rare, fair if too strong wind. We made a close fetch of it, carrying just a little jib and 2 reefs in the main. The boat bounced rather in the short seas but we were making 4–5 knots and always in the right direction. The glass was rising too and no trace of cirrus cloud which meant perhaps no gale for the next day or so. 3 hours later the wind had moderated to 4–5 and drawn almost on the beam but leaving a nasty lumpy sea.

28th Jan.   By morning Cabo Raper light was abeam, 10 miles off. We're now sailing north with a light wind on the quarter. As we altered course to the NE, bringing the wind dead astern the speed dropped to 2 knots. So it was on with the plonker and roll up the genny. The swell helped us along, but for us to make an anchorage by nightfall in Anna Pink we needed to average 5 knots. All day there was little wind, sunshine and clouds. In the afternoon, for ½ hour, I even had my shirt off. The sun shone through a haze of cirrus with a big halo. The barometer was steady, so I hoped for at least 12 hours before the next gale.

A comment in the Admiralty Pilot 'Shipwrecked persons in boats, instead of going by sea along this dangerous coast in search of help should make for Estereo Auxilio; thence they can reach Puerto Aysen or other small ports further Northward almost entirely by water'. They omit to add the boats would have to be dragged through shallow water at the head of Auxilio.

We made into Port Refugio at 9 p.m. A good fair breeze had just set in and the swell too was helping us do 6 knots. Inside we dropped the C.Q.R. just where I planned with a transit and bearing taken off the chart. We should have been in 10 fathoms. To my surprise it was only 4. But the anchor bit well, and we lowered down the anchor weight to be doubly sure. It is a well sheltered berth this, although a slight swell creeps in. This would probably be a lot worse if it was from the NW instead of due west.

29th Jan.   Scarlett had the alarm set for 6 a.m. By 7 the two of us had the anchor up and were motoring over the nasty swell at the entrance. We left Mike sleeping as with only the one anchor down two of us could easily cope. There was little wind and somewhere near low water so we should have a fair tide for 5 or 6 hours, which was the object of the early start.

We wonder if this bay gets its name from the pink, Anna, which was part of Anson's squadron. He was around here in 1741.

Just at the entrance to the channel is an island with grassy patches (Centro Island). I was told by a naval lieutenant in Puntas that there were wild sheep here and we would be welcome to shoot one. I could see no sign of them through the glasses so, while there looked to be an anchorage on the east side, since we had a fair tide, a falling barometer and fog swirling in from the sea, we zoomed past. After our rather plain food the mouth waters at the thought of real solid meat roasted over an open fire.

As we carried the tide up the channels we made great progress until, that is, we got lost. Ile Lucia we were headed for when the fog clamped down. The starboard coast trended SE. The helmsman followed it. The Island we were passing south of, I decided, had to be Barranco. This would lead us into a mass of shoals and uncharted rocks. A quick turn

81

left was ordered. Two minutes later, from a flat calm we had a fresh wind, which cleared much of the fog. On with the port engine to boost the speed back to 5 knots; the isle of St. Lucia came clear. We could then bring the wind on the beam and for a wonderful ½ hour could actually sail with no engines.

The next canal, Chacabuco, is where the tidal streams separate, so we had carried the flood and could now carry on with the ebb also in our favour. Alas, the weather turned really foul. A strong north wind and driving rain. So we went 5 miles south to Port San Miguel, a well sheltered anchorage. I used the Chilean chartlet and two transits to drop the hook exactly where it was marked 10 fathoms. It was only 8. After careful bearings, it was obvious that the chartlet should be looked upon as a sketch map and not accurate cartography.

30th Jan. It pays not to fight the weather for this proved to be a lovely summer's day. There was very little wind and while we could sail occasionally, most of the time we plonked on at a steady 5 knots. All the islands are heavily forested and while the mountains may be as high as further south, they look smaller clad in trees right to their summits instead of bleak rock and snow.

The afternoon was warm enough to sunbathe. Navigating between a lot of islands on the approach to Port Aguirre, I saw ahead what looked to be a black triangular buoy just sink. Sudden excitement when we realised there was a school of the dreaded orca or killer whales around the boat. One of them, the boss male, had an enormous fin, it appeared to rise out of the water for a clear 6 feet. They leisurely passed close by but took no notice of us.

Port Aguirre suddenly appeared through the islands. One passage was very narrow but even very close to the rocky shore there was plenty of water. Ahead of us was a quay quickly lined with people 2 deep. The current was setting strongly round it as a back eddy so of course we had the fenders out on the wrong side. Despite the audience I felt we made a very creditable come alongside.

The first thing was to re-victual and buy some meat. We had to count our communal purse. In all some 600 pesos (£8) were left, easily enough for a big chunk of meat and some vegetables. Two students found us and then an American, Ray, who helped in the translation of our needs. We were then invited for a beer followed by a game of volleyball. The evening was closed with a singsong in the school which had been taken over by the students and two chopper pilots. They were mapping the area. Many of the students were medical and during this, their summer holidays, were on a form of peace corps work, training the local population in rudimentary hygene and generally checking them over.

31st Jan.   Another lovely day so I got on with repairing the dinghy which had chafed badly on the chines. Unfortunately it did not dry out enough to fibreglass, and the forecast for the morrow was bad, a cold front coming through, so it was left covered on the foredeck. It gives us a good excuse for staying a few days.

This is an interesting settlement. The basic economy is shellfish, mussels, clams and abalones. They have hand operated air pumps mounted in a 20 ft open boat. The diver goes down in the traditional gear relying on his mates not to get tired. A very dangerous job. There used to be a canning factory here for the shellfish but the boss ran off with a government grant so it had to close. The local population relied heavily on this one factory so the numbers living here have halved to about 1,500. As most families have 6 to 12 children it means that there is not a great number of working men left.

We are tied up on the inside of the quay opposite Los Elephants — from where Rodrigo Azocar runs his shellfish business. He has a boat with a captain to collect mussels and oysters which he farms (the others collect wild) and an island where he has a man, Pedro, living to grow his vegetables, chickens and a few sheep. Rodrigo built his own sailing shallope, makes ship's models and puts them in bottles and is deeply interested in boats and sailing. With his wife and 2 youngest children we sailed to his island to collect vegetables. It makes sailing these waters very much easier with a pilot aboard.

Somehow or other we have gained a day, so instead of being the 1st Feb we have had to remain the 31st Jan for a second day.

To any yachtsman sailing this way I recommend a stop here. Tie up on the inside of the quay and you are well sheltered. Victuals, fuel and wine are available and any amount of shellfish.

2nd Feb.   Friday was a lovely warm day so I managed to do the fibreglass repair on the dinghy. Went swimming with Rodrigo and his family off a little island but we all delayed diving in until after a school of killer whales had passed out of sight and could be no longer heard. On a calm day you can hear them blowing at least 2 miles away — long before you can see them.

3rd Feb.　　Left Aguirre for Isle Teresa where Rodrigo, with his English/ Chilean partner, Michael Westcott, runs a mussel and oyster farm. The navy started this but it could not be run economically in the recent, troubled, past so was abandoned. They bought the concession 2 years ago taking over the houses and the buildings and laying new oyster and mussel beds. Unfortunately, now the Aguirre canning factory is closed they have to send their products all the way to Puerto Montt, 200 miles to the north. Michael and his wife, who are down on holiday from Santiago, showed us round and gave us a quantity of their cultivated mussels. These are better than the wild ones as the shells are easier to clean and the flesh fatter. Scarlett and I made supper of them (Mike turned in early needing to catch up after so many late nights at Aguirre) eating them with a bread dough made paper thin and then fried in hot oil. Jolly tasty meal.

4th Feb.　　A force 4 wind was blowing into the anchorage so we had to motor out under both engines for an hour before being able to pay off around the headland at the head of the fiord. From there it was a great sail. What a pleasure to see the speedo leap to over 6 knots and what a joy to feel the boat moving under sail as she was designed to do.

It was a lovely sail to Puerto Amparo. We had to go right to the head to find shallow enough water. The C.Q.R., as it has 30 fathoms of warp, was dropped first, then the fisherman close to the beach. We middled up and this gave us swinging room.

We made an expedition ashore for some timber to cut an oar. The jungle was dense but we fought our way through the bamboo, stumbling over huge rotting trees that had fallen through old age, and selected a tall thin tree about 6 inches in diameter. With axe and saw we felled it straight down our path, sawed off a suitable length, and staggered and stumbled to the shore with it. We axed and sawed at, but unfortunately had chosen a heavy, tough timber. To hack out an oar from this was going to take weeks.

5th Feb.　　Sailed up with a following wind to Puerto Cisnes where we went ashore with our few remaining pesos for supplies. The harbour master sold us 4 lb of best rump steak for £1.60 and with some eggs, tomatoes and onions we were once more adequately stocked for a few more days. We were shown over the small township which has a large school, a small hospital and a lady mayoress. So frequently someone who speaks English comes along and takes us under their wing. This time it was Carlos Gusman who had an English nanny many many years ago. The anchorage here is frightfully exposed and the boat was pitching to the seas as quite a fresh wind was blowing. We therefore did not stay the night but headed for the thermal springs just before Puyuguapi Narrows.

We beat into this charming little spot with a falling wind. There was a yacht by the small wooden jetty and five new chalets with brilliant painted roofs on the shore. Aird, a Scot, rowed out and let us use their mooring. The yacht belonged to Tony, the brother of Michael Westcott who had welcomed us at the mussel farm.

As soon as were were ashore, the owner of this Shangri La invited us to his chalet to meet his wife Daisy and daughter-in-law, Gloria. He, Ernesto de Hein, was the grandson of a German immigrant who settled in Puerto Montt. With his two sons, he runs a small charter airline for this area and had bought the thermals with the idea of developing it with baths and a few chalets and walks through the forest. It is really an enormous project as everything has to be done by hand. Even a tractor cannot cope with the terrain. To clear forest, he uses a team of oxen trained, with their strong necks, to lift out the timbers. The paths have to have wooden bridges every few yards and the baths and swimming pool dug by hand and the hot and cold water carefully channelled to give a constant flow through the pool at the right temperature. Any special supplies like cement and whisky can be brought from the north (Puerto Montt) and landed at Puyuguapi, five miles away, but mostly they have to rely on what is available on the land. . . It is great to see what, with a pioneering spirit and some capital, can be done here.

After a late meal, we were taken to the pool at midnight for a prolonged soak under the stars in a small, steaming pool. After an excellent meal, whisky and wine, a day's easy sail! What bliss, and what a contrast to those days of a week or so ago of waiting, frightened, cold and wet, struck by fierce williwaws south of the Gulf of Penas. Today has been how yachting really should be but so rarely is.

6th Feb.   A gorgeous sunny morning so we took our grotty month long dirty clothes to one of the early thermals and, succumbing to temptation and awed by the enormity of the washing task, left them to soak while we ajourned to the neighbouring pool to sip a midday scotch while soaking up the goodness of the thermal water. Ernesto is a great host. He had a boat towing job to do, bringing a 70 ft fishing/

85

cargo boat down from Puyuguapi. Tony was going to do it with his yacht but his engine, or rather shaft, had seized, so I volunteered *Ocean Winds*. After all, we have 14 hp.

Ernesto had a launch with a 20 hp outboard, so with Tony as pilot, we motored up to Puyuguapi. The rudderless boat was a small ship capable of carrying 150 tons of cargo. Unfortunately it was also a miniature mussel farm — the bottom being very very foul. However we on one side and Ernesto's launch on the other, with Tony high on the bridge of the ship to shout down directions, we managed, after hand hauling (9 men) the anchor up, to progress at 2½ knots.

The narrows are very narrow and it was fully dark as we approached. As my two diesels were, despite being 6 hp less, so very much more powerful than the launch's outboard, I had control of the steering. Tony, some 15 foot above the water, could see quite well and he would call down instructions like 'A touch to port'. All went well until our final approach to the thermals anchorage when, at the critical moment, Tony vanished. He had walked into an open hatch on the bridge and fallen 15 ft to the engine room below. By some miracle he was not a heap of crumpled, bleeding bones, but still bruised, badly shocked and a little torn.

7th Feb.   On the morrow we found our washing full of silt. Serve us right for being so lazy. Really a notable achievement having OUR washing come out of hot water dirtier than it went in. Daisy rescued much of it and put it in a cleaner pool into which we jumped and soaped them more or less clean.

They have a rainfall of 4½ metres a year. A month during the summer is usually good. Somehow we seemed to have arrived with the good weather. The view from the chalets is incredibly beautiful. Looking out across the anchorage, *Ocean Winds* gaily strung with our washing and beyond the mountains, tree clad (in fact jungle) on their lower slopes with snow and glaciers on the higher peaks and the sun shining down out of a clear blue sky and no motor cars!

Actually, 2 miles away across the sound, they were constructing the first road. It was to be a dirt road and to take 3 years to build at 5 metres wide. Aysen would then be reached by road from N. Chile without first going through Argentina as at present.

In the forests are a few wild animals; foxes, a small deer and others on which the puma preys. Ernesto had the skin of a puma which was shot locally. The farmers dislike them as they wreak havoc if they get amongst the sheep. In some of the valleys the land has been cleared and there are quite large farms of several thousand acres. Ernesto, as a pilot, sighted one virgin tract, and with Tony, is about to develop it. But this presents tremendous difficulties and capital. They are initially taking a man up there, with a machete, an axe and a bag of flour and fishing gear. He builds a log cabin and gradually explores and clears land for a base.

8th Feb.   After a leisurely morning and lunch, we said goodbye to Ernesto, Daisy and Gloria (who is both beautiful and beautifully pregnant) and in company with Tony and Aird in their yacht, sailed down the estuary. At the corner of the fiord they turned back and we carried on with, as extra crew, their two engineers, both named Jorge or George, as they could get neither flight nor ship out on the regular service for at least a week and so were otherwise stranded.

With our two diligent Jorges doing the steering, we motored under both engines down narrow fiords for some 20 miles to an anchorage that Tony had marked on our chart. As usual a pantomime with the anchors as again it was deep water until close in and one certainly cannot afford to drag onto these rocky shores.

9th Feb.   Another lovely cloudless day as we started motoring north. Around the corner was a thatched hut made entirely from the available materials nearby and used by the shellfishermen. They lash together a frame of saplings and thatch it, top and sides with marram grass. As we hit a tide rip just clear of the Islands, Jorge II went down with sea sickness. We managed to sail then, albeit close hauled with a force 2–3 wind. There were fine, snow clad mountains to starboard. One, in particular, Corcovado Volcan, 7512 ft, was spectacular, rising alone to an almost perfect peak.

The Golfo Corcovado, like the Golfo de Penas, has an evil reputation for sudden storms and bad seas. For us it was like a mildly ruffled millpond. Jorge remained, however, sick.

I picked out the light on Isla Tranqui but at 4 miles off. It was supposed to be possible to see at 8 miles. I took 4 bearings at one mile intervals then shut off the motor which woke Scarlett for her watch, and plotted a running fix. With the four bearings all tallying I was confident of our position so altered to enter through the banks for Castro, some 40 miles away. By the end of Scarlett's watch we should have been abeam of a 7 mile light and 4 miles off. While we could see shore lights, there was none flashing. We had a large shoal to port and rocks 5 miles ahead, but this supposedly marked by a lit buoy. The chart cautions 'Buoys are not to be relied on'. As the shore lights patently were not either I shut off the engines and there was just enough wind to push us at ¾ to 1½ knots which gave us steerage while we waited for the dawn. Jorge II had overcome his nausea and bravely stood the helm while I half dozed in the corner of the cockpit, looking out every 10 minutes to check all was well.

The position at dawn showed us to be where I thought, and the buoy marking Banc Vettor Pisanic was missing. Once clear of the dangers I woke Mike to take over the pilotage while I fell asleep for two hours.

We motored the morning through gently rolling hills on either side of the canal or channel. It almost looks like parts of Devon — as if you could go ashore to the first farm and say "A cream tea please'. But the shingle clad wooden churches were very different from our stone towered ones.

At the pretty town of Castro the two Jorges left after treating us to a meal at a very ordinary looking cafe. It was a super meal of abalones, sea urchin eggs (raw) followed by veal and cheese cordon bleu — a much better meal than you might get in one of our tarted up, super decor restaurants.

On Sunday we watched the firemen practise. As all the buildings are of wood, the local people are very proud of the skill of their 'bombadiers'. The service is voluntary and much like our R.N.L.I. in the speed with which they get operative. Sundays the various teams race, running their hoses over a high inverted V ladder opposite each other and then trying to blast the opposing team off their feet. The first to get their hoses operative had a great advantage as they could then delay their adversary's blast.

After the display, we went into the twin spired church, built of wood 430 years ago so it must have been here when Drake passed. The interior is amazing, particularly considering the few people there were in the area when it was built. It has a high vaulted roof and timber columns.

Scarlett's Alan met us here — he had spent a boring 3 weeks waiting for Scarlett. So Scarlett left, which was a pity because she has turned into a good, cheerful crew. Her cooking is good and she had a low tolerance of dirt, particularly in the galley and loo, so these places are cleaned before I am shocked into doing it. Some of her arguments and attitudes are, to my mind, screwy, but then I expect mine were to her. But our discussions were friendly.

We had some left wing economists from Santiago University visit us on board. I was not impressed as they were ignorant of the levels of inflation in Allende's day. It went up to an average of 300% and in 1973 the cost of living rose by 508%. So, as he is reputed to have gerrymandered the elections it is no wonder the military had considerable popular support in deposing him though people were shocked that it was done so brutally. As our Spanish is so limited, we can only talk with well educated English speaking Chileans, but I get the impression that the military government is much preferred to Allende but that it is very hurtful to their pride as a nation that they are no longer a democracy. The military are not everywhere in evidence as in Argentina. In fact it is a much easier and more comfortable feeling for us. No gun has been pointed at us since entering as was all too frequent by the uptight guards of Argentina.

13th Feb.   After victualling, which job I have taken over, Mike and I sail *Ocean Winds* off the buoy with Scarlett busily clicking away on her camera and waving us goodbye. Rain soon set in and then wind, so after some 12 miles we made for an anchorage. There was another yacht there but they obviously did not wish to speak to us as they vanished below at our approach, which is most unusual for we yachties are usually pretty friendly and like a yarn at the end of a day's sail. So not to intrude, we sailed well past before anchoring with our usual care. The wind increased and they started dragging their anchor so inadvertently left. I reckon he had his boss's wife aboard as 'crew'.

The wind shifted in the night leaving us exposed to a fair fetch. By 6 a.m. we had the anchor up and were gently sailing north between the islands which could be clearly seen in the moonlight. At dawn, we dropped the sails and let her drift while we hoisted in the dinghy to stow it in its 'ocean' position over the aft cockpit.

The channel became very narrow off Dalcahue, and the strong tide, which we had made sure was with us, zoomed us through. The countryside was looking beautiful, fresh green after yesterday's rain, with the smell of pinewoods and new mown hay wafting across. A lovely day's yachting and only for the last hour did we have to motor through an evening calm to Chacau — the ferry terminal for the isle of Chiloe.

15th Feb.   Through the straits out into the Pacific, the tide runs at up to 8 knots so you have to have it with you. So as we could not leave until 2 p.m. we had a lazy morning. I prepared a dumpling lamb stew for the evening and then the harbour master rowed out to check us. Years before he had been on a commissioning visit to England when a Chilean destroyer was being built at Barrow-in-Furness. I was a teacher there at the same time. He spoke some English and it was all very friendly as he checked our papers.

It was an easy motor through the narrows, with the tide just turned in our favour. It did not get really strong until we turned north for some careful navigation through some sandbanks into Bay Maullin. This was a sizeable short cut, and with our draught, not dangerous although there were some tide rips even in this calm. Then a light breeze enabled us to set a course close hauled for Isles Juan Fernandez, 530 miles away. The Pacific has welcomed us as her name indicated she would. We had but 2 hours sailing before the engine had to be restarted — there was no wind, just a lazy 7 foot swell. The stew was delicious.

At twilight Mike and I spent half an hour sussing out the stars as their positions are new to us here. Jupiter is very bright below Sirius. In the morning there is a good moon to cross with the sun.

16th Feb.   I find it always takes a few days to get back into the 24 hour watch system. At first, one's eyes seem perpetually heavy never getting a decent length of sleep. We are doing 3 on and 3 off with a 4 on and off watch during the daytime. Not that we go short of sleep even with just two of us. It means, with the extra work, that instead of reading a book a day it now takes 1½ days to read one.

In the early hours of the morning it was possible to sail again — close hauled on the starboard tack, not quite laying the course but getting well away from the land and any possible shipping. By the time the wind picked up to force 4 it was getting uncomfortable then a front passed through with rain. The sudden change of wind was too quick for the wind vane and so we were caught aback. The ship hove herself to, which pleased me as it gave time to leisurely don oilskins before braving the elements and sorting out on the new tack. It was now a beam wind and we went galloping along thrusting through the remnants of a head sea. Shortly after midday, the sky cleared and the wind died, so, rather than hang about it was on with the plonker to thrust on northwards.

18th Feb.   Britain is trapped in the jaws of a hard winter. I can imagine the complaints; the fuel bills; the flat batteries and the dozing in front of the telly. We are gently ambling along at 3—4 knots, wind abaft the beam light, but cool coming off the southern ocean. The moonlit nights are gorgeous. The atmosphere here is so free from pollution even the stars seem brighter. There is a big swell, some 14 feet, rolling up from the south but the barometer is high and climbing, so I believe the swell is generated by strong winds a long way to the SW and that the depressions will pass to the south of us.

19th Feb.   During the night we have galloped along at 5—6 knots with a force 4 trade wind. Now a wave pattern overlays the swell so occasionally the boat gets thrown off. Mike, who is young with little thought of the morrow, likes to keep the Autohelm on as well as Quantock Pete (the windvane) for then you never have to worry about occasionally correcting the boat. However we know we will eventually have several hundred miles of motoring through the Equatorial calms, so I insist that while we have a reasonable wind, only the vane may be used thus saving the electric autopilot's motor from wearing out. Now we have rigged secondary steering lines from the self-steering rudder to the main wheel. When the servo tab turns the rudder this now also turns the wheel a couple of inches.

For the night, and so as not to make a landfall in the dark, we reduced sail to cut our speed to no more than 4 knots. With the dawn appeared the Island. When I surfaced at 8 a.m. Mike had already altered slightly so that we would pass the Eastern headland on our port. It was beautifully outlined in the early light; the mass fading into the horizon and the jagged mountain tops in silhouette. Such a dawn island landfall gives me a real lift.

We have kept the same compass course since leaving Chiloe. Our sights showed we were mostly about 4 miles to the west of the course line.

We sailed comfortably round the east point of the main Robinson Crusoe Island. I think I prefer the old name of its discoverer, Juan Fernandez, but guess the Chileans need to catch on to the tourists and if renaming it after Defoe's book helps, who am I to carp? The wind followed us round to the entrance of Bay Cumberland, then changed and came screaming down from the mountains ahead. At the anchorage we first laid the fisherman, but before finishing our anchoring were invaded by the Port Captain and others. The gusts hitting us were very strong (50 knots on the ventimeter) and we started to drag. So we got down the C.Q.R. and held up our heavy reserve Holdfast anchor at a passing fisherman. He waved, and held up 5 fingers. Five minutes later he was back from the quay, collected the anchor, and dropped it well upwind. I later learnt that this was a notorious spot for boats, particularly yachts, getting adrift by dragging their anchors.

Interesting boats they have here. Basically a whaler of about 30 ft, with sails and a well which takes an outboard. This is a great long shaft affair with twin opposed cylinders. Most steer with an oar, a few with a rudder when under sail. The place abounds with fish, Mike caught a large yellow tail off the stern. They were hook shy, but he tempted them into a frenzy of feeding with ground bait.

We climbed up to Alexander Selkirk's look-out, a four mile hike and high, which subsequently made our muscles hurt. We accompanied a tall American, Silas Smith, who had already heard we were voyaging around South America. A National Parks worker, riding a docile mule, also jogged up the steep rocky path. That animal impressed me; I could not keep up with it although Mike could, and I did not have a fat Chilean on my back.

There is a bar/restaurant here that makes Cornish Pasties (he calls them empanadas) filled with lobster. They are superb. The best pasties in the world.

The Dresden was sunk in the bay during the First World War and three of the crew are buried in the grave yard. The Island has been designated as a national park and Chile has proposed that it, along with Easter Island, be one of the 100 under the patronage of the United Nations. There is a lot of flora and a little fauna peculiar to the islands. They have opened up paths and are busy planting trees to cut down the erosion. The wild goats on this main island have been got rid of as they destroy too much of the vegetation. A few domestic ones are still kept around the settlement at Cumberland Bay.

The goats and rabbits were introduced centuries ago. The island was used as a base for pirates and then for political prisoners, and they dug out caves overlooking the bay. Around the headland, in West Bay, Alex Selkirk first lived in a cave before building a house. He was on the island 4 years and 4 months before being rescued by a privateer. Defoe met him in a waterfront pub in London, and after hearing his story, rewrote it as Robinson Crusoe.

The population has increased from zero in his time to some 2,000 a few years ago but has now dwindled to about 400. They are mostly engaged in the crayfish industry, sending their catch back to the mainland aboard a slow old cargo boat called the 'Darwin'.

24th Feb.   Time had come to depart. In so far as we had down 3 heavy anchors and neither Mike nor I feeling particularly strong, we had a problem. But first ashore for a couple of bottles of wine. On the quay were two strapping lads camping on the island and could they please come and see the boat? Like a shot, we had them in the dinghy. With their help and a shanty we hauled up the two heaviest anchors, and it was still hard going with four of us. Back ashore I dug out the Port Captain for my clearance for Algarrobo. The passage is 350 miles.

First we motored to West Bay to photograph Selkirk's cave. Here was a pleasant green valley with mules grazing the hillside. As we cleared the island we were expecting a good reaching breeze but our luck had broken. The wind had backed SE and with a course of east we were close hauled on the starboard tack. Fortunately, on this tack, Quantock Pete, the wind vane, is clear of the downdraughts of the main so at least we do not have to steer at all. It does take a lot of patience and playing to get the boat settled down. You have first the wind vane to adjust which, by a servo tab, steers its own rudder. Then the main rudders have to be pegged just right and the sails balanced. Just a little too hard on the main and the whole balance can be upset.

I find it hard to sleep well at the start of a passage and bloody near impossible when thumping to windward. So sleep tends to consist of several 10 minute cat naps with disturbing dreams. Never mind, this close hauled bit is only for 3 days.

26th Feb.   This evening there has been a marked change. For the last two days the sea has been distinctly rough, the wind a good force 6. Gradually it has been pulling round to the beam and we had to reduce the sail to slow the boat for comfort. We are cutter rigged with a bitty jib, inner jib and deep reefed main — a total area of about 240 sq. ft. Still at times doing 6 knots, which is great when the seas are with you but if they are big and forward of the beam at times you seem to leap out of them as if trying to become airborne, and then smash back down with considerable force. In such conditions you do not feel much like cooking — last night it was just pasta twists with butter and cheese. But as I say, now we have a marked change. All of a sudden the seas have moderated to half their height. We are now 50 miles from the mainland and well upwind so can afford to pay off a little more, although we now have to allow for a north going current.

Mike's morning star sight did not tie up with the radio direction beacon. His sights are rarely as much as 5 miles out and it was a good triangle. From the chart it does not appear that the beacon bearing is deflected by land which might cause it to bend. But this was a 15 mile discrepancy. I decided to run two course lines on the chart on the presumption that one of them was right. Two days later I got a time check which showed that the chronometer was a minute slow which would give a 15 mile error to the sights position.

The wind fell light during the night and we could see the lights of San Antonio some 25 miles away. The trusty Volvos were started and we motored through vast shoals of fish which you could see darting away from our bows leaving phosphorescent streaks.

Our destination was Algarrobo, a yachting and holiday centre for Santiago. It was first charted by Fitzroy when he called with the Beagle. Now the Chilean navy has made a more detailed chart but we still managed to park the port hull on a rock right in front of the yacht club. We hardly felt it, and soon motored clear and tried another spot in which to anchor but it was all very crowded so, since we could see a new marina under construction in the corner, decided to try there. They made us very welcome although all they could offer was a pontoon and good shelter. Just what we needed. Also there was a quiet beach on which we could dry out to anti-foul, but first we would have to buy the paint.

I did a check of our expenses from Mar del Plata to arriving here. Sometimes there were 3, 4 or 2 persons sharing the cost over differing periods, so I divided it up to the single person cost and made a generous allowance too for stock stores consumed in the channels. It worked out at £10 (20 U.S. dollars) per week per person. This includes fuel, food and other general expenses but not personal spending. Of course this would increase with inflation, I guess by some 15–20%. So for 1981 the cost would be about £14 a week.

Down this coast there are not a great number of harbours unaffected by the swell so this marina is rather special. It is also nice and safe to leave your boat for a few days to visit Santiago. The penguins on the island, now joined by a causeway to protect the marina, are a species threatened by the encroachment of man into their territory. The authorities have fenced the island off and prohibited visitors in an attempt to protect them.

Mike and I left the boat here for 3 days and were driven to Santiago by Aird Cameron and his wife to stay at Tony Westcott's house —

a super bachelor pad, complete with swimming pool in the lawn and a daily maid to take the drudge out of being solo. Unhappily Tony had developed a skin allergy so was rather uncomfortable, but despite this made us more than welcome.

While we were in Santiago, Bill Bannister and his wife, sister and husband took us to the British Country Club for a meal. A visiting English cricket team had just won by 300 runs to 30 against a newly formed local team which made me feel rather embarrassed. The hospitality we receive from second generation British people, which both Tony and Bill are, is tremendous.

Time presses though, and as I was anxious to get on with the maintenance jobs, armed with anti-fouling paint, resin and fibreglass, we caught the bus back to Algarrobo. Bus travel in Chile is good and reasonably priced.

We beached the boat in the corner of the marina. Initially there was not enough range so it was bitterly cold water of the Humbolt Current into which we had to wade to scrub the bottom clean. The range of tide became a metre so was just enough for us to paint the bottom except for the bottom 3 inches of keel. I also modified the self-steering rudder by making its underwater area twice the size. This was quite difficult to make a good job, but I managed to buy a piece of polyurethane foam in Santiago, and by making up some filler with resin and, for want of anything better, flour (Mike commented — in extremis, we can always chew on it) fixed it on and then fibreglassed it. Now we have to hope the servo tab is big enough to work it.

By the time all the jobs were done and the anti-fouling finished my forearm was painful. It got worse over the next 3 days, and now creaks horribly.

12th March.   Sailed for Valparaiso with Aird Cameron and his wife Honor. Alas no wind so it was under motor. The first pelican was seen off here — they are huge, ugly birds. It was tight manoeuvring into the crowded main harbour of Valpo and the navy would not let us stay but insisted we went right out to Recreo Yacht Club at Vina del Mar. The club is very good, giving free use of their facilities but it is 5 miles up the coast and catches a nasty lop. The boat is never still so the dinghy thumps. I moved it to the lee side and then it thumped Mike's berth. He was furious and belligerent with me so we had a humdinger of a row. This has been long simmering. Since the channels he has not been happy, which he has made rather obvious, so I was quite ready to

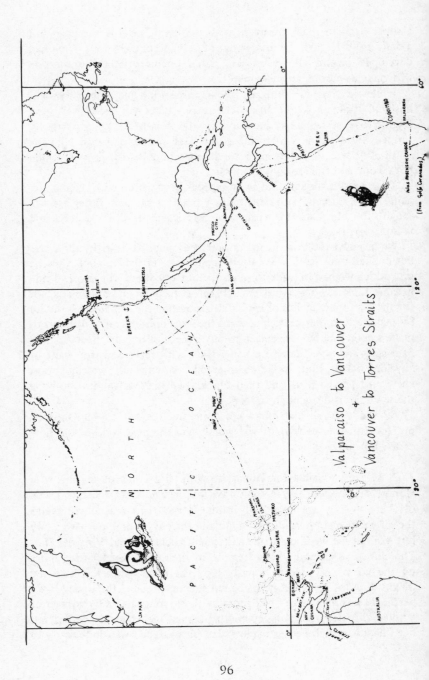

Valparaiso to Vancouver
&
Vancouver to Torres Straits

boil over. We talked it over next day nice and quietly. He has decided to travel back by land so I am lending him 500 dollars. He is quite excited with the idea of now travelling across a strange land — this has to be more adventurous than the next long trade wind sail. And I would rather sail single-handed than with a morose and unhappy crewman.

The consul here, Mr Kendrick, has been most helpful and invited us to his lovely home for drinks. He runs a large shipping agency. I am constantly impressed by the taste of the ex-British out here. It is quite aristocratic in the best sense.

Valparaiso is one of the oldest towns on the coast. It was pillaged by Drake 400 years ago and virtually destroyed since by earthquakes but there are several old buildings that have survived and La Matriz church which Drake cast his beady eye at for any surplus gold ornaments. Mules and horses are still used as pack animals; a double bed and mattress can be carried on the back of a pony but the poor beast cannot lift its head to see where it is going. The market is the best we have found since Morocco. Very reasonably priced and very colourful. It is on Av. Argentina every Wednesday. It is a roaring bustling city, but alas I could spend little time here. My arm hurt by evening so it was early to bed. During the daytime I was concerned with getting the victuals and changing money for Mike. He 'phoned his parents to let them know the change. In a way I feel responsible for him, but then remembering back to when I was 18, I too travelled alone across a continent.

15th March. Mike left with a back pack, catching a bus to the north of the town and then to hitch towards Peru. He is once more an enthusiastic happy person. Sailing is mostly boring and tedious attention to detail with interrupted sleep. It is, if well executed, not very exciting. Indeed, as the reader will note, we have had few adventures. In my youth I used to have many more crossing the Irish Sea from Barrow to the Isle of Man. So you have to develop an attitude, and above all you have to want to be there and doing it. It is also incumbent on the crew to suffer the Skipper and his fads. He not only has to make sure the ship does not hit anything, but also ensure the victuals last and are reasonably varied, that there is water and fuel both for cooking and the engines and that the maintenance is kept up and the ship kept tidy enough without it becoming a drag. While he must always consider the crew, they, in their turn, must not think that the ship is run for

97

E

their benefit. Their job is to help get the ship successfully from port to port.

It took an hour to get my 'Zarpa' or clearance from the Navy. They hiccuped when I told them the crew had left but there was nothing they could do as he had already gone. I wrote out a little letter for them saying he had left, which they duly stamped, told them it would take 5 days to Coquimbo (I expect actually 2, but do not want rescuing if the engines fail and there is no wind), hoisted the dinghy aboard and the anchor up all single handed. I was a bit concerned about my arm but have decided it definitely must be a strained ligament and not a break as it started after anti-fouling. It hurts like hell if I rotate it. Pulling seems alright. I have an elastic bandage on and use it as little as possible.

For the first 26 hours I kept the motor on as the wind was force 1–2, never more. Then for 18 hours there was a stern wind of force 3 which allowed me to have the engine off and sail just under boomed out jibs. The wind was not quite strong enough to work the wind vane alone so had to use the Autohelm as well. I got a time signal so know my chronometer is right, but both sun and star sights were worryingly bad. My star sight cocked hat was a 10 mile one. I suspect I am getting a false horizon as visibility has not been good.

17th March. Fortunately there is a good R.D.F. beacon on the Coquimbo headland, Point Tortuga, so I headed north until the radio bearing showed we were clear of the rocky headland 20 miles to the south of Tortuga, then I altered along the beacon line. During the two nights I have had reasonable sleep, dozing for about an hour, then up to check the course, any shipping and the wind. My sleep periods have been marked by vigorous dreams. I wonder if this is caused by the motion, tension, or both. Not that I feel particularly tense. Nor do I, at present, have any problems about waking at hourly intervals. The only upsetting thing is being so indefinite on the fixes. This is the first time for a long while I have been unhappy about my sights. I am glad I have a good back-up with my Brookes and Gatehouse R.D.F. (radio direction finding) set and a boat in which it can be used – that is, non-ferrous. It is an expensive business getting a useable R.D.F. set in a steel or ferro-cement boat.

2 miles south of Coquimbo is a bay called the Horseshoe of Guayacoe because it is shaped like a horseshoe so is very quiet on anything but a NW wind. There is a fish meal factory at the entrance and long iron

ore loading piers. In the southern part of the bay is a small yacht club catering for water skiers. Here I dropped anchor and my first visitor was a club member, Dr Michel Chambelland. What luck, he was the local specialist saw-bones. He felt my wrist and arm and immediately diagnosed tenosynovitus, which, whatever else it is, is not a broken bone. There is little one can do but suffer it and avoid twisting the wrist.

The Chileans are remarkably hospitable and friendly. Michel telephoned to the Port office to report my arrival. Later they telephoned back, and a charming young lady helped out with the translation. They wanted details of the radio carried etc. They always want that and have great difficulty understanding that while I have an emergency transmitter I never listen and never use it. The other question is for where am I destined. "Hell" was the immediate reply which had my girl translator in stitches and the little man on the other end more than puzzled. I explained I did hope to get to Vancouver first though, so that was written down. What an incredible load of bullshit all this paper work is, but of course it keeps an awful lot of people employed.

I was taken by the owner of the local paper to see the church at La Serena. Drake marched the 10 km to raid it, as also did the British pirate Sharp, 50 or so years later. The local priest was upset at the mention of Drake — crying out 'Malo, malo, malo'. Drake is a hero to the British and a foul despicable pirate to the Spaniards and S. Americans, two views that take some reconciling. I pointed out that times and moral attitudes were different and were not the Spanish as bad, for did they not pirate the gold and silver of the Incas?

Michel's wife took me round for cooking gas. This is often a problem as the liquid gas filling stations are, for safety reasons, usually located well out of the built up area of town. Then there is the problem of persuading the operatives to fill my British bottles. Taking a lady along to do the asking is the answer. Here was all sweetness and light. She also helped me with my clearance, but despite her charms, this still took the Navy over an hour to make out.

The whole Chambelland family, complete with strong attractive maid Maria, came to help me get sailing. So while Michel and his wife hauled up the second anchor, Maria & I swung in the dinghy along with encouraging shouts from the foredeck like "He needs a crew Maria." It would even be worth tangling with the Navy again to get her to come along for she is a super cook as well as having muscles, but I guess her husband would be fast behind us with a meat cleaver.

99

I waved goodbye to these very hospitable people and with a gentle breeze, reached out of the harbour under full sail. As dusk fell, so did the wind, and so once more was it on with the engine and autopilot. There was an island up ahead so I had to remain awake until this was safely passed; after making a running fix on its light, a slight alteration in course, check my own mast head light was shining brightly and no shipping around then I could get my head down for an hour or so.

21st March. All morning there was not enough wind to sail but with the afternoon came a gentle breeze from astern. The sky cleared, so I stripped and messed about naked on the deck setting the twins and handing the main. Once more we were sailing well; by evening making a healthy 5 knots with Quantock Pete doing the steering.

22nd March. It was a great sailing day, gradually the wind freshened to a full force 4 and *Ocean Winds* heaved herself over the bosom of the ocean with great aplomb, with Quantock Pete at the helm. I spent the day just writing, reading and cooking. The night was particularly fine for there are masses of phosphorescence in this part of the Pacific, and with the boat surging along at 6 knots the wake was sparkling with a further flash well astern where the generator turbine was revolving.

23rd March. A good fair breeze rarely lasts and while we managed 130 miles by log, noon to noon, the speed is once more down to 4 knots. Quantock Pete likes a good force 3 or more to work well when running so, if the wind falls lighter, I have to keep a beady eye on it and frequently leap up to make a helm correction.

26th March. It has become an incredibly placid passage. If I am lucky the wind picks up to force 3 which gives a wave height of a foot and us a speed of 3–4 knots. Much of the time we are struggling along at 2 knots. At times it is very tempting to use the motor and I do when even the Autohelm, due to the water passing the rudders so slowly, cannot cope. The occasional booby (much like a gannet but with sexier eyes) circles; more often a pair of petrels pattering over the calm waters. They are called Petrels after St. Peter because they so often seem to walk on the surface of the sea.

Yesterday evening, while cooking, I saw a ship on the horizon, the first one for 5 days. It was a good 2 miles off. I do not worry about being run down. During the daytime I reckon I will be seen and during the night I put on the all round white light and hope I will be. But even if I ran a black ship, in this part of the world there is so little shipping I do not think it would be a very big gamble. I sleep the night dozing in the saloon, now getting up 3 or 4 times to check the course and conditions. I notice as the passage progresses, my periods of sleep are getting longer between each waking.

I checked my sextant this morning and found some errors. Took over an hour correcting them, and as I had to use the sun to take out the side error, will not have eliminated it completely but perhaps will be able to tonight using a planet or Sirius, the brightest of the actual stars. The noon lat. showed we had only done 75 miles so no current is helping us. As the water is quite warm I guess we are outside the Humbolt current.

28th March.   Now in the latitude of the start of Peru. The last two days have been quite humid and then yesterday evening it started raining. I was asleep at the time so all hatches and windows were open and the place got decidedly damp. It has rained all night — which is most rare for this area by all accounts. I took the sea water temperature and that is $27°C$ (it should be $21°$). So coupled with the fact that there has been no helping current, in fact probably an adverse one, I have reluctantly had to conclude that I have been unlucky enough to cop an 'El Nino' current. This is an unpredictable warm current that in some years, from about Christmas to mid April may replace the cold Peruvian current. It kills off a lot of fish, brings rain and flooding to an otherwise arid coast and generally upsets things.

Yesterday morning I had a 9 inch flying fish in the cockpit, I suppose another sign of warmer water, which made a tasty breakfast fried and laid on a bed of rice. There was another this morning, but since it was only 1½ inches I gave it a burial at sea.

Yesterday also saw three tropic birds (sometimes called bosun birds). These graceful white sea birds have a long thin tail. The only other birds seen have been boobies, petrels and one species I have been unable to identify. One's library should include well illustrated bird, fish and dolphin/whale identification books.

Since it has been raining the wind has slightly increased and now, for much of the time, the speed is 5 knots which, with an adverse current, is a great relief.

I have a bucket under the gooseneck and the boom topped up with the topping lift to make a gulley at the foot of the mainsail. I am trying to catch enough rain water for a hair wash. Plenty has fallen, but I was a bit late putting the bucket out. I have also given serious consideration to stripping and having a natural shower but since I can stand the smell and others do not have to, dirt has prevailed for another day.

29th March.   A good sun and cloud day. I used the water, first a hair, then a me, wash. With the water remaining I soaked my dirty clothes. Must stir my lazy self and give it a rub and rinse. But since I wear so few, if any, clothes, there is no urgency for more clean ones. A small school of whales passed but otherwise it has been an uneventful day.

30th March.   Only about 90 miles from Callao. I managed to wake in time for a dawn sight. As one of the stars chosen hid behind a cloud, I used Venus instead. Coupled with the stars, Peacock and Vega this gave an excellent cocked hat. There are also 2 radio stations for direction finding which is satisfying as I like to be able to make regular fixes when approaching port after a passage of several days. This has been a slower passage than expected but even so have averaged just over 100 miles a day.

Yesterday I made up a large bowl of shell pasta and had some left over. So for breakfast it was a treat of pasta, with on top a slice of bacon and a fried egg. The eggs, at a ration of one a day, have just lasted. The bacon, bought in Algarrobo, was expensive. It is in a slab and smoked cured and can be eaten raw.

The sea temperature has dropped to 25°C and the colour is now sort of dirty moss green. The boat is foaming along with the genny boomed to starboard and the working jib to port. Sometimes the jib gets blanketed by the main, but most of the time it is pulling allowing the speedo to show 7 knots.

As dusk settled in I could see the Isle of Lorenzo which shelters Callao, clearly defined 15 miles ahead. It was now a reach under genny, inner jib and main. There were a few fishing boats and some ships about. The wind was a comfortable force 4. I thought there would be a lee under the island. The reverse happened. The trade wind was funnelled down the valleys of the high isle. All at once I was hit by a force 7. Made for an interesting and exhausting few minutes. I cast off the inner jib and pulled it on deck. Then eased the genny sheets and rolled up half the sail. How glad I was for the Cooney reefing

102

gear, this certainly makes life a lot easier, especially when single handed. In the dark, I could make out a black lump to starboard. Surely no rock, for the chart showed the N end of the island steep to. I guessed a fishing boat, but paid off to be extra safe. Around the isle, the lights of Callao materialized. The airport light flashing alternately white and green was easily identified. With the lights of the town behind, the other navigation lights were more difficult; as I approached I decided they were impossible. So I crept up to some anchored warships and judging from their marked anchorage on the chart, took bearings of the various lights. One frigate had to light me up with a search light, which temporarily blinded me. My chart was just a year old. The harbour lights had all been changed.

I motored slowly into the big commercial harbour not knowing where to go. There were some coastguard vessels tied up alongside the far quay so alongside them I went much to their surprise. An officer, with his car, whisked fruitlessly around the various offices (it was 11 p.m. and most were closed) and in the end dumped a petty officer on board with instructions to show me where to moor. He took me outside the harbour near where the navy moor their picket boats. Ernesto (the P.O.) had a couple of drinks and a yarn, then hoisted out the dinghy and I rowed him ashore at 2.00 a.m.

31st March.   Ernesto came back at 9 a.m. with a P.O. of the navy police. I was just getting up. First of all, what photos had I taken of their navy ships? As I had arrived in the dark and as I was just getting out of my bunk when he arrived I persuaded him that I could not have taken any, and promised that I would not.

Next question was how much marijuana had I? I showed him my vitamin C pills.

Did I want a girl (his sister?) sending on board after my long solo trip? Very tempted, but he was fat and ugly, (also his sister?), so despite 9 months celibacy, declined.

What pornography had I on board for him to see? I had given my last *Playboy* away in Algarrobo.

Had I a gun? His face lit up when I said yes, and showed him the shotgun. Alas, a shotgun was allowed, he meant a handgun, so I had to disappoint him on that score too.

He had me at last. I had no courtesy flag. He would sell me one. (Later, it being the week-end, the navy stores were shut and he was unable to steal one from anywhere else so we failed there too.)

After making a cursory search he left with my passport promising me I would be able to collect it in an hour from the Port Captain's Office. I eventually managed to prise it out of them at 5 p.m. and then moved to the more salubrious anchorage off the yacht club which is just below the conspicuous white tower at La Punta. This proved to be, as is usual in South America, a very hospitable yacht club and gave me free use of its showers and other facilities. In their guest book, an early entry was H.W. Tilman on his way home after making the first crossing of the Patagonian ice cap. Eric de Bisschop called with the 'Balsa', *Tahiti Nui* in March 1958. In 1974 Tristan Jones passed on his record of vertical sailing — starting at the Dead Sea and finishing at Lake Titicaca. The barque *Marques* enacting H.M.S. *Beagle* for a BBC film was here last year. Even our first sea lord, Sir Peter Norton has 'humbly' signed in. August company indeed; I made a sketch of boat and route in their leather bound visitors book.

Apart from La Punta, Callao is a grotty dump with a peculiar odour. Vegetables are cheap off the barrows and there is a small town market four blocks off the main drag. There I was warned by several ladies to watch it. Some of the teenage louts had eyed me up and the ladies thought they would roll me without their protection. There I bought some Charquie (jerky) which is traditional Inca dried meat and looks revolting but is supposed to keep years.

Lima is a half hour bus ride away. The buses quickly fill up and run about every 5 minutes. The fare is 10 cents or 5p. In Lima there are a few old beautiful buildings but in general it is like all the other horrible big towns, noisy, crowded with too many vehicles rushing hither and thither. Carpets and silverware are often cheap and well made. I bought a pornographic drinking vessel, a well made copy of an old Inca one for £4.50. All along the streets people were selling artifacts, leather work, brass, rocks and beautifully marked gourds.

In 1911, Mr Hiram Bingham was tracing the old Inca road system when he found Machupicchu, the lost city of the Incas, which even the Spaniards never found. I would dearly have liked to visit there but did not feel happy about leaving the boat unattended for 3 days.

5th April. Having watered, fuelled and victualled the day before, I got up with the dawn and struggled with the anchors. Oh for an electric anchor winch. I motored out in a calm followed by the whole of the Peruvian Navy evidently just starting an exercise. I obtained my clearance the day before, after only a little bother. They first wanted me to get it on the day of departure but I explained why that would mean a 4 hour delay and that I was only a little yacht and not really worthy of their notice. Then he asked for payment of 500 soles (2½ dollars) so I demanded to know what for. This was not followed up. As soon as he stamped and initialled 2 of the bits of papers I said thanks and left the building fast. This stupid bureaucracy is so wearisome and time consuming. On this voyage in total, I have wasted weeks of my life in wretched offices. Peru comes a close second to Argentina as the most painful. Here is a hoping we never have a military government in England.

The navy have here, as their school ship, a fine 70 ft schooner, ex-Noah's Ark. An American sailed her in here to buy a cargo of drugs. He was sold some fine cocaine and good hash by, all three different people who told me about it believed, someone in the pay of the police. The police then raid, throw the Skipper in jail and confiscate his boat.

7th April.   Midday, and the wind had freshened to force 4. The boat was surging along at 5–6 knots. In the last 24 hours we have covered a comfortable 130 miles by log and a little more over the land as we have a helpful current. The pilot warns how this current can shift unpredictably either towards or away from the coast and counsels caution on maintaining a check on ones longitude in order to avoid hitting Isle Lobos de Afuera. I did my best despite a poor horizon shooting the sun in the afternoon. Twilight star shots were unobtainable as thin cloud spread across at dusk. However I was sure I would not arrive before dawn and as it has a strong light I should be able to pick it up an hour or so before then, which I duly did.

I was upset to find my mast light out. I checked the fuse and the connections but all appear okay so presumably the bulb has blown and I have no spare. It has meant keeping the side lights on which consume more electricity and are not as visible to other shipping. For a stern light, I left on the nav. room light. There was quite a lot of shipping about so my kips were limited to half hour ones. To charge the batteries I am towing a turbine which turns an alternator. The otherwise excellent engines have no hand start facility so it is a constant worry avoiding a flat battery.

Labos de Afuera is a guano island (where they mine bird shit for fertilizer) and as we passed it, flocks of pelicans lazily flopped out of our path. They really do look prehistoric. With the morning the wind dropped somewhat and with it, our speed down to 3½ knots. It has been 2 days now and I have hardly touched the sheets and only had to make minor adjustments to Quantock Pete.

A calm but pretty sleepless night as there was a lot of shipping. If the snatches of kip were added up I might have made 4 hours. I picked up one light where no light, and certainly not one of that characteristic, should be and decided it might be an offshore oil rig. I suspected a strong westerly set and at dawn shot Vega, Antares and Venus. My suspicions were confirmed, we had been set 8 miles offshore.

A breeze got up with the dawn and this time it was a close fetch. (Wind about 65° off the bow). As the land hardened up I had great difficulty deciding it was what it ought to be by the description in the pilot. Ile Foca looked longer than the one mile as described. However all eventually resolved itself after I got my vivid imagination to work on the problem.

2 miles off the island I passed a solitary man fishing from a balsa raft with, 30 yards astern, a solitary pelican waiting for offal. These rafts have a beam of about 4 feet and a length of about 12, a mast and a centre-board for lateral grip. The wind was up to force 5 and the sea quite choppy when I passed one 3 miles offshore having to scull. He was making surprisingly good progress too. Doubtless the owner did not like the idea of being blown any further offshore as the land under his lee was 6000 miles away.

At Paita I handed the sails and motored around looking for a berth. The fishing boats were packed together and the men could see my problem and waved me to a place that was too cozy for my liking. I did not want to be thumping another boat in the middle of the night, so I went a little shallower and dropped the hook into clayey mud, disturbing 10 pelicans perched around the gunwhale of an open boat just ahead. Fancy having that lot shitting on your decks!

Half way through clearing up, bagging sails and coiling ropes, a launch came alongside with three men. One was captain of the coastguard, one from the Port Captain's Office and the other a shipping agent expecting employment. In the cabin, the agent explains I need his services and for me he will do it cheap — 20 dollars (£10). Of course there will be another 20 dollars for the Port Captain.

"No thanks," I says, "Never use an agent."

"Ah, but here you have to."

"Why?"

"Because of all the papers, your ones from Callao die here." Says the agent taking the papers away. He also tried for my passport.

"Not necessary." I say, grabbing it back.

I get out a bottle of the local drink, Pisco, and lemons, thinking this might help smooth out the argument. The coastguard Captain explains it has to be done by an agent as here there is no yacht club, and he smiles. He smiles a lot. But then, if every other tooth is a gold one, you would too. I am not impressed and the agent seems to understand my comment about "A rip off" — obviously a slang expression he has heard before. I told them I had never used an agent and was not going to start now and that the Port Captain's fee of 20 dollars was totally unreasonable and I will leave Paita here and now. Have another Pisco. (This is as strong as scotch and I was dishing it out in treble measures. The C.G. Captain smiles and says yes. The agent looks crestfallen and refuses. The Port Captain's minion just holds out his glass and helps himself to a sweet out of the packet on the table.

Finally they decide no agent and tomorrow morning I see the Port Captain in person and argue the cost of his bits of paper out with him personally.

The fishermen in the adjacent boats are very friendly and helpful. Refuelling off a barge was the easiest of the voyage. I managed to get a bulb to suit the masthead tricolour light; changed the engine oil then had a bottle of beer and listened to Beethoven's violin concerto before turning in for what I hoped would be an uninterrupted night's sleep. A crash at 2.00 a.m. woke me. The boat next door was shoving me out of the way as I was over his anchor and he was off fishing.

I typed out a general declaration, 3 copies and 3 crew lists then went ashore to spend the last of my soles, and argue it out with the Port Captain. After waiting 10 minutes outside his office I thought 'What the hell', told the sailor on duty that an exit paper did not interest me, and wandered off to find more fruit (oranges and limes), eggs and tomatoes. No angry sailor followed me down the jetty so went back aboard. I topped up the batteries, checked the boat over, started the engines and, with difficulty owing to the good holding, broke out the anchor. Still no official on the jetty. Friendly waves to the fishermen and I motored out, carefully checking out all the moored boats to see if there were any coastguard ones. None were.

I kept the motors going for though the light breeze was fair, I was anxious to get out of official range as soon as possible. Soon though, the wind picked up enough to sail merrily along at 5½ knots. The land was fast disappearing. I was relieved. No doubt cocking a snook at Peru's ridiculous bureaucracy means vast fines and prison sentences, but I am very tired of it all and to want me to pay for the pain of it all really hurts.

12th April.   We have sailed 155 miles in 24 hours since leaving Paita, and very pleasant sailing it has been too. The sails have been boomed out wing and wing with a force 3 stern wind. Now, out of the shipping lane I do not keep a very good watch, popping up only about 3 times during the night, and then more to check the compass course and the set of the sails. The sea is a beautiful blue with the occasional whitecap; Quantock Pete is steering and I have just scoffed a good breakfast of 2 eggs, bacon and 2 tomatoes.

13th April.   During the night, crossed the Equator. The wind dropped too light for Quantock Pete, so in order to sleep with the boat keeping her course, I used the Autohelm. With the dawn it developed cramp. The old bother was diagnosed so I stripped the motor out and soldered two thin pieces of brass over the worn fingers of the bronze brushes. Unfortunately I trapped the feedback line and this broke. It took another hour to open her up again and patiently work out how the line was fitted and what it did. It now seems to be working alright again and I am going to need it in the doldrums when I will be under motor.

14th April.   Just as I finished working the morning sun sights I saw an enormous white body approaching to port. Christ! I thought, a great white. Then two, then three. Then a dorsal cut the water. They were orcas, mottled black and white. A big school of them and showing what I thought was too much interest in *Ocean Winds*. It was only a few hundred miles away that the Robertsons were sunk by such a school. Well I have a low terror threshold, or to put it another way, scare easily so, following the advice of the Baileys who were also sunk in this area by whales, started the engine to let them know I was not edible. One leapt clear of the water and seemed to be suspended before sliding back into a wave. They all appeared to be predominantly white except for a big black daddy bringing up the rear.

15th April.   As it grew dark I was having a little doze in the saloon. I was woken by banging sails. We had been hit by a sudden squall from the north. I wound up the genny, and having the inner small jib set, I brought that aback and hove the boat to on the starboard tack and went back to sleep after ensuring that all the windows were shut as it was pouring with rain. 3 hours later, the squall passed, the wind boxed the compass and then fell calm leaving an evil short lumpy sea. So we motored for 2 hours. That, I thought, was the last of my beautiful southerly, but no, back it came again, force 2 then 3. All day long the wind was up and down like the proverbial lady's drawers (I am having to wear mine as my bum has got a trifle sunburnt). The sky has been mostly cloudy with a weak sun coming through from time to time. My dubious sights indicated we are well to the east, so I have altered course by 10° to compensate. In the afternoon, a squall came up from astern so I grabbed soap and shampoo and deodorized. My, but that felt nice.

As evening fell, so we became becalmed once more. I motored until the Autohelm once more went haywire. Stripping it down, I saw that the feed back line had broken. It took me half an hour to work out how to replace it just the right length. With some 300 miles of possible calm ahead it was either solve the problem or steer the ship. Such a threat concentrates the mind — I solved it. All night me motored, during which I saw two ships. The stern light of one indicated that it must have passed quite close while I was asleep, but it should have seen my light and radar image. The sun is only 4° to the north, and with no wind it is getting distinctly tropical.

16th April.   A very mixed day starting off becalmed then head winds, rain and when that has passed, a following wind. Real doldrum weather. I managed a sort of longitude shot; there was thin cloud over the sun, but the sun disappeared at midday so could not get a latitude. Indeed I have not managed to get a latitude since the evening of the 13th. If I had an unknown current of 1 knot, in 3 days this could alter the latitude by as much as 70 miles. By my dead reckoning land should be some 80 miles to the north. Bashing on in the dark I felt unhappy. I was sorting out the genny sheets on the cabin top; it was a very dark night. Close, very close to starboard, it seemed only feet away, a dark shape shot out and above the surface of the sea and smacked down with a hell of a splash. Then another just beyond it. I shot back to the safety of the cockpit, trembling. Were they giant rays jumping clear or whales flicking their tails? It was too dark to see. At such times, a yacht seems a frailly built thing.

Ahead was a glow in the sky — lights reflecting off low cloud. Experiences told me it could be one of 3 things (the Northern Lights not showing at these latitudes). It could be a liner lit up on gala night; if so, its bearing would change. The bearing did not. So it must be either a large fishing boat like a factory ship or a town. If it was a town, bashing on towards it, I could well hit the coast first. I thought probably a fishing boat but decided, as I was tired and uncertain, to heave-to for the night.

17th April.   At dawn I started the engine but she would not go into gear. The lever had been getting stiff for 2 days now. While I was stripping the control down, a helicopter circled and the pilot waved. Christ! Where did that come from? I later saw two tunny fishing boats (the glow in the night sky), the chopper was their spotter. Not being able to repair the gear lever control I disconnected it down at the engine and moved the engine into gear at the gear box. I decided I would strip it all out in Costa Rica, if necessary calling on the Volvo agent there.

The sun came out and I dripped with sweat. It gave a good longitude but it was a latitude I needed. Just before local noon it clouded over. Curses. 10 minutes before noon the cloud thinned, so I started shooting ex-meridians. In the end I reckon I did get a noon shot which showed I had suffered an adverse current and was some 30 miles south of my D.R. position. It is very hot. My thermometer chickens out at 34°C (93°F) (I feel like doing likewise) so I do not know how hot it is.

18th April.   Dawn, and I could see Costa Rica some 25 miles away. Virtually no wind, so plodded on under engine. During the day a Marlin leapt clear of the water close to starboard. What a gorgeous looking fish — it must have been 7 or 8 feet long and shimmering blue and silver in the sunlight.

Managed to get latitude and longitude sights. The Costa Rica current was pushing me strongly westward. Saw a yacht to starboard but too far away to speak to him. Reached Ile Cano at dark, this left some 24 miles to Puntasarenas. Then the weather changed. A little thunder, a lot of lightning and a fresh head wind. As I did not want to spend the whole night beating back and forth across the Gulf of Nicoya dodging a lot of fishing boats, I decided to bash straight into it with both engines and try and make an anchorage by midnight. I dropped the hook off the town, hung a light in the rigging and crashed out for some well earned sleep.

Puntasarenas, as its name implies, is built on a sandy spit, the deep water to seaward where the big ships lie. Between the spit or finger on which the town is built and some mangrove swamps is a 2—3 fathom channel where the fishing boats and yachts moor. As I motored down this channel at 8 a.m., I was surprised to see more multihull than monohull yachts. One big tri I recognised, *Lorelei*. This was being built at Wadebridge in Cornwall 12 years ago when I was there building a 42 foot cat. Since I last saw the owner, Andy, and his wife Jeanne, they, with their 3 children (now taller than me) had sailed both the Atlantic and the Pacific from Australia to Canada.

Jeanne showed me where to start the hassle of clearing in. It is usually quite good in Costa Rica, but unfortunately I had no Peruvian Zarpa (clearance).

"We will fine you 20 dollars," says the guy.

"30 dollars," says the voice over his shoulder obviously thinking about these inflationary times. So I went back on board, hunted up my old Chilean 'Zarpa' that had carried me from Puntas Arenas in the Straits to Coquimbo and had lots of anchors stamped all over. Changed my last port from Paita to Coquimbo, Chile, and everyone was happy.

Puntasarenas is a good port and behind the spit the holding is excellent. You can water and fuel with the minimum of trouble. Unfortunately the booze, namely rum and gin are very cheap, particularly when bought from the government liquor store in 2½ litre jugs.

Found out here that I have passed the bay Drake actually stopped at; it is off peninsula Osa. I headed for the wrong Ile Cano, there are unfortunately two, one here at Bay Nicoya and one at Bay Coronado which I passed in the night.

There are a number of people looking to crew to various places. One guy hoping to get to Ile Cocos, others going to Panama. Owing to the fighting in Nicaragua the road is now closed for tourist traffic so two young American surfers from San Clemente jumped aboard my ship. Denis (20) and Carl (21). Good willing workers too. We immediately went across the Bay to the beautiful Hacienda de Nicoya to beach the boat on sand to scrub off the anti-foul. A Canadian doctor, Clare and his wife were also there working on their cat on the beach. With his electric drill, he helped me fix my gear shift control. This is a super little place, a few avocado pears, coconuts and limes to pick up, a bar which sold not only cold beer but also excellent hamburgers and salad for 2 dollars. In fact all around the Gulf of Nicoya are some idyllic anchorages and fish abound. The waters at night are alive with their phosphorescent trails.

Denis and Carl did most of the victualling while I obtained the clearances. We motored across to Hacienda de Nicoya again to spend our last night in this lovely anchorage and to collect off the trees some mangoes and limes.

It was afternoon by the time we managed to get away, sailing with a fair tide. After rounding the point, the first 30 miles were evil. As soon as we got out of the lee of the islands, there was a nasty tidal lop we had to bash straight into. This ruined all our appetites, and while none of us actually threw up, it spoilt the start of the voyage. The sky was black and as the sun set behind the thunderheads it became ominously red. We managed a little sailing but most of the time were motoring. In the early hours, Denis had to kill the motor as the alarm went signifying that the engine was overheating. Fortunately we soon had a pre-dawn breeze so were able to sail. At daylight, I took out the water pump impeller. I could have sworn I had two spare but could not find them in the engines spares box — they must have been left behind. Actually the impeller looks okay and is, so to speak, passing water. The exhaust is black so I guess the injectors need attention. We still have the port engine, but with maybe 900 miles of calm ahead, I feel I ought to get it fixed, so plan to head for La Union in the Bay of Fonseca, Salvador, which is just opposite the NW end of Nicaragua.

As the Nicaraguans are not welcoming to yachts passing close, and even are known to pirate, it means paralleling the shore about 50 miles off. At Puntas, a couple in a 42 ft ferro yacht were telling us how they were threatened by a Nicaraguan gunboat just as they were crossing into Costa Rican waters. As they refused to stop or go back to a Nicaraguan port a gun was trained on them. The lady held up the baby, who innocently waved to the man behind the gun. He sheepishly waved back. They then told the Nicaraguans, "You are in Costa Rican waters so cannot stop or board."

As we left Costa Rican waters we could see the lights of what we thought was probably a fishing boat, keeping up with us. So I put out our nav. lights just in case, and altered to get further offshore. We lost our companion in the mother and father of a thunderstorm, so I hove the boat to for an hour while it rained and blew.

The sea here abounds with life. Marlin and sailfish are seen jumping, but not at our lures, though Carl did get one bite. Rays leap clear and make a mighty splash on re-entry. Dolphins frequently play around the bows. Even turtles, many with hitch-hikers on their carapaces in the form of a sea-bird, leisurely float by.

30th April.   Again a magnificent sunset but showing no green tonight. It is very black over Nicaragua promising rain later. The galley started to walk. Denis, I feel, exaggerated the size of the worms crawling about the counter top. We had to throw out one length of our expensive sausage and a salami and some fruit and vegetables. This is the sort of problem that must have beset Drake, and he could not fall back on a reserve store of tinned and packeted foods.

Carl made a delicious guacamole with avocado, peppers, tomatoes, cheese and toast.

In the night, at the onset of a thunderstorm, Carl had a problem when the wind boxed the compass. He accidentally pushed the wheel pin in thus locking it. He became disorientated and in a panic called me as the boat was going round in circles.

During my watch we passed through the centre of a heavy storm. The lightning was overhead and the thundercracks and rolls prolonged and deafening. I was, as my American crew would say, scared shitless. I was on the verge of dropping all sails and rushing below for the crew to hold my hand. However British pluck (boneheadedness) prevailed, and I bashed on getting wetter and colder in the torrential rain. It was a watch remarkable for its fear and discomfort. It just cleared at the change for Denis. From nervous exhaustion, I slept solid.

The morning sun showed we were 10 miles to the west of our dead reckoning (D.R.). Land appeared shortly after noon, along with a hammerhead shark. I have no large scale chart of the Gulf of Fonseca and this stupid modern system which leaves the ports and gulfs blank just saying 'see chart 21521' is all very well if you have that particular chart, but otherwise the old ones were much better as they showed some detail of the major hazards. They were not, though, like the new ones, printed in pretty colours and were much more reasonable in price.

On the approach, we were nearer Nicaragua than any other country. At the sight of a boat closing us, we hauled in the fishing line so there would be no official reason to stop us, and loaded up the shotgun in case it was a private freebooter but the vessel passed well to our starboard. Probably we were blowing up the danger out of all proportion but the country has a terrible reputation. It is also in the middle of a revolution.

A dugout canoe came out from Salvador and went racing past at over 10 knots driven by a 15 h.p. outboard. They have beautiful dugouts here.

113

There was a lot of surf off Punta Amapala. We approached in the last of the light too late to find our way up to La Union without a chart. We followed a dugout canoe around the point to calm water and anchored where he indicated then asked the fisherman alongside for a rum. Two hours later a breeze got up from the east and turned the swell around the point. This changed our quiet anchorage into a very unquiet one. Carl and I put out a second anchor and I did anchor watch until it eased around 2 a.m. when at last I was able to sleep.

As it turned out, it was an easy passage up to La Union with just one reef off the most easterly point of the mainland. At La Union we anchored off a jetty and a petty officer came out and took our Costa Rican Zarpa. At the mention of an engine problem, and confirming that I expected to pay, he had a couple of his mates, engineers from the marine, out in 10 minutes. They could do nothing but charge 10 dollars which the P.O. shared. We got fuel and beer then looked for somewhere for a meal. They were celebrating May 1st and all the restaurants seemed closed. Somewhat reluctantly, a gentleman did direct us to the only one open, a hotel near the barracks. There we were served a good shrimp meal by lots of lovely waitresses. They kept changing, coming along and waggling their pert bottoms. Then it dawned. We were in the local whore house. Not only were the waitresses pretty, the food was good.

Salvador was a very friendly place, though it appeared to us expensive. There were not a great number of gringos to rip off so that they have to take advantage of the few that do visit. We baulked at being asked 4 dollars to take the fuel back 400 yards to the quay so carried it. The place reminds me of the Cabo Verde islands although the poverty was not quite so extreme. Pigs on the shore, cattle instead of goats tethered under the trees, people passing in the street always smiling and speaking.

2nd May. An early start ashore, Carl and Denis to the market for fresh vegetables and eggs, I to tangle with the authorities. The sergeant on duty smilingly asked for 8 dollars for the clearance. I, unsmiling, replied something about robbery and asked for my old one back from Costa Rica. I had to wait a quarter hour for the captain to arrive. He ordered his sergeant to give the zarpa to me free. They quite understood my reluctance to part with 8 dollars for a piece of paper. Of course they had me over a barrel, I would have had to pay if they had stood their ground, but I guess they were pleasant people anyway.

114

We got good vibes from Salvador.

Late afternoon sailing 5 miles offshore, briefly spoke the trimaran *Audacious* from Los Angeles headed in the opposite direction. Then ahead of us, 3 trawlers with their beams out either side looking like cats whiskers, fishing the shallows for prawns off San Sebastion. Our line is trailing astern. About time we caught something.

3rd May.   Carl woke me, saying we have a passenger boarded. There, on the starboard bow was a young booby preening. Denis sat a foot away grinning at it. It stayed, as our deck made a super lavatory, for 3 or 4 hours. A sailfish jumped clear of the water by at least 6 feet, and gave several repeat performances and as we passed, made a tentative strike at our lure then thought better of it. The sea was smooth as glass. The sun beat down. We have a canopy over the cockpit to give very necessary shade. The deck is too hot to walk upon.

The afternoon heat over the land drew in a sea breeze. With this we could sail at 3 knots or, helped with the port engine (stb. one still u.s.) motor/sail at 5½. As this gave an appreciably stronger wind to cool us as well as much better progress, we opted for the latter.

4th May.   Quite an eventful day. On the radio I heard that Britain had elected its first ever lady Prime Minister. The morning became hotter'n hell, with the sun almost directly overhead. Sweat just ran off us. We stood on the foredeck and poured buckets of sea-water over our heads to cool off. Denis had his first shit since leaving Costa Rica. This blocked bowel syndrome often happens and can be very dangerous. I put it down to holding one's stomach muscles taught all the time against the boat's motion.

We passed Guatemala and into Mexican waters at dusk. There is a new artificial harbour at Pt. Madero with leading lights and light buoys, none of which were in my 1978 list of lights. However I did a running fix on the main light and then we were in the Bay of Tuantepec.

It was my turn to cook, so it was mashed potato, bacon and pineapple. The sweet was some over ripe bananas fried in batter as fritters. The boys had not had banana like this before and the fritters went down a treat.

5th May.   This morning I was quite excited landing a fat little bonito of about 2 lbs. Just right for lunch. Then we lost two lures, the second one to a large marlin which ran the line out, jumped clear and snapped

115

it. It was a magnificent fish and far too big for us to ever land so it is as well it got away. Now we have heavier tackle out.

Scotch girdle or drop scones were made for an evening treat. Half way through the cooking, I had to hand over to Denis as we were in the middle of a shrimp fishing fleet and all seemingly converging onto us.

6th May.   The wind piped up during Denis' watch to just about gale force. It was around a thunderstorm so it was also raining stair-rods. The rain really hurt. We rolled up half the jib and deep reefed the main, then the boat was very comfortable. The bay of Tuantepec has an evil reputation for these strong winds, sometimes reaching up to hurricane force. This is why small vessels are advised to creep around the shore so you are not affected by the bad seas the winds whip up if you go directly across. I was really too far off at 10 miles, so put in a tack to close the shore to just outside the breaker line, by which time the wind fell right away.

Carl had just prepared lunch when his fishing line ran out. It was a 3 ft 6 in. dorado. Brilliant yellow when landed, then darkened to dull green and in its final death throes changed to white all over with dark spots. Carl is now on the foredeck cutting off large steaks. It is going to be a treat tonight.

7th May.   Shortly after the sun rose Guatalco light was fine to starboard. As we approached, below it on the rocky shore we could see a blow hole spewing spray vertically as each swell hit. A young sprightly dolphin played around, skipping along apparently on its tail while its mother, more sedately, swam alongside. The very lovely bay of Santa Cruz opened up. The entrance lay between the island, Pedra Blanca and the headland. It is deep and clear of dangers. There were 4 yachts at anchor. The village was beautiful, a number of thatched shacks and verandas with hammocks slung under. The holding is good once you can get your pick dug in. We had 3 goes, I did not realise it was a hard clay and should have used the fisherman. As it was, Carl had to dive down and physically dig in the point of the C.Q.R. before it would hold. Fortunately Carl is a very good swimmer.

One guy was in the local jail — about the size of a large privy, with a wooden barred door. A chain led from his leg through the bars of the door to a stake in the ground outside. He had been knocking off some goodies from a neighbouring village's church.

The church here is an open rectangular building with a roof, altar

116

and bell. The first bell was stolen by Francis Drake 400 years ago, when he called to pillage and water. His visit is not remembered, but from the account, it must have been a more important place in his day. We had a pleasant day's stay, had time not been pressing, I would have spent longer here as it is a lovely spot. Spent the evening aboard the other English yacht *Wizard*, a very posh 50 footer.

8th May.   Left just after dark with an almost full moon. Outside good force 4 head wind so put a long tack in offshore. After 6 hours we tacked, and the wind died off so with just the port engine, we had to motor into quite a lumpy sea.

During the day, the breeze set in from the SW so we gradually had to alter course towards the land, motor sailing to keep the speed at 5 knots while very close to the wind. Just at dusk we managed to identify Point Galero which tallied with our dead reckoning. A surprise, as we had had no fix for 70 miles.

10th May.   A bad day. The head wind increased to force 5 and the waves to 10–12 feet. To keep the boat plugging against them fast but very close, I motor/sailed using the port engine. We were about 45° off the true wind. This is okay in sheltered waters, but out at sea in those waves it is purgatory. The galley quickly disintegrated into an evil greasy mess, and come evening time, none could stay down there long enough to cook a decent meal, so I fell back on the emergency food – Complan. This cup food, a concentrated mix which becomes a light meal when mixed with water, is excellent for such conditions and was much appreciated.

11th May.   25 miles from Acapulco, and the sea and wind gone down, so we could motor/sail a mile offshore, cook a decent meal and enjoy our last day's passage together.

Acapulco is a beautiful natural harbour and the yacht club is in the west corner of the large bay. As it was 10 dollars a day at their marina, we dropped the hook 300 feet away in 40 foot of water. No one seemed to mind us rowing to their jetty and using the club's facilities. It was also a very easy clear in. *Wizard* got rooked 20 dollars by migration and health officials as they came to the club and visited anyone on the pontoons. As we were at anchor we had to go into the town and do it all at the office where they reluctantly completed the forms for free. It was the least hassle of anywhere since Cabo Verde.

117

Acapulco is a great sprawling mess over 50 miles across in places. The bay is still lovely though and caters for tourists, mostly Americans. A lot of street vendors offer a variety of goods, but you have to haggle for bargains.

Anchored just ahead of us was a red steel French Canadian from Montreal. At the turn of the century, a hardy guy, J.E. Bernier made a two year expedition to take part of Arctic America for Canada. Real Bouvier, after much research, sailed across to Greenland (with the charming Marie-Eve, and three others) and then through the NW passage. It took him three summers to get to Vancouver. I was particularly interested in the navigation problems for without a giro compass how do you manage sailing almost over the top of the magnetic North Pole? He used the sun's shadow on the pins of a pelorus. He worked out the sun's azimuth every few hours and changed the bearing on the pelorus every 15 minutes.

"O.K. I can understand that while you have the sun, but what about when it was overcast or foggy?" I asked.

"Ah" Real replied, "I think I will write a book about 'By guess and by God navigation', I am now ze expert."

He is a great guy. Not surprisingly the Canadian bureaucrats did their best to dissuade him from attempting the passage, even trying to forbid him. He is fond of saying, with a charming French accent:

"The life of an adventurer is not an easy one".

He does not mean getting stuck in ice, navigating with inaccurate charts, facing storms at sea — they are minor problems. No, it is tangling with the authorities, obtaining 10 mm bolts or merely getting diesel. As he says, get to sea and your worries fall away. He sailed out of the harbour on Monday 14th. I have not much mentioned his companion, Marie-Eve, with her laughing twinkling eyes, but she impressed me as being a very capable lady.

My two crewmen also left, getting berths as working crew on a 45 footer being delivered to San Diego. Much to their surprise they were offered a 1000 dollars so are going to arrive back home with more money than when they left. The boat has a big engine so it should not be too tough a passage either.

I had to wait 4 days for the Volvo agents in Acapulco to air freight to me two water pump impellers, the seals and the 2½ in. long shafts. What with phone calls and collection fees these cost 100 dollars, and they were for the wrong engine.

19th May.   I was up at 6 a.m. filing out the bore of the water pump to take the new shaft. It had to be done carefully to avoid ovalling the bore so took me two hours. By 9 I had the motor functioning once more. Then it was the usual pre-sail chores of filling up with diesel, topping up the water tanks and spare 5 gall. reserve ones and into the city for victuals. After a shower, I made a tour of the boats in the marina to swop as many paperback books as possible, and then an early night.

20th May.   Just after first light, the anchor was weighed and we motored out in a virtual calm. Nautech had sent a new motor for the Autohelm but the British postal 'go slow' and the exigencies of the Mexican Post meant it never arrived in time. I had checked the unit out and found the build up I had done on the brushes still good. I had stored the unit on its side in the tropical heat, and the silicon grease used to seal and weatherproof it had melted and run down the compass thus insulating the electrical pick up points. Cleaned with alcohol it once more worked well.

The bloody wind and sea was all wrong for going west. I could make long and short tacks up the coast, but the seas were such as to stop the boat so progress under sail was going to be minimal. At which point I banged on both motors and thumped towards Zihuatanejo, 130 miles up the coast. There I can replace the fuel and it is reputed to be a pretty place and it is where Anson hid waiting to knock off the Manilla Galleon back in the 18th Century.

I had an evil throat which bothered me. Was it the start of a cold, laryngitis or something worse? I decided to take a course of tetracyclin as when sailing solo you cannot afford to go crook.

It was fairly lumpy going north and the wind took a long while to die in the night. A couple of ships and a liner passed; I slept in half hour snatches. Coasting, and in a shipping lane to boot, is no joy for single handers. Even so I did not feel too tired when approaching Zihuatanejo next morning at 9 a.m.

The Princess, a British cruise ship that passed me in the night, was in for a short stop and was re-embarking as I was going ashore. Again it was a very hard bottom and I had trouble getting the C.Q.R. to bite, but once in, the holding is excellent.

There was a little surf on the beach so landing was quite thrilling. The second time I did not make the right approach as there is a technique to landing in surf. The dinghy broached, went up to an angle of 90° and I toppled out. The dinghy righted and surfed in with me dripping and cursing staggering up the beach behind it. Surprisingly the camera, in its bag, remained safe and dry in the dinghy. Fortunately my glasses have a retaining cord for they tried to go adrift. However, getting soaked in this climate is of no great moment.

At every place I have been in Mexico, they have been sold out of diesel and awaiting delivery. Here the delivery came in the afternoon and as that made a 4 hour wait, I decided to spend the night here despite the urgency of getting out of this area before the season starts for the tropical revolving storms or hurricanes.

It is a well sheltered port, with a lot of shops and a sandy beach. The bay is alive with fish — the most I have seen anywhere. A Canadian met ashore suggested I hit the town with him that evening. A night in the local cathouse, he pointed out, was only 10 dollars. Although tempted, the thought of a dose and 3½ thousand miles before I could get a shot of penicillin was too sobering so I hoisted in the dinghy (damned hard graft on my own) to remove temptation and went to bed at 8.30. A disturbed night, as a voracious mosquito avoided my murderous intent. It actually rained during the night, the first since Tehuantepec.

22nd May.   Away at 6.30. Thank God it was the lightest anchor — it still made me puff. There was very little wind but a nasty head sea so I motor sailed WSW to get offshore. Ahead, perhaps 50 feet or so, a ray with black and white underbelly, about 4 feet wide, leapt vertically well clear of the sea and turned a complete somersault, for all the world like a first class gymnast, before diving back into the water.

For breakfast, I fried up half a cooking banana. These are bigger, longer and a slightly different shape from the variety you eat raw. They are excellent fried in oil and best kept until they go black.

When the wind got up just before noon it forced the course to be only 15° west of south, but at least that was getting us well offshore. As I have to sail well out into the Pacific before being able to go north for Canada, the westing I need. I set the QME, Quantock Pete, to steer as close to the wind as possible and so it followed when the wind backed or veered. I just read.

23rd May.   The wind died by midnight and so I used the starboard engine and, as there was the occasional ship about, had on my all round white light and the lower port and starboard steaming lights.

With the engine running, the battery drain did not matter. I am not happy with my mast head light as I have been unable to obtain the correct bulb replacement. The bulbs should be brighter to give the required 2 mile range. I expect to be out of the shipping lane by tomorrow.

The day, now some 60 miles from the coast, has been calm. We must be out of the influence of the land heating and cooling. The course has been set at 20° north of west which only very gradually diverges from the coast. In 24 hours of motoring the engine has used up 9 imperial gallons of diesel. My plan is to sail WNW until I can pick up a wind which I hope will allow me to sail out to 120°W, (noon position today, 17°N 103°W) and about 20°N where, according to the pilot chart, I should find the trades. They start NNE but as I haul out to 130°W they should veer to NE allowing me to clamber, thump and shudder NNW. Hope, springing in its eternal fashion, is that the wind Gods agree with the Admiralty pilot charts.

Days like today are very conserving of clothes. The sun sights did not take long, sitting on the deck out of the shade, an important consideration, as otherwise I would have had to put some sun tan cream on my chopper.

26th May.   All day on the 24th motored through a calm then on the 25th came a mid-morning breeze. At last the engines could go off. The speed was only some 2½ knots but picking up to 4 in the rare force 3 gusts. Of course we were hard on the wind. This fell away to nothing during the night so motored. Today again a morning breeze which almost allows us to lay the course for Ile Socorro, 180 miles away. I cannot quite climb onto the chart I am using. Fortunately these American ones have a wide bottom margin and for the last 100 miles have been plotting my position on that. All the time we are plugging west, making 80–90 miles each day. I keep hoping for the start of the northerly trades but no, what wind there is keeps coming from the NW. There is a slight swell from the same direction. I still have over 50 galls. of fuel left. We have come over 400 miles since leaving Zihuatanejo and used up 25 galls.

28th May.   At dawn, the D.R. position was 30 miles from Ile Socorro. According to the pilot, on a clear day it can be seen 70 miles away. It was a clear morning, and there was no sign of it. However an hour later I could make out a smudge on the horizon which slowly took shape.

The peak was mist enshrouded until after midday. The wind picked up to force 4 and at times we were reaching along at 7+ knots so quite soon came up to the island. Fortunately I had a large scale chart. There is a cove immediately to the west of Bay Braithwaite with leading marks and a threatening swell breaking on the rocks to port. A fishing boat was at anchor, so I went further into the cove and dropped my hook. Later, on the advice of the commandant, I went right up to the head but had to drop stern anchor as well to stop the back eddies blowing the boat onto the rocky shore. The water is very clear and you can see the anchor in the sand 5 fathoms below. Multicoloured fish abound. The Navy have recently charted the cove and marked the 5 fathom points with orange buoys.

It is a naval outpost of Mexico. There are about 200 personel. The Captain speaks English, more or less, and proved very hospitable, supplying me with eggs, biscuits and a leg of lamb which was deliciously tender. He also let me have some diesel. He is only allowed to let voyagers have enough to reach the nearest port (some 300 miles away) so now all my spare containers are topped up. He could not take payment, so I passed over a couple of bottles and 150 pesos (7 dollars) donation for the sports fund. *Playboy* magazines and bottles of whisky are usually the most appreciated gifts at such places — but carrying a big enough trade store is the problem, unless you count NOT drinking the whisky yourself also a problem.

29th May.   I took advantage of the washing troughs by the well to do a few clothes, topped up the water tanks, and had a last swim. It has been a very worthwhile stop. Then the hard sweat hauling aboard the dinghy using the main-sheet off the end of the boom. It is really a bit much for one person, particularly since it now leaks and gets waterlogged. Then it was a question of getting the two anchors up. While I was doing this, the Mexican Navy sailed in with a supply ship and anchored in the entrance. Weighing the 35 lb C.Q.R. made me sweat — the 45 lb Holdfast made me fear a heart attack. But still, no more anchoring for 3000 miles. I motored out giving the Navy a wave and hoisted sail. The island was affecting the wind strength and direction but once clear, on a beautiful sunny day, we chomped along at 5–6 knots with a few rolls in the genny as quite a fresh wind was blowing. The best course, hard on the wind, I could lay was just south of west but at least this kept us well clear of the unlit Ile Roca Partida, a small desert isle passed sometime in the night.

There is another isle of the group, Isle Carion, lying 200 miles west of Socorro. As big as Socorro but uninhabited and rarely visited by any vessels so not a place to be wrecked. It can be quite worrying sailing with no look-out and an unlit rock or isle ahead. I got a noon latitude sight and an afternoon longitude one so I was sure we would not be up to the island until after daylight.

31st May.　Sure enough, 2 hours after light, I picked it up about 20 miles fine on the port bow. In fact we sailed past without touching the sheets or steering and a good 15 miles to the north of it. And now no more land to worry about hitting until Canada.

I have the sails sheeted in fairly hard and the QME set to keep us on an average of about 55° off the true wind. Any closer and it gets uncomfortably lumpy. We have been averaging 4—4½ knots, making good just over 100 miles a day. Unfortunately we have been sailing due west but soon the wind should pull round more and let us go NW. We have before us a windward leg of 1,500 miles.

2nd June.　It is pretty depressing making such little progress. Occasionally I motor for an hour which increases the light head wind and makes me think we can sail. At the moment we are making 3 knots (well almost), slightly south of west. According to the pilot chart the wind should be coming out of the north now instead of out of the NW. I suppose it is not really too bad as we are making about 80 miles a day towards an area where the wind should be stronger.

Yesterday I noticed 2 seams going on the leech of the genny so in the calm of the evening handed the sail and restitched all the suspect seams. Today I was surprised to see a V.L.C. carrier hull down to starboard. I have been sailing at night without lights (a black ship) as I thought there was unlikely to be any traffic whatsoever in this stretch of ocean. Guess I will run the masthead light at night from now on even though we are well out of the shipping lanes.

5th June.　Lolloping along with a force 2—3 wind. It is never worth pinching too close to the wind as then even a little sea stops you. The speed varies between 3 and 6 knots and the course also with the wind shifts to between SW and NW. I actually want to go NW and according to the wind roses on the pilot chart should now be able to lay the desired course. Alas, the wind Gods do not read pilot charts.

I have been reading a book a day and doing very little else. After dark, I listen, if I can find a reasonable station with good reception, to the radio for an hour or so before turning in for the night. Occasionally the U.S. stations have some interesting talks but generally I do not think their standard as high as the BBC overseas programme. Some Bach and Vivaldi came through well yesterday on the Dutch station, Radio Hilversum. The BBC also has some tuneful music on occasionally but alas the witty quiz game, 'My Music' was spoilt by poor reception. I wonder why 'Voice of America' only play asinine pop? They do have good talks and discussion programmes though.

I have laid a seat cushion athwart the companionway on the bridge-deck, originally so my ear was immediately below the engine alarm when motoring. Now I find it is a good berth when under sail, particularly at night. If the sails start flapping that wakes me, and, with the hand bearing compass at my side, I do not need to get up to check the course, so now rarely get out more than once a night for a look-see. Progress might be slow (about 90 miles a day) and often 30° from the desired course, but at least it is not arduous.

My pickled meat has gone off and had to be thrown out. Two large chunks of rump steak. It was laid down in the second week of February and was still good a month ago. One really should follow Mrs Beeton's recipe and hang it to dry after two weeks or so of pickling, then eat it as jerky.

9th June.   Engine on. 4 hours later, engine off, light breeze, speed 2+ knots. It has been like this for 3 days. It is all most frustrating. What a relief that I managed to top up with diesel in Socorro.

Yesterday I crossed the sun's declination, when it was dead overhead. This allowed for a beautiful fix at local noon. I took a page of sights. To find the geographical position (G.P.) of the sun at each sight (i.e. the spot on the earth it was vertically above) the declination (from the almanac) gave its latitude and exact Greenwich Mean Time converted into arc (1 hour = 15° longitude) plus the small correction from 'equation of time' gave the longitude. The corrected sextant altitude was subtracted from 90° which equalled about 0° 30'. Each minute equals a nautical mile, so I was 30 miles from the sun's G.P. With a compass set at 30 miles we must be on the circle scribed with the G.P. at the centre. As the sun's G.P. moves rapidly, 4 sights taken within a few minutes of each other gave a beautiful cross.

11th June.   During the past 3 days a big northerly swell built up, from trough to crest about 12 feet. This morning it had gone and now the swell is only 3 or 4 feet. When the swell was running we were able to make up on our northing but now we are going more west. So far, in the last 12 days, the wind has not been above force 3 and all too frequently below force 2. The last days have been a little better and we have sailed over 100 miles in the last 24 hours all under sail so things are gradually improving. With the sun so nearly overhead one would expect it to be bloody hot. In fact it is distinctly cool; I am dressed in long trousers, shoes, socks, shirt and sweater and am rapidly losing my sun tan. The sea coming down from the north and probably some upwelling off the Californian Coast, cools the breeze down. The cabin temperature is 26°C.

13th June.   In the trades at last. At evening the wind picks up to a good force 5 and I first roll up part of the genny and then a little later, bend in a deep reef in the main. We bounce on through the night making about 5 knots. In the mornings, the wind moderates to force 4 so the reefs are shaken out and we hammer to windward at 5–6 knots, occasionally 7 if she gets her head knocked off by a wave. It is quite a lively ride but progress is being made — 140 miles each of the last two days. Unfortunately we are still going more west than north. Vancouver is 1,200 miles to the north but it looks as if we will have to sail about 1,800 miles to get there. When ocean sailing, you must not look ahead for arrival; rather just exist for the day itself. Not that there is much to the days. I try to sleep through the 10 hours of darkness, rising at first light. First a couple of cups of tea, and run up the ded reckoning position. (Ded is not misspelt, but comes from deduced). It is very satisfying seeing a jump on the chart of 40–50 miles.

I have taken to frying up some spiced soya bean hamburgers with an egg and potato for breakfast then nothing to do but laze and read until an hour before noon when I take a longitude shot which I cross with a latitude sight at noon. The sun is so strong, it pierces the thin clouds. After plotting that lot on the chart, I think about lunch. I have a tin of asparagus tips which I am going to save to be a celebratory treat as soon as we actually start pointing towards Vancouver. So today, I guess it will have to be rice with chopped onion and open my last tin of ham. For the evening meal tonight I will make a spaghetti as have not made one for a while. For the meat sauce I am having to use soya bean dried to resemble meat.

16th June.   Now at last off the the coast of the U.S. — the same latitude as San Diego, but 1,000 miles to the west. A ship passed in the night a mile away. The first seen for 2 weeks. This will be the 7th day in which we have sailed over 100 miles. The distance covered has gradually been dropping. 3 days ago it was 145 miles, then 129 and 127 and today looks like about 115. The barometer has risen to 1026 m.b. so we are almost up to the Pacific high. The course is NW. Ideally it would now be due north for 500 miles and then NE and being a perpetual optimist, I keep looking at the compass in the hope that the wind has veered, but it is getting difficult to keep my hope bubbling up.

The tabling on the leech of the big jib has come unstitched between the seams and must be causing a bad eddy. The sails need the attention of a sailmaker. With only 1½ thousand miles to go I am keeping my fingers crossed hoping that they will hold together. The problem is that the stitching of the seams chafes through although the small inner jib and the main both have small chafe holes too. However, as soon as the wind becomes fair, the strain on them will be much less.

18th June.   At 10 minutes before each hour on the U.S. time signal station, WWV, a weather synopsis is given out. Bloody depressing it is too. The Pacific high is very intense and centred about 6° further north than is usual for this time of the year. I am in a position where the headwinds should be dying off but owing to this, must expect them to continue for another few days. So, while the wind has dropped to a comfortable force 3, and the seas likewise moderated, I still cannot head towards Canada. If you were to draw a 1,100 mile radius circle centred on Vancouver I would be going around the SW edge. Every 100 miles sailed gets me no nearer my destination. It is no good coming about, for while I would at first shorten the distance from Canada the wind would become very bad and I would soon suffer a stronger adverse current. With luck I should be able to tack in about 2 days time.

The wind is awfully cold and I have been wearing, day and night, a furry synthetic exposure suit. But I am feeling uncomfortable so today intend to use some precious fresh water for a flannel bath, then don a clean shirt and knickers. That is, if I do not fall asleep beforehand and put it off until tomorrow. Mind you, it is developing a modicum of urgency as the cook and crew are objecting to the Captain's smell.

The Captain finds his cook and crew distinctly malodorous too.

During the night I was awakened by a squall. Started rolling up the genny when I heard her rip. By torchlight I could see she had gone 4 panels down from the top. I rolled her up as best I could which proved later to be a bad mistake. Under just main and inner jib our speed was down to 2 knots so, after donning oilskins and clipping on safety line, I sat up on the heaving foredeck clipping on the No 3 jib. This sail I had never set before on the boat, but carried for just this emergency. It is 135 sq. ft and proved just right for the force 6 wind.

19th June.   In the daylight during the first quiet spell, I tried to unfurl the genny to hand it. Alas, shreds of terylene (dacron) have somehow locked it at about one third out so since I cannot fully unfurl her I cannot get her down. This would not matter except that a yard of the top portion is flapping free and beating hell out of the other sail on the adjacent stay. Now I realise I should never have rolled her in the night but handed her as soon as she split. Of course the big mistake was not taking her down when I first noticed that the tabling had become unstitched. Had I done so and repaired her then it would have been a case of a 'Stitch in time saving 9'. The trouble serves me right.

The No 3 was handed and the No 2 hoisted. This is the other 'twin' and is 225 sq. ft with the full length of the forestay for a luff. It sets well and is a good sail for getting to windward which is just as well for it looks as if this long beat is going to continue for a while yet. It is now back to the traditional way. Donning oilies, then up forward to change jibs in the squalls.

20th June.   Again during the night a squall woke me. I eased the sheets to take the pressure off the sails, then donned oilies, clambered out, and deep reefed the main. There was a thin driving rain and a force 6 wind which had veered nicely so we were headed almost north. Once more below and the oilies off, the squall passed. Blow me, it was a virtual calm. Sod it, talked I to myself, the reef can stay in until morning. For the rest of the night the wind was up and down; at times we sailed at 2 knots, and at others, 5. I am beginning to feel a bit Flying Dutchmanish. It is now 3,000 miles or 31 days sailing since Acapulco.

21st June.   The yard of sail flapping in the breeze was worrying. Where it was beating against the No 2 jib I could see it had already chafed through some stitching on that sail. Somehow I had to get a lashing around it, but it was 30 foot up the luff. If I could hoist the forestay cover, that would do it, but I had no spare halliard. Gradually I realised there was no other way. I was going to have to climb the mast and reeve another halliard. How I would have managed without the mast steps I do not know — with them was bad enough. It is above the cross trees that you really get jerked to hell and back again. I got a spare halliard reeved through a stainless steel eye on the masthead cap. Then, with patience and curses got the jib cover on. Even then it was not good enough. Too much of the sail was still free and the line at the top would not tighten. So hey-ho, back up the mast. Tying knots one handed is not easy — at the top of a madly jerky mast it is not only incredibly difficult, it is also bloody frightening. Eventually I got the job done with only a little of the sail stuck out. I have to hope it will last without jerking free. Only a little more than 1,000 miles to Canada.

22nd June. The worst 24 hours run for over a week, and the best. We have only sailed 83 miles but mostly in the right direction so now am actually nearer Vancouver. Much of the day has been calm so are motoring north. The swell is coming from the NE instead of the NW. There are occasional fog patches, light drizzle and even the odd sunny period. I have stitched up the chafed stitching on the No 2 jib and been reading in the cockpit with my shirt off. Altogether a good day.

23rd June. After motoring for little more than 2 days, came a light breeze. The Autohelm had just packed in too. The breeze was hardly enough to operate Quantock Pete, particularly goose winged (yes — a following wind!) with the jib boomed out to port, but it is such an improvement the occasional gybe only made me swear. I have put in an hour trying to fettle the Autohelm. I have got it working again, but the commutator on the motor is so worn it cannot last long so I will save it for use only when under motor. It is a marvellous instrument, but everything is so small and my fingers so big and the boat heaving in the swell it is amazing I have repaired it rather than done it irreparable harm.

The barometer has started to fall slowly, so I should be over the hill and for most of the way should have a favourable wind to Vancouver Island. Even so, I shall keep to the NW of the direct line so as to have something in hand if the wind does back northerly again. It is 850 miles to the Straits of Juan de Fuca.

For the past two days a sooty albatross has been gliding around.

Odd that they should cross the Equator in the Pacific but not in the Atlantic, for you never see Albatrosses in the North Atlantic. There are masses of small sailing jelly fish. They are oval with a chord of about 4 inches and 2 inches. Their sail is diagonally across and inflated. They do not have trailing tentacles like the Portuguese Man o' war, just a purple collar. There are literally millions of them. Where they bunch up, the sea changes colour — at first I though they were large oil slicks.

25th June.   Woke up in the morning and saw by the hand bearing compass that we were 40° off-course. I dragged myself up, and lo and behold, a ship passing but a mile ahead. We were crossing the great circle route from the Philippines to San Francisco.

The wind was very light. I had to hand steer in between booming out the jib, then gybing and handing the pole a couple of times — all to try and get her to sail at 2 knots. When the speed eventually dropped to 1 knot I called it becalmed and started the engine. The Autohelm then steered while I read 'The Worldly Philosophers' which deals with the birth of political economy. I notice that most of these early economic experts were pretty incompetent at managing their own affairs.

When the wind returned it came with the fog. It was also a head wind so it was a tack to the north and tack to the east. Then at 3 p.m. came a welcome wind shift as the wind quickly freshened from the ESE. At last laying the course and making good progress. Alas the wind kept increasing with driving rain, so I donned oilies and reefed the main. It was starting to get nasty, so I handed the No 2 jib intending to change it for the No 3. However when I got the No 2 to the deck, I had plenty of sail up with just the inner storm jib and the deep reefed main set, so I just lashed the No 2 at the bottom of its stay. It was now blowing a full gale; in the gusts we were making 6 knots. Whether it was fog or thin driving rain, visibility was right down too. As the wind had got up from a virtual calm in just ½ hour, initially the seas were not bad but they soon increased to 8—10 feet. Then, as suddenly as it started, it stopped. It continued to rain hard and the seas were nasty but the wind had died. I was about to leap out and put up the No 2 jib again when I thought 'perhaps this is the eye of a small depression'. So I thought it best to wait a little and put on a brew of tea.

The rain cleared, but soon the wind was whining again, force 6—7 off the starboard bow. It was uncomfortable and looking so black up ahead, was going to get worse. Soon it was again blowing a full gale. Gales which get up quickly, usually drop as quickly, and it was so with this one. Within 2 hours the wind fell to a light breeze but the evil sea that remained, virtually stopped the boat. It took some 20 hours for the sea to calm down.

27th June.   The following day I woke realising something was wrong. We were headed SE instead of NE. It was now a run, fortunately Quantock Pete could just cope with the steering. By mid-afternoon it fell calm and we had to start the engine. There is 30 gall. of fuel left and 500 miles to go, so we have to sail at least half the distance.

29th June.   For the first time last night I had to keep constant watch on the helm for 8 hours. She would hold her course for long enough for me to put the kettle on or make a stew. Down in the galley, I keep the bearing compass by me so I can see if she has gone off course by more than 20°, then it is a case of rushing out and correcting her up before we gybe. We had to motor for a long period then in the early hours we had a light beam wind. Quantock Pete could just manage so at last I could fall asleep. This morning the wind has picked up to a nice breeze and is broad on the beam which is ideal. The speed is 5 knots and we are 330 miles from Juan de Fuca straits.

I am in range of the U.S. medium band radio stations so can listen to the weather conditions on the mainland. They have a heat wave with appalling smog in Los Angeles and drizzle, fog and 20 knot winds in Washington and Oregon. It is better weather where I am.

Drake came up here from his last stop in Mexico (Guatulco), and for him, too, it was a long sail, but in his case without charts or knowing where he might expect to land. His boat must have been getting foul and so unhandy to sail as well as slow. He must have been wondering at his chances of ever getting back to England with his booty laden ship. At least I know I am only 3 days away from land and, while today I have had to throw out the last of my potatoes as they are now all bad, I know where I can get some more very soon. When Drake reached a similar stage in his voyage for him to have to throw out rotten food must have been a major calamity. For me, with the engines and terylene (dacron) sails and wire rigging and at all times having adequate charts, the trip has been arduous enough but bears no real comparison with Drake's achievement.

The sailing jelly-fish have at last been left astern. The ocean has been littered with them for the last 600 miles; in total there must have been many millions. At times they were so close together they discoloured large patches of sea.

30th June.   By afternoon it was drizzling and the barometer falling. A trough was obviously passing through. At midnight the wind suddenly veered, gaps in the cloud and a force 7 wind. I deep reefed the main and had just the storm jib set on the inner stay. It was cold, with the wind from the NW.

During the morning the wind moderated; progress was good and I was beginning to think it was going to be a pleasant easy passage for the last 200 miles. What a hope. By afternoon it was drizzling again with a falling barometer. A clear indication of another depression and so close to the preceding one. As the jib furler was out of action there was the wet, uncomfortable job of changing down to a smaller headsail. But at least it passes the time and gives you something to do.

Nightfall and a sudden wind-shift to the NNE, a full gale to boot with cold, piercing rain. Up on the foredeck, as I struggled with hauling in the No 2 jib, I could make out a ship's red light close to port. I wonder if he saw me in the murk. Handing the jib and deep reefing the main was rough. I put her on a close fetch of about 60° off the wind with the sails just drawing which slowed us to 2—3 knots so that we did not bash into the seas and yet more or less maintained the course.

I had just got my head down on cushions on the saloon floor when banging on the deck told me that the lashings on the jib had come adrift. Ah well, back on with waterproofs, safety line and brave the elements on the pitching foredeck. It is so so cold.

In spite of it all, some of the night I slept. At dawn twilight something was wrong, we were way off course. I tried to adjust the self-steering, then realised the control line had parted. Repairs had to wait an hour for more light. Fortunately the wind moderated a little, down to force 7. The job meant leaning over the stern held by a taught safety line, pitching up and down with sheets of cold spray lubricating me and with cold fumbling fingers trying to thread the control line through its leads. It kept jamming, but patience was eventually rewarded. What a relief to get it working again. The wind had also backed a little so it was now a reach at 5—6 knots in quite vigorous conditions. I retired to rest and thaw out.

Full morning and the gale was blowing as hard as ever. A weak sun shone through the scudding clouds. The seas were magnificent, I suppose about 20 feet high and streaked with foam. It is an awe inspiring (frightening) sight and one I would gladly miss. *Ocean Winds* has been riding the seas admirably and making good progress. We are under deep reefed main and storm jib which is set on the inner stay, so all sail is close to the mast and centre of the boat, which I am sure is best.

I have often heard it said that ketch rig is best for ocean voyaging. I do not think so for boats under 40 feet long. Certainly a mizzen and jib would have the same area as we have set, but the pressure on the ends of the boat would tend to hold her down so I think a ketch would tend to be wetter and take more punishment. And when under full sail, generally a ketch is at a disadvantage because then it is a less efficient rig.

During the day the wind slowly moderated. I could plot the position by radio bearings. The seas were too big and there was too much spray flying around to try for sun fixes but fortunately there is a plethora of radio beacons.

As night fell it made a change for me to be increasing sail. By midnight I had picked up two lights on Vancouver Island. We were about 10 miles off, so I backed the jib and hove-to for 3 hours while I slept.

At dawn, I had to force myself to get cracking. We motor sailed. We were 90 miles from Victoria, the port where I intended clearing into Canada. A breeze got up from the worst possible direction — dead ahead. It brought with it fog and a cold drizzle. Altogether quite miserable. I did not fancy the slog up the Straits in those conditions so put a tack in across to the Washington State side and into Neah Harbour. There a little man came out and instructed me to anchor and wait Customs and clearance. So I did. 2 hours later I am still waiting — pissed off, because now it is getting late and the shops will be shut so it no longer seems worthwhile going ashore. I was really looking forward to getting some bread, eggs, bacon and cheese and have had to make do with a bowl of soup and pasta shells. What a let down.

Three hours later a lady customs officer was brought out by the coastguard. She was very pleasant, but as I was not going to land in the U.S. her clearance was pointless. The evening was developing beautifully as she left.

If I had a crew, I would have left too. Sod it, I said to myself (lone

132

sailors talk to themselves a lot — even long discussions and arguments). I have some 'keep awake' pills which I have had for 12 years and never used. The weather could well deteriorate tomorrow. I was a bit shy on sleep, only having had 5 hours in the last 24, but such a calm might only last the night. I argued it back and forth and then, muttering something about 'affairs taken at the flood' hauled in the anchor. The sun was setting beautifully in the west.

It was a spanking night. Crystal clear; of course cold, but I had on 4 pairs of socks, polar suit, 2 shirts, sweater and my sheepskin jacket. My tootsies were still cold, but then they had not been warm for a week.

There was 25 gal. of diesel left so I used both motors to give me an extra knot of speed. It was calm; pegging the wheel she would steer herself for long periods which allowed me to keep stuffing myself (alas — the tin marked custard contained rice pudding, but with a tin of gooseberries heated up, it did me twice). I sailed right down the middle of the traffic separation zone and this entailed frequent plots using the various lights, so kept me occupied and time passed quickly. To keep fully awake I took a pill every 4 hours; these did the trick nicely with no apparent side effects, although I did not feel a 'high' either.

As a rule I am not much given to night passages but this one proved exceptionally pleasant and interesting. It was a quiet sunny morning too. Approaching Victoria after a 16 hour passage (more foul than favourable tide) clothes are drying, polar suit is off at last and even my feet are not quite so cold. But my eyes are beginning to feel heavy.

3rd July.   Victoria, British Columbia, a super port. I tied up at the jetty beneath the customs house virtually in the town centre. The customs let me in with no fuss — took about 10 minutes and then ashore for some food. This is a magnificent cruising area. Hundreds of miles of sheltered waters strewn with islands and anchorages. Many places there is a Government wharf to tie up to for a low charge. Fishing is good and there are shellfish and crab for the catching. In summer, there is usually little rain and pleasant, warm, sunny days. The waters are too cold for civilised people to go swimming though.

It was a good 3 days stop over. Met some folk-singers who were doing their thing on the streets. They came aboard for a drink and stayed two nights. Then I visited a local fishing boat for a drink and a yarn and to swop books. Staggered off that ship clutching a four foot salmon.

5th July.   From Victoria I motored and sailed as wind allowed up to Salt Spring Island. Beautiful scenery and gorgeous weather. I have a brother, John, and sister-in-law, Marion, living on this island so I telephoned them from Fulford Harbour to come and collect me before the salmon gets high. Then I spent, after a long soak in a hot bath, a night in an actual bed. All very strange.

The boat I laid up at the head of Ganges harbour and left her in the safe hands of Chuck, the boatyard owner, while I flew back to Britain for a two month spell to see if my own boat business was still operating. It took a year to get half way round the world, and a day to get back.

2nd part of voyage — Vancouver to Plymouth

Returned — dragging with me for a 2 week holiday, wife Ethel. She was so shocked by state of the boat she insisted on painting the saloon out. She made a good clean-up job of the galley too. We had a difficult launch, with only just enough water at high tide, but several of the local yachties mucked in, and gave us a shove. The yard were very moderate in their charges. People here have been so helpful and considerate from the commodore of the yacht club to the passer by asked for directions.

We took John and Marion up to Princess Louisa inlet which can only be reached by water. Alas, Marion got sicker even quicker than Ethel — the least motion upset her. I hope she thought the trip worth it for it is an exquisite fiord. In a tree perched a bald headed eagle. Otters popped their heads up and watched us pass their territory, while a black seal leapt alongside clearly happy to see us. The falls at the head were impressive. On the way out we were stopped at the narrow entrance by a 7 knot tidal current rushing in. So we went alongside a wharf and visited the impressive timber built lodge there. This lodge, once built for the jet set, is now maintained as a non-denominational Christian holiday centre for American children.

It proved a hard passage back to Vancouver as the weather turned foul. We took shelter in various coves; Smuggler's cove, a marine park, was exceptionally pretty. We fiddled our way into the inner cove and moored alongside a log boom.

At Vancouver, we had an introduction to Dr Makepeace of the Multihull Association, so tied alongside his Catalac — called *Peacemaker* — at the end berth of the rowing club. Dr M. and his wife entertained Eth and me to a gargantuan Chinese meal and had a long yarn about boats in general and catamarans in particular.

We took on replenishment booze here. Neither the customs nor the

137

chandlers were used to dealing with yachts and their small orders but we got our three cases with only a little bother.

Leaving Vancouver early in the morning, Ethel just spotted a dead head in time at the entrance to the harbour. By the way the waves were rising up and down the end we could see I reckon the butt was aground, and this was in 12 fathoms. But for Eth's eagle eyed lookout we would have hit it and been holed. These dead heads and floating logs make this otherwise idyllic cruising area too dangerous for yachts at night. Fast power boats are frequently holed.

It was 70 miles to Anacortes, U.S.A., so we could not hang about, so despite the light favourable wind, increased our speed to 6+ knots with the help of an engine. Crossing the border a pod of killer whales passed us going north.

We reached Anacortes just as it was growing dark and tied up at the visitors' berth in the boat haven. An English ship, the *VEGA Seal*, was waiting to discharge at the port and had the customs on board, so we had to wait until the morning to clear in and obtain our licence to cruise U.S. waters. This licence to cruise is very important to obtain, and has to be checked at each new customs area you visit. If you omit to do this, they fine you between 500 and 1,000 dollars.

Ethel flew back via Seattle from here while my son, Pip, and a young lady named Sue joined to crew across the Pacific.

5th Oct.   Doc MacKintyre of Seattle sailed in last night, and thought so little of my fishing gear that he made me up a trace he guaranteed would catch fish. We cruised around San Juan island as directed and caught an ugly spotted member of the bass family. It was just big enough for the three of us and very tasty. We reached Port Angeles just at dusk and tied up in the Boat Haven with plans to refuel in the morning.

6th Oct.   A very quiet day so motored along the Washington shore of the Juan de Fuca Straits to Neah Bay which we reached soon after dark. Fortunately there was a full moon as, even here, there are still a lot of floating logs and even the odd dead head.

7th Oct.   The hooting of the island fog horn had us awake at 7 a.m. Not quite so cold was the general conscensus. After a cup of tea, started the engines, and for the first time since fitting it, tried out the electric anchor winch which I bought in Ganges. It grunted a couple of times when it came to break the anchor out, but not as much as I would have done. It makes weighing the anchor a much less painful operation — let us hope it keeps working. With the electric auto-pilot, diesel engines, jib roller reefing gear and now this electric winch, this sailing lark is getting to be a real old man's game. But then, I am getting to be a real old man.

As we approached Tatoosh Isle at Cape Flattery off NW U.S.A. (beg pardon Alaska) there was a good big swell running. We passed with Tatoosh Isle to port and Duntze Rock to starboard, each no more than ¼ mile off, then altered course for the south and butter melting warmth. At noon we were overtaken by a magnificent Ocean Racer, *Windward Passage of Portland*, bound for San Francisco, our destination, but first, we wish to go into the Quillayute River if the bar is passable. This big swell could make passing over the bar nasty.

This gave me the opportunity to use, for the first time, my new VHF radio transmitter. From 3 miles away I called up the Coastguard on channel 16, after first practising the tongue twisting Indian name.

"Quillayute River Coast Guard, Quillayute River Coastguard. This is Ocean Winds, yacht Ocean Winds. Over."

I got an immediate response:

"Ocean Winds, Ocean Winds, this is Quillayute River C.G."

"Q.R. C.G., this is Ocean Winds, do you have channel 10 over".

"Ocean Winds — negative, channel 22 — over."

"Q.R. C.G. negative, channel 67 — over."

"Ocean Winds, channel 12, over."

"Q.R. C.G. affirmative, switching 12."

"Q.R. C.G. this is Ocean Winds, do you read me?"

"Affirmative Ocean Winds, what is your problem?"

"Can you give me a bar report?"

"Ocean Winds, there is about a 5 foot swell over the bar. Tide is full. Navigate with caution as there are net fishermen off both banks. What was your port of entry into the United States? Over."

"Q.R. C.G. My port of entry was Anacortes."

"Thank you Skipper, please stand by this frequency for a while. Over."

"C.G. Confirm, will stand by this frequency. Over and out."

He came back to me 10 minutes later, after having made a check with customs. I was very pleased with my new toy. From seaward it is difficult to judge how dangerous the river bars along this Coast actually are so the Coastguards have their lookouts positioned to get a good sight and can always tell you how dangerous they are.

The end of the breakwater was covered but as I crept in close to the protecting island, Pip spotted the right entry which was between two Indians in canoes fishing just where the swell ended. It was, in fact, a very narrow entrance. It is on the ebb that these bars are so dangerous, but we had arrived just before the tide commenced to run out.

This is an Indian salmon fishing village. Overnight, many of the boats would bring in 20 or 30 salmon, mostly about 2 to 3 feet long. They would throw them out onto dirt shore just as if they were any old fish. The village itself had a look of decrepitude. Cars scrapped, old cookers dumped; even the Sheriff's car parked with 3 flat tyres. Is there still a war between the Indians and the Sheriff?

The object of calling here was to cable in insurance brokers, Morgan & Co., accepting their quote of £900 for an insured value of £20,000 (with a £1,000 excess) for the next 12 months voyage back to the U.K. Up until now I have been uninsured, and hesitated at such a high premium but felt that if the worst did happen, at least the family back home would not lose out. However I found it was a public holiday, 'Columbia Day', so the post office was shut. I then tried a collect telephone call from a booth. I caught wife Ethel at 6 p.m. (10 a.m. here) just before she went on duty at the hospital for her night shift. She would arrange it with Morgan's by telephone in the morning.

8th Oct. Out over the bar at 11 a.m. Dolphins were chasing salmon which, in frenzied attempts to escape literally the jaws of death, were jumping clear. We towed a lure, but of course had no luck — unlike, I am sure, the dolphins. It was a flat calm, so we motored until the evening breeze allowed us to sail.

9th Oct. A super day; running under twins to a nice force 4 making a comfortable 5 knots. In the evening spoke a Coastguard vessel, *Resolute*, who gave us the weather forecast. Good weather to continue with N to NE winds. Hours later we were close hauled port tack 30° off course with fog and a head wind, which gave us a nasty, uncomfortable night.

Even all bad things have to come to an end, and eventually the weather changed and once more were able to sail due south. Listening to a forecast from Eureka, Humbolt Bay, promised fair for the day but becoming southerly by the following morning. Oh, to hell with bashing against another head wind and sea. Eureka was not too far away, so homed in on its radio D.F. beacon. The bar was breaking

140

quite badly but down the deep channel close to the breakwater was quite reasonable.

Inside, at the Boat Haven, we discovered one or two other yachts on passage south. A pair of Canadians, Dennis and Bob, were waiting to get their engines fixed, and somehow we ended up drinking a couple of bottles of wine and eating with them. The trouble was, the bottles were gallon ones.

14th Oct. The morning dawned thick with fog. That, coupled with a certain fragility on the crew's part, decided me to remain another day. A strictly rest day, and no more than one glass of beer.

Like many best laid plans, this one too got upset. The local yacht club had had a big race and were that evening celebrating with a wine tasting. Someone thought of inviting us — what an evening! It ended up with us all in a car port in a hot tub somewhere in that aptly named town of Eureka!

Monday 15th Oct. A lady named Fred (well, this is California) took us out to an enormous supermarket where the beer was 2 dollars 30 cents a dozen. After that essential re-victualling, we headed out of the harbour. The harbour bar was not just moaning, it was crashing and thundering. All most impressive. *Pearly Shell,* a U.S. yacht, followed us out. It was a beautiful evening, clear as a bell, then an hour later thick fog rolled up from nowhere and blotted out Cape Mendocino and Blunt's reef buoy. The starboard engine overheated — water pump I guessed. Ah, the joy of two engines. Instead of having to fit a new pump immediately while still not recovered from the previous night's excesses, we could just keep going under the port plonker. There was virtually no wind. Harry, on *Pearly Shell,* offered to hold back but I assured him I was okay and would put into Fort Bragg if I had further problems, but was otherwise headed for Bodega Bay.

16th Oct. Pip had a fright on his morning watch. The fog was thick. Suddenly from ahead loomed a container ship, just port side open. He gybed to port and this ship passed some 50 yards to starboard. It was an Evergreen Line motor vessel registered in Panama. No one saw us — there was no evidence of a look-out, and when I called them up on the VHF, no answer. But it *was* breakfast time.

Gradually, with the increasing wind, the fog cleared. In fact it developed into a good sailing day. Alas the crew were still either

141

recovering (slow convalescence) from Eureka or had not yet developed their sea legs so this, another one of my 39th birthdays, was allowed to pass with little celebration.

In the evening we handed the main and just sailed on with the wind dead astern, under boomed out genoa. Passing Point Arena, I reckoned at our present speed that we would arrive at Bodega Head before dawn as we were surging off the waves at 8 knots. We reefed the genny by 8 rolls. *Ocean Winds* was still making better than 5 knots.

At dawn we were an hours sailing from Bodega Head, but the wind fell right away and the fog rolled over the headland completely obscuring the land. This made for an interesting bit of navigation, dodging shoals over which the swell breaks dangerously. To find our way to the Channel entrance we used bearings from the radio beacon and a line of soundings. A coastguard open boat led us up the channel to the port, where, as both yacht harbours were full, we tied up at the fish quay.

We are just getting into 'Drake Country'. Some claim has been made that Bodega could have been the 'convenient and fit harbour' he found, but this is not generally accepted. The three favourites are:
1) Drake's Estero, just under Point Reyes.
2) Bolinas Bay, halfway from Point Reyes to the Golden Gate.
3) The Bay at San Quentin, more or less where the prison stands, and inside the Golden Gate.

We sailed across Bodega Bay and up Tomales Inlet. The bar was breaking right across occasionally so I ordered the crew to don life-jackets. We were fortunate, and went across in a quiet spell although I am sure *Ocean Winds* would have surfed in safely anyway as she has such good directional stability. Had it looked really dangerous, I would not have attempted it.

At the head of the inlet is a village called 'Inverness'. We tied up to the yacht club pontoon. No one minded and the commodore and members were all very welcoming. In Canada and the States, the small clubs are always better than the big posh ones towards voyaging yachts. As the club had no showers, the commodore, John Bryce-Smith, took us to his home where we had a general de-odorizing session. What a beautifully planned house he had, set in a few acres of woodland; the quail, and many other birds eating off his patio.

As the wind had turned southerly and we might not be able to anchor in Drake's Bay, we walked some 10 miles over downland to Drake's Estero. This is a National Park so grazing, apart from cattle, were small herds of deer of three different species. There were birds of many species. An interesting and worthwhile walk even if my calf muscles did hurt for the next three days.

21st Oct.   Getting out over the bar proved more exciting than coming in. It looked as if we had chosen a quiet spell, then 3 breakers hit us, one after the other and slowed the boat right down to 2½ knots, making the engines labour.

I had intended anchoring under Point Reyes in the corner of Drake's Bay but a southerly swell was setting right in so I decided not to risk it. The white cliffs reminded me very much of the 'Seven Sisters' near Dover in the English Channel. So much so, I could well understand Drake naming the country, of which, incidentally, he took possession in the name of good Queen Bess, 'Nova Albion'.

It was dark by the time we reached the Golden Gate. Luck was with us, for the tide was fair; an important point as it runs through under the bridge at over 3 knots. We tied up at St. Francis Yacht Club as befitting someone following in Francis Drake's wake, but when next morning, found they charge over 11 dollars a night we moved to the quay beyond Fisherman's wharf to Pier 39. There, for short stay was 5 dollars or if over a week, only 2.5 dollars a night. Sometimes here a short set comes across the Bay and gives the pontoons a bit of a rough time. They have a breakwater made of old rubber tyres chained together, which absorb a lot but by no means all of it. But you are fairly central here and I reckoned it was worth putting up with the creaking and groaning of the pontoons as Pier 39 was quite a fun place to be — full of shops and restaurants; with shows of high divers and jugglers.

One of my first calls was to the Indonesian Consulate to get visas and permission to sail through their waters. They were most unhelpful. Yachts were obviously not encouraged. They suggested I write to Jakarta. Which I did, express airmail and requested (but humbly) a quick reply. What a hope. Three weeks later, as there was no reply, we looked at the alternative of sailing east about round Papua New Guinea. We trotted along to the Australian Consulate for visas and to see what problem there would be. The ladies there were charming and helpful although insisting on a mug shot for their records.

The starboard engine was smoking a lot and we were suspicious that a piston ring had broken. After much 'phoning around I eventually located a firm at the south end of the Bay which said they would immediately order the rings to be flown out from the east coast and

143

had a gasket set in stock. So we sailed down to Burlingame Marina, and stripped the engine down. Or rather Pip did, marine engineering being his trade.

The rings, while not actually broken, were gummed up with carbon and had lost their spring. But the American Volvo agents were unable to supply new rings. So we had the valves ground in and the injectors checked, put the old rings back and reassembled the beast. America, I decided, is not the super efficient place it is cracked up to be. The locals were not surprised. Many were the comments like "Told you so when you first arrived — cannot get any replacement parts nowadays, have to buy new."

Drake possibly careened his ship near where the San Quentin penitentiary now stands (the actual site is much disputed amongst American Drake enthusiasts). If he was spot on with his latitude (with the instruments he had that must have been difficult though he was a superb navigator) he was at 38°N. Well as I wanted to change my props for ones with less pitch, we motored and sailed to this latitude, just above San Quentin to a place called China Camp. In the 1860's this was a busy shrimp fishery but was now a pretty derelict historical monument. It suited our purpose excellently. We also had a visit from an academic friend of my brother who arrived toting gifts of alcohol and fruit. So we all went sailing to Angel Isle for a walk and a booze. One of the great things about this sort of trip is the people you meet. Next night, at Sausilito, a couple from another yacht came aboard for a drink. Hal, with two Australians, once bought two canoes, lashed them together to make a catamaran, and descended the Amazon. Rosita told of a terrible experience of when she was a hippie and returning to the U.S. from Mexico being brutally stripped and searched at the border.

We crossed back to pier 39 for a final sort out and to obtain Customs clearance for Hawaii. That was a pain, filling in the stupid forms. The snotty little little man got quite uppity when we handed them in all wrongly made out, and made me do a completely new set. They charged 2 dollars as well. At Butlers, the chart agents, I at last discovered the fabulous American efficiency. I bought charts of the Marshalls to Papua New Guinea. The first chart agents I have ever been to that had all my requirements in stock. Being American charts, they were half British chart prices too. Mind you they are not as good and printed on rubbishy paper but still generally quite adequate for the job. ·

144

14th Nov.　　Bound for Hawaii, 2,200 miles away. The weather forecast in the paper augured well; NE winds for the rest of the week. And indeed, they were great, pushing us through the Golden Gate at 5—6 knots. But once outside they dropped to zero so we motored as far as the Farallones, islands from which Drake revictualled with a load of seals. We were disappointed in not seeing any. A light head wind was now setting in — so much for the forecast.

15th Nov.　　We were close hauled on the port tack with a force 4 wind, and it was getting uncomfortable. Sue was sorry she had come, Pip still undecided. I was awakened just after dawn by some terrific bangs. O Christ! what had happened? I find my glasses, struggle out, and there is Pip, grinning from ear to ear with a fat 3 foot blue tuna beating hell out of the cockpit sole. It weighed about 30 lbs. Pip gutted and scaled it, foolish youth. With no refrigeration we could use but a fraction of it. I just cut 6 big steaks out of its back and threw the rest to the sharks. What a terrible waste. It was a beautiful fish and fed us for the next 3 days and even then we had to throw one of the steaks away. Mind you, Sue was on a slimming kick and had stopped eating all but the odd slice of dry bread for 2 days. Judging from her pallor, I think she would have liked to stop living too.

16th Nov.　　A bad and frustrating day. It rained so we collected hair washing water in the bucket beneath the goose-neck. This fell over before we had a chance to use it. The head wind increased so we deep reefed the main and half furled the jib. We could head west towards Japan or SE towards the sun. We did neither but instead hove-to with the jib aback, just letting the boat gently ride the increasing sea.

　　Four hours later the front passed through and the sky rapidly cleared. The wind became a reach; once more the boat was sailing on course. There was a nasty head sea left so we kept the reefs in to slow us down to 4 or 5 knots otherwise she hit into them very hard, which while unkind to the boat would have been unbearable to my fragile crew.

17th Nov.　　At last — gorgeous weather; reaching along and I, at any rate, am glad to be alive. Pip is perking up too.

18th Nov.　　Sue has decided to rejoin the human race — tentatively at least. She has even coped with tuna and rice and beans for lunch and toasted tuna sandwiches for tea. Give her another two days and she will

145

be back on 'mother's ruin'. We are running with the twins set and mainsail as well making 120 miles a day plus another 10 with the south going current which has brought our average up to over 100 miles a day. We are, I guess, some 50 miles south of the great circle route for Honolulu so I see no shipping. Occasionally a school of dolphins come playing around. Today, over a hundred of the darlings were leaping clear of the water and chasing through between the hulls.

19th & 20th Nov.   At last, after a good twilight fix, able to make way. We are actually on course for Hawaii. During the night we motored a lot through the calm but with the dawn were able to close-haul, sailing at 2−3 knots. Not much in the way of progress but a hell of a lot better than the last few days. According to the pilot chart, such winds as we are experiencing never occur in this part of the ocean this month.

24th Nov.   Actually sailed 100 miles in the right direction even though hard on the wind. Midday the barometer stood at 1026.

25th Nov.   Bent in two reefs at the watch change, and still making 5 knots. Good old Quantock Pete doing all the steering. All day the glass has steadily fallen, now at midnight standing at 1014.

26th Nov.   In the early hours of the morning, completely rolled up the genny. Frequent rain squalls and at 5 a.m. with the barometer at 1009 Pip hove-to under reefed main and backed storm jib. By 8.30, I decided it had moderated enough to get her sailing again on a close fetch with a spitfire jib, storm jib and double reefed main. The wind was 5−6 and we were bouncing along in grand style. Two hours later I started to get frightened again so handed the storm jib and just backed the pocket handkerchief size jib up front, pegged the wheel, and she lay nice and quiet. It was I guess, force 7. By 3 p.m., the barometer had fallen to 1000 millibars. It was now blowing a pretty consistent 7−8 with the occasional force 9 gust, from the SW. We were very uncomfortable. I decided to hand the main. Lying across the boom, lashing the main down, I realised how strong the wind was. The seas were estimated at 18 feet and getting bigger all the time. The breaking seas were blown to leeward and it was all pretty horrible. With only ½ sq. yard of jib held aback and the wheel pegged she lay pretty quiet again. The wind is whining in the rigging, the washboards are in the door, so even if we do ship a sea over the top, virtually none should get inside. Up until now, the worst has been seas smashing into the side, then spray and some water washing over the deck and even right over the dog-house. The Pacific weather forecast tells us that the centre of the depression is about 500 miles away to the NW, with the storm quadrant in the west. This should miss us. It is quite bad enough as it is, thank you. Bar. 998.

The barometer only dropped another millibar and then started to rise. Apart from the odd squall, the wind was moderating too, so we got all hopeful. When the barometer had risen to 1002, it decided enough of a good thing and started to drop again. Of course the wind quickly picked up to a full gale again, and the seas were rough. We were lying beam on, as I did not want to lose ground. Sue found it very exciting. At least, until the seas started to hiss towards us and crash into the sides like a sledge hammer. The boat would rocket sideways and books and oddments hurtle off the shelves. Fortunately this only happened when we were caught by a breaking wave, maybe every half hour or so. From the shock feeling, you would think the boat would be broken into pieces, but apparently no damage.

28th Nov.   After lying ahull for 2 days, I got her underway an hour before dawn. The crew were sleeping. There was an evil residual sea from the SW which the wind would have allowed us to sail directly into, but that would have been murder to crew and boat, so I broad reached off due south. Even so it was bumpy. Then by midday, the wind had gone so we had to start the motors. The sea was gradually diminishing, but taking its time.

29th Nov.   At last a fair wind, blue skies and warm sunshine. The log reads at midday:

'28° 09'N. 140° 29' W. Yachting! Skipper de-odorised.'

I stripped off and had a seawater bucket bath on the foredeck. The crew were either too modest or preferred to remain grotty. It is great to be knocking off the miles again in warmth and easy motion. I have put the ship's clock back 2 hours and changed the watch system to 4 hours on 8 off giving myself the dawn and sunset 4—8 o'clock watches. This so I am on watch at twilight to shoot the stars. Susan seems fed up with the watches — she spends her day reading and sleeping and really resents it if there is not enough wind for Quantock Pete thus making us hand steer. I can sympathise, for I hate hand steering too.

147

1st Dec. A day of frustratingly light winds, a goodly proportion of which were on the nose.

2nd Dec. A fair NW wind and started going places. Little did we realise that place was smack in the path of the next depression. The glass did a steady slow fall until midnight, and then it fell at the rate of a millibar an hour.

3rd Dec. At 2 a.m., Pip and I handed the main and continued under storm jib and about 75 sq. ft of unrolled genny. We were making good progress reaching south — it was getting squally, at times, full gale. The sea was building up.

8 a.m. and a humdinger of a squall hit. The seas were now very big, clouds of spume were being blown in sheets to leeward. All the surface of the sea was foaming white. This was by now a strong gale with storm force gusts. Pip was handing the storm jib when I saw a dangerously precipitous sea rushing towards us. I spun the wheel down to get her to bear off but too late. The sea came tumbling over the starboard quarter. I was saturated, only dressed in jumper and trousers. Pip held grimly on up forward. He was fixed to the ship with a safety harness. That sea badly frightened me, so as soon as Pip had securely lashed the jib, I yelled for him to bring aft the 2" warp stowed in the forward locker. While I steered the ship dead down wind, he brought out my jacket and safety line. Pip let the warp out in a bight astern, tying two rubber tyres in the middle. Just before Pip had finished, one giant sea came cascading down on us in a welter of foam and smashed against the port quarter and shot up under Pip's oilies to his waist. He effed and blinded something rotten, but I could see at the same time he was exhilarated with the excitement and apparent danger despite the discomfort of a wet crotch.

To maintain steerage it was necessary to keep a small amount of jib set, otherwise, once she got broadside, she just lay there not paying off. This still happened even with the warp out astern. Of course, it was the helmsman's job to ensure that she did not get broadside to the sea, but a moment's inattention and it was likely to happen. Towing the warp and tyre, and pulled by the 50 sq. ft of jib and keeping the wind on the starboard quarter, we were making 4 knots. The seas at times, were terrifyingly steep and easily 30 feet from trough to crest. The water was warm indicating we were now in the tropical current which would be against the seas and probably accounted for their steepness. *Ocean Winds* behaved magnificently. It was a drag hand steering. At first we each did a half hour stint to get accustomed to it in daylight, then, for through the night, one hour on and two off. At least that was the plan. Two hours off is not enough, but longer than one hour at the helm would, I thought, be too physically tiring in such conditions. However by 10 p.m. the wind had moderated to force 5—6 and the seas were no longer shock-like. So we let her lie broadside making SE at about a knot under her own devices.

4th Dec.   The glass slowly started to rise. The U.S. met station broadcast told that the depression was more or less stationary and was centred about 200 miles to the NE of us. We had obviously run south of the worst and were left with a huge NW swell and force 5—6 westerly winds. All day long we lay hove-to making a knot or so SE. It was my day to cook. The other two buried themselves in books while I experimented with a yeast dough and fried it ½ inch thick over a low heat. It rose to about an inch and tasted like muffins.

Hilo lies just over 600 miles to the WSW. It is certainly no good trying to hammer into the present sea and wind.

5th Dec.   At dawn I got a fix on Sirius, Procyon and Jupiter. The wind had dropped right off leaving an uncomfortable sea as it usually does after a gale. The swell was still huge — somewhere between 25 and 20 feet with a nasty popple on top. I got under way with sail and port motor with the crew still sleeping unsoundly below.

All day, and much to the chagrin of me and my crew, we had to hand steer. In the evening the sky, or rather the cumulus clouds towering astern, were periodically lit up with sheet lightning. Quite a fantastic sight. It was as if they were being lit from inside by flood lights.

7th Dec.   For half the night we motored and then had a stern wind and were able to sail at 4 knots. Pip cursed Q.P. as he could not get him to work. The wind, from dead aft, was not quite strong enough. There were a lot of rain showers so I topped up the boom and just before going off watch had a bucket bath in fresh water — quite a luxury.

8th & 9th Dec.   The Gods have relented. Made good better than a hundred miles each day in pleasant tropical weather. The days are getting quite hot, reaching 90°F in the saloon. Because the water is so warm, 76°F, even the night temperature does not drop more

149

than a degree or so below this. Each morning I have been able to fix our position with the stars. Actually the moon is so bright we could shoot the stars the night long.

10th Dec.   With the dawn, there was Hawaii ahead. 20 miles from Hilo the light wind headed us. So we handed the sails and started both engines. What a Godsend those little diesels are. Without them it would take a long long while to sail 20 miles against a light head wind.

We dropped two anchors and backed up to the quay at the head of Hilo harbour; the part called Radio Bay. The first 3 days are free but after that it is 4 dollars a night back to day one plus 3 dollars. So stay 4 nights and it costs you 19 dollars. It is not too convenient being 1½ miles from the town centre and the public transport leaves a lot to be desired. During the day it is noisy with containers being loaded. But there are cold showers on the quay and a laundry a block away.

We started our many jobs, but found the heat wearing. Brian, a guy that lived in a van, gave us a lift back from town so naturally we invited him aboard for a drink or four. Next day, with his girl Andrea, he took us up to a volcano past an enormous recent lava flow. The forest just stopped and there was this black expanse of broken lava blocks. The road had been wiped out and subsequently rebuilt. Our hosts, like many in Hawaii, were pot smokers, so the reefers were regularly passed around. I found I much preferred the high one gets from alcohol to that given by marijuana. I wonder which does you the least harm?

At the end of our free days we left towing our neighbouring yacht, an Alaskan, Chris, who was sailing his engineless boat back home from Bora Bora. Our hippie friend Brian, Anthea and friend Bob had jumped on board for a sail across to Mauii. We stopped first at the old whaling town of Lahaina usually well sheltered being on the lee side. Our luck was out as one of the nasty 'Kona' winds set in from the west. Our guests had to quickly depart and we weighed anchor to look for a more sheltered port. This was a pity, as Lahaina is one of the most attractive ports in these islands. But there was already one yacht on the reef there, and I had no intention of being another.

We sailed around the north end of Mauii with its magnificent cliffs and scenery keeping a good lookout for the humpback whale as this is one of their breeding grounds. We reached down the east coast of Mauii to Kahalui, the commercial harbour for the Island. Either side of the harbour entrance the surf was terrific. The offshore breeze was blowing

150

the tops back and with the sun striking through it was as if the spray were rainbow clouds.

There was quite a scend coming through the harbour piers which meant one has to anchor a fair way from the shore to keep in deep enough water. We anchored between two other yachts, Mike and Marvellee on *Time Out*, Pamela and Kirk on a ketch. Beyond them was a third large racing type sloop.

17th Dec.   Pip took the dinghy to surf ashore while Sue mended sails and I wrote an article for P.B.O. After lunch, Pip had not returned so Sue and I decided we would swim ashore taking our clothes in a new plastic bag blown up to a balloon and securely tied. This was a mistake. We did not realise it, but before the sandy beach there is an underwater reef of dead coral which causes the swell to break as surf. As a wave broke over me, the water pressure burst the blown up plastic bag. It was a walk through town in wet clothes.

Returning towards evening we were greeted with a sight sailors dread. There, pounding on the reef, was the big white sloop that had been anchored beyond us. He had been trying to sail out, not realising that just beyond *Time Out* a finger of dead coral lay 5 feet below the surface. Pip had returned earlier and had already laid out for him my and Kirk's spare anchors. Mike, from *Time Out* was helping Barry, the owner, to winch the bows round and as she was picked up with each wave, they were gaining feet at a time before she was smashed back down onto the reef. Then the cables parted. All that had been gained was rapidly lost as she was pounded closer inshore with the waves breaking clean over her.

Using my super little dinghy, Pip and I rowed a warp out to the channel marking buoy about 600 feet away. This, Mike and Barry led through the bow fairlead and aft to some mighty sheet winches using two by crossing the cockpit. To a kedge anchor warp, slightly forward of the beam and well away from the boat, Pip and I took the spinnaker halliard. We had just got the kedge warp and halliard together, Pip swimming and I rowing the dinghy, when a series of enormous waves came roaring towards us. The yacht disappeared in a flurry of spray. Pip clung desperately to the halliard. I just managed to breast the crest. Then the second wave was upon us, again somehow we all survived it; by this time I had been pushed near to the yacht, and saw the two aboard waving seaward and shouting a warning. Looking over my shoulder I saw a monster of a wave, already breaking and about to

151

hit.

I had the bows directly into the break but the dinghy was being carried backwards as I was rowing up a steeper and steeper wall of water. The sky was blotted out. I was in a tunnel with strange green light. The wave was breaking beyond the transom of the dinghy. It was fantastic. I am going to make it, I thought, but then it was the finish. I was hurtled out of the dinghy clutching an oar. I was under the water for what seemed a lifetime. I made the surface on the back of a wave, gasping for air. The two on the yacht later said that they had lost sight of me for so long they thought I could not survive. Pip, too, had had an exciting few minutes. He had been swept away from the line to which he had been clinging, but being a strong swimmer and diver, had managed to swim through the wave. Meanwhile the dinghy was floating the right way up, albeit half full of water, close inshore. So I beached it and swam back to give Barry a hand aboard the yacht.

We winched the bow line taut, Mike and Pip on the mast winch, heeled the boat over to some 40° with the spinnaker halliard. The waves would sweep the boat from bow to stern. As each wave passed she shuddered as she crashed on the coral. . . But that was when we made ground. At first we were inching her off, but then we were gaining feet at a time. It was essential to keep the boat well heeled. It took us three hours sweating at the winches, soaked by each succeeding wave but eventually we had her free and moored to the channel buoy.

She was a fibreglass yacht with a bolted on lead keel. The way she had been thumped and pounded on the coral, one would have expected terrible damage. A third of the rudder had been broken off but she was still steerable, and incredibly, she was taking no water. Her bolted on keel had taken all the punishment. As to damage to us humans, Barry had had his nerves shattered, Mike had hurt his hand, Pip tore a toe and I had bruised a leg. Barry had also lost 700 dollars when he first went aground, as he swam ashore with the money tucked in his waistband, and was bowled over in the surf. He was going to use the money, all his funds, to bribe the harbour tug skipper to tow him off. But no money, no tug.

Barry had sailed from Seattle in a bit of a hurry as he was being chased for child support (a few thousand dollars owing). On the way across he lost his self-steering gear in a gale, ran out of food, got his water contaminated with sea-water, used all his diesel up and got air into the system so his engine would have to be bled before it would again work, and had no charts of the islands. The guy had been sailing for 20 years, much of it, or so he claimed, as a delivery skipper.

With the surf in the harbour stiring up the sand the water visibility was only 2 feet. We had to dive and try and find our anchor chain and warp in ten feet of water. I thought we had little chance of finding it. Amazingly, Pip, on his second dive, discovered the chain. We had to buoy it off, as even using the buoyancy of the dinghy we could not get it up. We would have to use *Ocean Winds*.

19th Dec.   We got away at 11.30, shouting goodbye to Mike and Marvellee, she being the first true Hawaiian vahine we had met. Pamela, off the ketch, joined us to sail back to her home on Molokai, the island to the north of Mauii. We motor sailed as to make port in daylight we needed to make a good speed. All around these islands you keep hearing stories of people parking their boats on the reefs when trying to enter the harbours at night. All the islands have a fringing coral reef through which you have to pass to enter the harbours.

North of Mauii, we had the thrill of seeing a mother humpback with a calf surface a few times. Sometimes these huge creatures leap clear of the water.

We spent the night in the main port of Molokai, Kaunahakui, which was easy to enter and had plenty of mooring space. This is important for the more popular harbours are often very crowded if not full. Mike had told us of Kolo harbour, 7 miles from the SW corner of Molokai. This was, until recently, used for shipping sand to Oahu but the works had now closed down. I asked in Kaunakakui, but few had been there so was told it was dangerous and not to be visited. I wanted somewhere quiet with clear water, and preferably shallow, in order to scrub off. Eventually I found a fisherman who had been there and was not talking from imagination and hearsay. He told me that the entrance was not difficult and that there was one shoal corner that might be suitable for scrubbing off.

We were motoring towards this harbour when we saw a yacht ahead virtually becalmed. This was *Time Out*. As we overtook them, Mike dived overboard and swam across for a beer, so Sue swam across to join Marvellee. They had been sailing overnight and had been ghosting along making little progress for the last 12 hours. They joined us in Kolo harbour and helped scrub off the goose barnacles which were feeding on our anti-fouling. This had only been on for 3 months but was now useless.

153

20th Dec.   *Time Out* had no engine, so we towed them through the morning calm half way to Oahu, dropping them with the onset of a good trade wind at midday. They were bound for a port on the north side of the island while we were bound for the town of Honolulu on the south side. It was then a lovely sail, sparkling sea, force 4 beam wind, Diamond Head up ahead and a school of pilot whales coming up astern. In the bay there were a lot of sailing craft, many of which were catamarans — we were no longer a peculiar type of boat.

We stopped first at the Hawaii Yacht Club where you can sometimes moor. They had room until they heard I was a cat (O.W. is about 4 ft wider than modern monohull of similar length).

"It is not the club policy to allow catamarans."

Snotty yachty bastards. We managed a berth nearby in the adjacent yacht harbour, but such treatment (not having experienced it before while sailing half way round the world) does bring one up with a jolt. Even so, most places people are nice rather than not, and after a day here we have met some very pleasant people. Last night we joined a yacht making a tour of the harbour singing carols and today Helen, a lady from Newport, R.I. wandered over for a yarn and as someone who realised the needs of voyagers, invited us to use the washing facilities of a condominium. A condominium is not a special contraceptive or a country bi-laterally governed, but, at least in the U.S.A., a block of flats with amenities.

A hole had been blown in the exhaust elbow casting on one of the engines, so from Mauii I had telephoned through to the Volvo agents in Honolulu to get one for me flown out from the main stockists. They were just as bad as the mainland agents, not having bothered to process the order and now, with Christmas near, and then the new year, could not get me one for at least two weeks. I thought I would get it welded, but, being cast, this was a specialist job. On the off-chance, took it to the boat yard in the harbour. There the boss expressed his disgust and said he would make me up a new one out of standard water pipe elbows. The result was not the most elegant of exhaust elbows, but it worked just as well. Just as one begins to despair, up turns a happy, obscene and delightfully practical man who gets things done.

A colleague of my brother, Robert Paull from Australia, is doing research on the freezing of fruit at the university here. He introduced us to traditional Hawaiian food and trained us in the skill of eating with chopsticks. We also ate Thai and Japanese style. The Japanese food was a great success, and being a boozy crowd, we voted the hot sake a winner.

We greatly enjoyed using Bob's 3 ft bougie board for surfing. This spurred Pip to take some lessons and try and master the art of riding a full sized Malibu board. Bob drove us all over the island's well tarred roads crowded with thousands of cars. Off one beach, a few guys were sailing 'Windsurfers' over the reef through some big surf. At times they got wiped out in a flurry of foam, board, sail and bodies.

Christmas Eve we were Rudy Choy's guests aboard one of his Aikane catamarans to see the hula dancers and sunset over the Islands. This cat is a trip boat and carries over a 100 tourists. It had dancing space and a five piece band, and for 15 dollars, guests were taken out for a splendid evening with an Hawaiian meal and booze included. The skipper of Aikane was pure Hawaiian, and he had been sailing with Rudy since he first made a beach cat back in 1947.

We were then taken to Rudy Choy's house for a Christmas Eve party. Rae, his lady, had prepared delicious Hawaiian dishes, some wrapped and baked in ti leaves. We ate with chopsticks to the surprise and delight of his other guests who were pleased that we so accepted their culture. Rudy and I talked a lot of catamarans and design. He is one of, if not the, pioneer of modern catamaran design. He designs very sophisticated asymmetrical hulls, and apart from his tripper boats, which are of course large load carriers, his designs are very fast cruiser racer catamarans.

Christmas day Mike and Marvellee came and collected us to sing carols at a hospital and distribute gifts from a group called 'E.S.T.'. They later had a party where all contributed drink and eats and talked about their experiences at all the Oahu hospitals (including the prison one) and how they related to the patients. They were nice people but I was unsure of the merit of going around doing good once or twice a year for the kick of making themselves feel good. But perhaps that is the real reason for doing good works and talking about it afterwards, while lacking in modesty, is at least honest. It was a good Christmas.

My leg had not discoloured with a bruise, but had developed a low lump and was becoming progressively more painful and waking me up at night. I decided it would be sensible to get it checked out at the hospital. After I had signed forms to say I would pay whatever the cost, a doctor saw me and diagnosed a haematoma. This is blood clotting deep in the muscle. Under a local anaesthetic, he put an inch long and an inch deep slit in the leg and removed a lot of clotting blood, then put in a foot long piece of one inch tape to drain it. When the local wore off it was painful, so I had to spend the rest of the day on the boat.

The following day, with Pip's help, I went along to the shower to remove the drain, lubricating it all with running water. I pulled the drain out very slowly and tenderly. Christ! I thought, I am going to feint — then looked at Pip, and thought he was. With the drain out, the relief was enormous and I was soon able to limp around without the aid of the broom as a crutch.

I had planned to sail on the 28th but due to the leg, postponed it a day. Meanwhile Pip and Sue victualled. The aim was to get enough tins and staples to last us to Papua, that is, 2—3 months. So after spending 200 dollars on food and 60 on diesel, we set off at midday bound for the Marshall Islands.

29th Dec.   Trade wind sailing with the twin head sails boomed out to port and starboard. All so easy and comfortable. Even so, Sue managed to contract sea-sickness. Pip staved it off — just, with 'stugeron' tablets.

31st Dec.   The wind backed around to the west; the glass fell more than the diurnal norm (in the tropics, the barometric pressure rises and falls twice daily by about 4 millibars. If it falls more than that, a storm is approaching). We were on a close fetch, pounding into a head sea. I had paid off 30° to due south to make life easier and progress away from the disturbance faster. As it turned out, this was a wise move. Hawaii, according to the radio, was hit by gales and heavy rain for 2 days but all we experienced were fresh winds.

1st January 1980
The trade winds are back again. This is the right way to start the new year — long may it continue.

3rd Jan.   The bottom bracket of the self-steering rudder had become loose. We were going to have to fit some new machine screws, and this meant one of us was going to have to work from underneath the bridge-deck. Pip almost volunteered. We handed the sails and lay beam on with the main rudders hard over to give him a foothold. Pip went over the stern and poked the bolts through, cursing in the best sea-going way when a wave slammed him up under the bridge-deck. I was in the lazarette to put nuts on as quickly as possible. These I doubled with lock-nuts, but it was impossible conditions for Pip to hold the screwdriver

156

on the machine screw heads, so it was not a perfect job. It seemed rigid enough, and Quantock Pete was back in action doing a far more dedicated job of helming the boat than we would.

We are back in our book a day routine except, that is, for the one reading 'Shogun'. That is so thick it takes 2½. We were getting worried in Honolulu that we would not be able to change enough of our library. I usually manage to change with other yachties 10 or so books at a time, but in the Ala Wai yacht harbour, when Pip and I went round with our box of books, all we could find were crews smoking reefers, stoned to the world. Just before we left, Mike and Marvellee turned up with a boxful, and the rest we changed at a book store.

4th & 5th Jan.   Rocking and rolling gently along under twins. At night the air temperature drops to the same as the sea temperature, 80°F and climbs, during the day, into the 90's. Gradually the wind lightened. As our speed dropped below 3 knots, we hoisted the ghoster to increase it back to 4. But we really need a huge spinnaker to give us that extra knot. By my watch in the afternoon, we were again becalmed and had to use both engine and Autohelm.

6th Jan.   I had just shot the dawn stars, including Acrux – the brightest of the ones in the Southern Cross, when the winch whirred. The fishing line had been struck. I put the engine in neutral and switched off the Autohelm. On the line was a beautiful yellow dorado; 3 feet of strong fighting fish. We had off him two lovely fillets. Sue cooked one which did for both breakfast and lunch, and for dinner, I cooked the other sweet and sour, which we had with fried cabbage.

With the aid of the ghoster, actually managed to sail for 5 hours. The ghoster kept collapsing and eventually snagged and tore. I was called to give a hand, as this sail, made of such light cloth, easily tears. The great thing about sailing in the tropics is when you are called in the night, you can leap out naked from your berth, and go straight to work without the bother of donning clothes.

9th Jan.   Sodding doldrums. For some of the day there has been a light SW to W varying between force 1 and 3, the stronger wind whenever we get a shower.

In the heat of midday we were hardly moving so a courlene line was streamed out astern and we all stipped for a swim. Remembering

George Millar's story of when he and his wife, in a Mediterranean calm, swam off their boat and a light wind then blew it out of reach leaving them naked, lonely and frightened, I decreed that one person must always remain on board. So Sue and I had our swim, then Pip dived and inspected our bottom. It is still beautifully blue and clean. Sue's, I noted, as she struggled out via our rubber tyre boarding ladder, was a blushing red. No wonder she says 'Oo' when she sits down.

We had been motoring a lot. An odd noise came from the engine. Pip was very quick to stop it, but not quick enough. The earth cable had fractured at the copper connection, breaking the circuit. Pip repaired it, but as I feared, the alternator had been damaged. With an alternator, a complete circuit has to be maintained at all times while the engine is running. Fortunately we have the towing turbine, so we can keep the battery adequately charged.

Shortly after messing with the engine, we were caught in a heavy shower. We all grabbed our shampoo and vigorously showered, each trying to find the heaviest drips off the sails. We also collected a gallon of water for the washing tank. But what a frustrating business this doldrum sailing is.

I made a very successful loaf using ¼ pint of brown ale, yeast, flour, salt and water. Well kneaded just the once and allowed to rise in a greased pan. We have the stacking camping type of saucepan, so used the large one with the pressure cooker's trivet in the bottom to give an air gap for the oven, and with the bread inside the smaller one we cook it on the gas ring for about an hour.

10th Jan.   By the time I took over the watch in the afternoon, the wind had picked up to a gentle sailing breeze. I asked Pip, what was the boat off the port bow? What boat? he asked, looking up from his book. We altered course to pass close. At first I thought it a small fishing boat. As we closed, we could see nobody on board. The mainsail was roughly handed and the jib had been used as a shelter up forward. The aft sun shade was bent and two boobies were sitting on top. The whole boat stank of bird shit. . . On the roof was painted S.O.S.

We handed our sails. There was no response to our yells. Obviously someone had to go aboard to check even though it looked abandoned. There was an 8–10 foot swell and the wind had picked up to force 3. She was lying broadside to the wind and waves so was rolling a fair amount. I could not go closer than 3 feet, for if we hit, it would surely damage our topsides, so Pip had to leap across. And that, out at sea, is much more tricky than you would think.

It was a roughly converted steel life-boat with the name *Little Ark – Marshall Islands* painted on the sun shade. It also had an Hawaiian registration number on the bows. Pip first did a quick check, and yelled across "No one on board".

That was a relief, for while we would rescue anyone alive, the presence of the birds indicated that only corpses would be aboard.

There were hardly any personal effects, so we presumed the sailors had been rescued. She still had 3 feet of freeboard, despite a flooded engine room, so should not have been abandoned for a life-raft. We did rescue a few 4 gallon stainless steel water containers off the deck and a few tools. There was a VHF radio transmitter firmly bolted to the canopy but this canopy was dangerously loose, so Pip had to leave it. We were about 700 miles from the Marshalls. The wind was drifting it south at about a knot and current carrying it SW at ½ knot. I reckon it was doomed to drift in the ocean for a long while yet. We could not ascertain who the crew had been or when they abandoned as there was no log or other papers.

It was a tricky job picking Pip off. Sue and I had spotted what we thought were sharks (admittedly only about 3 or 4 feet long) swimming around, so were anxious that Pip should not miss the jump. Pip reported that the boat was a mess with little of value on board. No charts, two broken plastic sextants and a book on acupuncture which he 'rescued'.

We left with the advancing dusk. The trades now settled in and soon we were broad reaching towards the Marshall Islands with Quantock Pete once more back on the helm.

11th Jan.   Just after midday, a large school of minke whales kept us amused for over an hour. They were diving under the boat — occasionally poking their heads out to look at us. They would pick up on a wave and surf past, easily doubling our speed of five knots. These are a common whale but the first I have ever seen. As yet, they are not a threatened species, but man could soon alter that. They seemed particularly fascinated by our turbine astern, which is just a 12 inch propeller revolving a line to the generator. We just hoped there was not a 'thicky' in the group who might decide to taste it. But, unlike man, perhaps all whales are bright and intelligent. Fortunately they just looked and hovered alongside it.

We are now running with twin headsails boomed out and the main also drawing as the force 4 trade is just a little to starboard of dead astern. Now this really is ocean sailing.

12th Jan.   This morning crossed the 180° meridian. A confusing business because this is the date line. Drake took a careful tally of the days and he was surprised, on arriving back at Plymouth, to find he had lost a day. If he had been going the other way he would have gained a day. There is a logical explanation if you can work it out. Be that as it may, we now have it all rationalised. When going west when crossing 180° longitude you jump to the next day, and vice versa when going east. So I jumped a day and made a complete cock-up of my sights. Ship's, or local time, had to jump to the 13th, but G.M.T. was still the 12th. With a lot of exercise of the old grey cells, I worked it out and had better be right as the atolls towards which we are headed are, at best, only visible at a distance of 16 miles.

16th Jan.   The trades are blowing at force 4—5 and bowling us along in grand style. Generally the swell is running at 12—14 feet but occasionally we get a real big one roar past. I was at the nav. desk running up the noon plot, when she surfed down the face of one of these extra large waves. Even as heavily laden she is (I estimate her weight at 6½—7 tons) she made 9½ knots.

The big swells make shooting the sun and stars difficult. As you are seeing the top of a swell on the horizon, you need to fix the star when you are on top of one too. This is easier said than done, as the boat always gives a jerk when the crest passes. The noon to noon run was 140 miles. We have reduced sail to slow her down as we want to arrive at Majuro atoll at about midday.

17th Jan.   At 0030 hrs were about 40 miles NE of Majuro so we reduced down to 50 sq. ft of jib, trailed a tyre astern and slowed the boat to 2½—3 knots. I called Sue at dawn to steer while I shot the stars. This gave a good plot some 30 miles from Majuro, so we hauled in the tyre, let out the full genny, and were once again tramping along at 5½ knots.

Visibility was down to less than 10 miles so we did not pick up the islands when expected. Eventually we spotted two towers 2 points off the port bow. These tallied with two on the chart, which we later learnt were no longer in existence — these were two new water towers 2 miles away. The entrance through the reef is 20 miles to the west of the little town. I expected the entrance to be exciting with the big swell running and the wind blowing straight in but as we approached it all quietened down and there were only 4 foot waves over the shallows. It was breaking well on the reef's either side though, and sending up clouds of spray which accounted for the poor visibility. As we were coming in, Sue shouted.

"I can see the bottom." The echo sounder was reading 12 fathoms! She could also see some large sharks down there.

Once through the reef, we found we could just about close haul up for the town, so hoisted the main and reefed the genny, for while warm, it was still a very fresh breeze. As we approached, we saw some yachts so headed for that anchorage, then some children in a dinghy waved. We motored up to them — they were trying to get back to shore with an apology for a paddle and a tin can to bale with. We towed them in with us, as otherwise they would have fetched up on the other side of the lagoon some five miles away.

Clearing in was not a great bother. In fact, as it was near knocking off time, immigration hurried through the forms and left a number for next day. This turned out to be a holiday so we never did get properly entered, missing out on visits from the Dept. of Agriculture and of Customs. The details of *Little Ark* we gave to the Port Captain.

An Australian boat in the anchorage, a 42 ft ferro cement wishbone schooner, came via Ponape. There, because they had not previously applied for immigration permission, they were not allowed, other than the skipper to buy essential supplies, to land. I did not want to be similarly treated, so I immediately wrote to immigration and sent cables to the governors of Ponape and the Isle of Kusai requesting permission to visit.

On the 3rd December, Majuro atoll was swept by some large waves. 6,000 people were made homeless out of a total population of 8,000. They are now living in tents supplied by the U.S. Government until the houses are rebuilt. Trees were uprooted. The wall of the bank was breached by an enormous coral block and giant clam shell and the yacht club was launched into the lagoon and sunk without trace. I can think of at least one other yacht club I should like that to happen to.

About the only industry for all these Pacific atolls is making copra. This is the one cash crop, and all it is, before processing, is the white meat out of the coconut partially dried in the sun. They have a processing plant here which we visited. They collect the copra from all the Marshall Islands and also the Gilberts and Ellice group. Even so, they can only get a quarter of the copra they are able to process. They extract the oil by steam heating the chopped up pieces of coconut and pressing them. The shredded remains, or pellets, are shipped to Hawaii for animal feed while the oil goes by tanker to California. They can make 40 tons of oil a day. When the Japanese were administrating the Islands, they managed to get the Islanders to produce more nuts and generally managed the plantations better, so, before the war, production was much higher.

I was disappointed with Majuro, it was not at all like the Pacific atoll of my dreams. Like most of them, it was built up of coral on the rim of a submerged volcano. The inhabited Island is some 30 miles long, but in places, less than 50 yards wide, and much of this has been turned into a rusting, rotting machinery dump. The big wage payers are the U.S. Government so there is little drive for self-sufficiency. But then the people with their expanding population and 25 cent taxi rides up and down the main drag all seem happy enough.

25th Jan.   Friday; superstitious and wise sailors never risk their luck by sailing on this day. After 3 hours walking backwards and forwards between the Port Captain's office and immigration, we finally got our clearance for Kusaie and Ponape. We loaded up with some useful supplies like Australian canned cheese and tinned butter and beer. Hoisting the dinghy aboard, the topping lift broke and the dinghy fell back in, giving Pip only a glancing blow on his shoulder. Not at all put out, I climbed the mast to reeve a new topping lift, a five minute job. I thought I had better give the mast head a quick visual inspection as well. What good luck the breaking of our topping lift proved to be. The forestay had almost broken clear of the mast head crane. After a few hours sailing it is certain that this would have parted and then the mast would have fallen down.

It took Pip and me, working as near flat out as we could in that heat all day to rearrange the forestays which included enlarging a hole with a file in 3 mm thick stainless steel which is a rotten job when working at a bench. Doing it while hanging away from the mast head by a safety harness is 10 times worse. Pip and I took it in turns as we found we could not work up there for longer than half an hour at a time. The repair done is temporary, but I think it will last until we get to somewhere like Darwin where we can take down the mast and the mast cap off for a proper machine shop repair.

162

26th Jan. Sailed at 4 p.m. and so just managed to clear the islands in the gathering dusk. The trade wind has dropped to force 3 and owing to our stay problem we can no longer set the genoa, and so are reduced to the number 2 jib as our largest one.

30th Jan. It has been an easy passage up until today when the wind freshened to force 5. Coming from astern that would not normally have bothered us, but unfortunately we are now in the Equatorial counter current and with the wind blowing against the current, the seas have steepened cruelly. Pip has been feeling sick all day and I felt delicate after scoffing some rather ripe bacon. It is very sticky and humid out of the cooling wind, and too hot out in the sun.

We lost the turbine of the generator today. I guess the towing line has chafed through or perhaps a shark has taken it. Fortunately I have brought along a spare.

Pip and Sue do not get along well together and, since Pip is such a useful crew member, I have asked Sue to leave, if possible, at Ponape. She took it very well, but I guess she must be unhappy with us for we rarely chat amongst ourselves and her only chance of real companionship is when we get into port and meet other people.

I have shaved around my mouth a la Solzhenitsyn. The aim is to stop my mask leaking when swimming. Sue says it makes me look 10 years younger. Shave it all off and I will be back to adolescence.

31st Jan. The previous evening's sight indicated that we have been pushed to the north by the set of the current. We altered course by 15 degrees. At 3.30 a.m., there being a full moon, I shot 4 more stars which gave a 7 mile cocked hat still showing us too far to the north. The sight was good considering the seas, which, while having moderated somewhat, are still big. Also the sights were taken between scudding clouds and rain showers. We modified the course another 10 degrees, put out a rope astern to slow us to 4 knots and expected to sight Kusaie at first light.

With the dawn there was the island mistily appearing in the early light, dead ahead and 15 miles distant. As I had had such a disturbed night, I put Sue on the helm while I dozed on the saloon seat, popping up every half hour or so to take bearings and make sure our approach. We were about 2 miles from the island when she screamed.

"Pat! Pat! quick, whales."

I grabbed my glasses, shook myself awake, and staggered out, expecting just another interesting sight, despite the panicky edge to her voice. I looked over the starboard side — Christ! An enormous leviathan was surfacing alongside — we were running over his tail section. My heart stopped as I awaited the bump of us grounding on him. It was a sperm or cachalot whale, and gigantic. I could have stepped off the boat and onto his back; how we missed him I do not know. I got Sue to start the starboard engine in the hope that the vibrations might dissuade them from hitting the boat. That is one theory anyway. I was concerned in case there were others near. 3 months ago, near the Ellice Islands, a yacht was sunk by sperms when the calf got curious and the adults decided the yacht might be a threat. You may have theories about the whale being so intelligent and not, therefore, a threat to yachts, but some are so damn big that when you get out there looking at them you realise it would only need an accidental flick of their tail to give you your come-uppance. Anyway, the way man has massacred them, they deserve to get a bit of their own back.

Kusaie (Kosrae) proved a delightful island. We went into Lele harbour which you enter through a 200 yard gap in the reef which fringes the whole island. We tied up to an old U.S. army barge, which, though giving us a risky jump to the shore, saved the bother of launching the dinghy. Also it is easier for visitors, which sometimes, particularly if these are all the village children, may not be an advantage.

Many of the locals visited us, notably Eli, a young member of the legislature who brought gifts of oranges and bananas, and Ted John who worked with the historical society. Ted took us to see the village canoe builder. This was under the shade of some coconut palms looking out over the reef. He was working on three canoes of various sizes, with two very small grandchildren sort of helping to plane up the gunwhale.

Each group of islands and atolls makes a different canoe. Some places they make symmetrical hulls, in others, the lee side of the main hull is almost straight and all the hull curvature is on the weather side. This asymmetrical shape is to give grip on the water when sailing. On Kusaie they use a symmetrical hull shape but build the gunwhale up by about 3 inches. The outrigger was a small solid shaped length of hibiscus.

Here, the builder was making an 8 man paddling canoe for the historical society out of a large breadfruit tree. It is taking about 6 weeks to build at a cost, including materials (these are actually free but he has first to cut a tree down and transport it) of 250 dollars (£125). Everything is made from locally available materials, including the lashing string which he makes up by rolling fibres from the coconut husk on his leg.

He knocked down for us a few green coconuts, dehusked them on a pointed stick and, with his machete, sliced off the top of the nut. The white meat was just starting to form, so inside was virtually all liquid, slightly effervescent and a very refreshing drink.

While we were there, it came on to rain heavily, a real tropical downpour. With so much rain, good soil and the heat there is a terrific rate of growth. The staples are bananas, breadfruit and fish with coconuts for a cash crop. A lot of taro is also grown. Then there are citrus fruits, paw paws (papaya) lots of pigs, chickens and a few goats and dogs. On this island there is no shortage of food, it just takes a little effort to gather and hunt, and not too much of that. It has the great advantage of being a high volcanic isle and not an atoll. Atolls have little soil being made up almost entirely of coral sand over coral rock.

As we were being driven back along the reef road, there was laughter and shouts as, inside the reef in the lagoon, five women, breast high in the water, their brilliantly coloured skirts floating up around them, netted a school of fish. At Ted's house, his wife was sat on the floor grinding tapioca root, his six children and their many friends wandering in to look and stare at us. His neighbour's wife squatted in the shade of a tree, busily knifing out the flesh of coconuts and spreading them out in the sun to dry. All very busy happy ladies, while the men worked at a more leisurely pace doing the masculine jobs, of which there were not so many.

We got good vibes from this island. The people were so friendly and happy we were surprised to learn that a rape case was pending. Then an attempted suicide was flown out to Saipan. A 16 year old high school lad, after a family argument and too many beers, had shot himself with a .22. So there were tensions and hassles in this idyllic isle, but it is still a long way from New York or London standards. They have 6 policemen — too large a force I was assured. Not many places left in the world where the police force is over manned. The locals have all warned us about Ponape. There, according to Kusaiens, traditional enemies of Ponape, the people are much more violent, and we were to be careful, especially at night.

There are some fantastic ruins here, no one knows how old. A huge fortification built of basalt logs (rock like that of the Giant's Causeway in N. Ireland) brought from the other side of the island. There had been canals or moats, but these were now just marshy areas, all densely

165

overgrown. A 4 foot lizard, unreal darkish yellow with black spots, unblinkingly watched us for a few moments before darting off into the undergrowth. The Japanese had introduced them to eat the toads which they had introduced to eat the mosquitos. Surprisingly the lizards are not eaten by the locals — this one looked very meaty.

2nd Feb.   Saturday night, Ted brought us breadfruit baked in hot stones of the central fireplace in their cookhouse, and also a mangrove crab caught by his sister. For on the voyage tomorrow, he gave us tapioca wrapped baked bananas. It has been very interesting eating the ethnic food.

3rd Feb.   We motored out of the harbour dead to windward through the reef. We had just cleared the narrow pass when the weather fell to pieces. It blew force 7 with torrential rain which cut visibility to 100 yards.

We motor sailed for the 3 miles to the north point, then freed off for Ponape Island, 300 miles away to the WNW. The weather was very squally; during the stronger ones we were sailing at 8—9 knots with reefed main and jib. The lively motion made Pip feel sick, and I was not too comfortable, nor, I believe, was Sue. It rained virtually all day, but only during the squalls was it really heavy. Then the rain flattened the sea and visibility was reduced to as bad as thick fog. Fortunately there are no islands to hit until tomorrow by which time we hope we will be back in sunny tropical weather again.

5th Feb.   A fast, but uncomfortable passage. Reefed right down, we were, at times, still surging off at up to 9 knots. Then as the wind eased, I wondered whether or not to shake out the reefs. I certainly did not want to have to reef in the torrential rain so we were often sailing undercanvassed. Fixing our position was essential as the small atolls of Pingalap and Mokil are in a direct line between Kusaie and Ponape. With the frequent heavy rain so reducing visibility, and at the speed we were sailing, we would be on the reef before we saw it. I had set the course to skirt the islands by 25 miles, but not knowing what currents were affecting us plus our leeway, kept me on tenter-hooks. Luckily the clouds cleared enough for two quick sights, 3 hours apart. This confirmed that we had once again had a strong northerly current and were well clear of the islands so could run straight for Ponape.

Ponape, a high island, should have been visible at a great distance, but was sighted when we were only 15 miles away. The radio bearing I was getting from the air beacon was badly bent which indicated we were well to the south of our actual position. Fortunately a fuzzy sun was trying to show, so a position line obtained from that cleared up the uncertainty of our position.

With a falling wind, it was touch and go as to whether or not we would reach the pass through the reef before dark. I would not attempt it in the dark. A fisherman zoomed past with a dory and high powered outboard. We waved, and said we were going in, so he kindly piloted us in through the reef and around the coral heads by the main channel before heading back to his village. It was quite dark by the time we had tied up to a barge along with 4 other yachts in the main harbour.

The immigration here are paranoid. They were all for banning us from entering, but I showed them the receipt for the cable sent from Majuro and the copy of the letter requesting permission to visit — both of which they knew nothing about, or so they claimed. Which means they are incompetent as well as paranoid. Actually their leaflets say you only need a U.S. entry visa and card. However, they claimed we require a special permit because we were in a yacht. Eventually they capitulated and gave us a month's permit.

Sue left here to fly back to England.

The main 'town' is Kolonia. We chickened out of sampling the night life — by all accounts, pretty rowdy — as there was quite a social round amongst the yachties moored to the barge. The main street of the town is a wide, potholed, dirt road with rusty tin shacks either side and looking, to quote their brochure, 'Like a Western back lot at Warner Bros.' Despite the Kusaien reports, the people proved friendly.

The shops were well stocked with liquor and tinned goods but very little in the way of local produce. It is an incredible place for growing food, plenty of rain, good soil, heat and sun. They do grow plenty of the root for making 'sakau' (Kava, in Polynesia). This is a mild narcotic drink and the poor man's booze.

This island is reputed to be the wettest place in the Trust Territories. Using the canopy as a rain catcher, we soon filled all our tanks and containers. During the downpours, the colander, left out on the deck, filled with water.

Where we were moored was right in the lee of the town dump, so we were inundated with flies. Our pet gecko, captured in the bar in Majuro, had the feast of a lifetime. Our gecko is a lizard about 6 inches long, with a tongue that darts out with amazing speed to capture flies and other bugs. We hardly ever see him, he vanishes behind the books and, we trust, scoffs the multitudinous bugs we have on board. I hope he is partial to cockroaches, as we seem to have a fine crop growing. I am not sure when they first came on board, but we have been killing the odd one or two regularly for the past week.

Pip is a bit under the weather with a lot of festering tropical ulcers on his legs. We have tried a course of tetracyclin and now have changed to ampycillin. His left foot is badly swollen.

10th Feb.   Sunday. Left Kolonia at 10 a.m. with the intention of motoring around inside the reef to the eastern harbour to visit the Nan Madol ruins which are similar to the ones on Kusaie. The chart did not show a complete pass, but we were told by several people that a way had been blasted through and that drawing only 3 ft we would have plenty of water.

The coral patches in the lagoon were marked with stakes so despite the odd squall reducing visibility to less than 100 yards, it was much easier eyeball navigation than I expected. The first pass that had been bulldozed was just wide enough. An open boat was coming in the opposite direction, so I waited to let him through first, for there was not enough width for the two of us. This was 6 foot deep. The next pass was a long cut, again just wide enough with a few feet to spare on either side. We had a strong following wind, and the current was with us so I could not go as slow as I would have liked. Once entered, we were committed, as there was not turning room and I could never have reversed for three cables against that wind up such a narrow channel. At first, all was well with 8 feet showing on the echo sounder, and I was just beginning to breathe a sigh of relief nearing the end when it suddenly shoaled to 4 feet. Then we were through and into a 20 foot deep pool amongst the coral. The way out of the pool looked very shallow so we swung up to the windward edge of the pool and dropped anchor. Pip rowed the dinghy across to the exit, and with a pole, sounded across. It was 6 feet deep. He had had a hard struggle rowing back against the fresh breeze so we had a cup of tea while he recovered enough strength to hoist in the anchor.

That was the last tricky bit, 2 miles on was Nan Madol, but there, with the swell coming in the east entrance and the poor chart (the best then available), I reckoned it too risky to anchor where you land to see the ruins. We sailed another 3 miles to the head of the harbour

168

Magellan Straits

Making a Cairn.

A day it got less cold in the Straits.

Mussel collecting — Caleta Burgoyne.

Bay Anna Pink

Off for water at the fall.

Notable tree – Caleta Connor.

In the Channels.

Bringing back the water — Port of Islands.

Pedro - the bread maker giving Scarlett a lettuce.

In the forest
cutting a tree
to make an oar

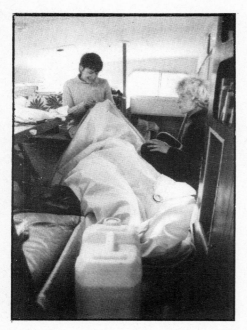

The constant problem.

Sailing to Puyuguapi.

Aguirré — Note diver's boat in middle with hand pumps.

Anchored at Hot Springs — Puyuguapi.

Washing clothes in Hot Springs. Scarlett & Mike.

Friends at Puyuguapi.

Riding out a strong gale with a warp on our beam.

Hove-to in the Pacific
measuring the strength
of the wind.

Making paddles.

Breadfruit tree cut for canoe hull.

Kapingamarangi Atoll — Outrigger canoe.

Working out a sight.

Pip & Henri
showing broken bracket
for self-steering rudder.

Refuel — Darwin.

Brenda struggling with the bananas.

The ruptured clevis that made us stop at the Ashmore Reef.

Swimming at the Ashmore before being chased by the snake.

Setting the Genoa again.

Becalmed —
swim in 6,000 ft deep ocean.

Tom & Brenda sail mending.

Tied up at Rodrigues.

Leaving Rodrigues, adjusting self-steering.

In the cold S. Ocean
off S. Africa.

Tom & Brenda leave.
Tim & Allan III join at Cape Town.

The water-driven generator — running before in good trade wind.

where it was sheltered but shallow. We anchored on mud in 4½ ft. The spring tide range is 4 feet and the neap tide range 6 inches. We were on neaps.

We discovered we had anchored just below a forestry experimental station where Salis Peter, from Pingalap atoll, was in charge. He was helped by two peace corps workers, Glen and Mary, and they all showed us around. They can grow teak here to a marketable size in 15—20 years. With the heat and the rain it is one continuous growing season. They were also growing a eucalypt and a mahogany. That evening they joined us aboard for a yarn and a drink which was very pleasant.

12th Feb.   Motored out at 9 a.m. but the starboard engine kept overheating. It would work for short spells of about half an hour at a time. There was plenty of water coming out of the exhaust so we diagnosed thermostat trouble. The bellows were corroded through, and were not shutting off the bypass when the engine got hot. I covered the hole with epoxy putty so now, at all times, the engine cooling water has to circulate around the whole engine, before going out via the exhaust.

When we got clear of the island, the weather greatly improved and the showers and rain squalls were nowhere near so heavy. With the wind on the starboard quarter, we set course for Nuku'oro atoll, 290 miles away but making sure we missed Ngatik atoll by at least 20 miles as we would pass that in the night.

14th Feb.   After a clear night, clouds formed at dawn to make getting a fix difficult. However I managed to shoot Vega, Rigel Kent, Mars and one other star I was, at first, unable to identify. Then I thought of Saturn, and that worked out fine. It gave us a position 32 miles from Nuku'oro bang on course and 10 miles ahead of our ded reckoning, so we must have had a little current helping us. The wind was force 4 NE.

We sighted Nuku'oro from eleven miles away. We later learnt from the teacher that as we sailed past, everyone was excited and she took the children out to see us, as they get few visitors to the island. The entrance through the reef looked decidedly narrow, but again we were lucky. A local boat with an outboard was passing inside the islands and saw us through the gap so came out to pilot us through.

This is a lovely place of palm thatched houses with palm thatched privies built out over the lagoon. The anchorage is deep, 8 fathoms

169

H

close inshore which rose up quickly to the narrow coral shelf of the island. The coral heads teem with multi-coloured fish.

The policeman came paddling out to us to tell us to bring our passports and see the chief magistrate. These formalities were soon over and we were then offered drinking coconuts by a tall distinguished looking greybeard, Narlik Lekker, the second son of the last king of the island. Narlik and the policeman showed us round the island. At the school, the U.S. Peace Corps teacher, an attractive girl from Minnesota, brought the school out to find out who we were, where we had sailed and to where were we going.

These islanders, like those of Kapingamarangi, are ethnically Polynesian, but are governed from Ponape which is Micronesian. The ethnic difference of build, temperament and culture is quite marked. We were inundated by friendly men wanting to trade. The store had run out of batteries and the next supply boat from Ponape could arrive next day or in three months time so our spare stock were soon distributed. Everyone brought shells, a few, interesting craft work. Fishing line, cigarettes, fish hooks, soap and above all, hard liquor — the latter we refused, pleading our own desperate shortage, which is almost true — were all in demand. People were curious and agreeable although one guy, a Ponapayan, was rather a pain.

15th Feb.   It rained hard all day so we did not go ashore as planned. This did not stop the locals visiting us. Karen and another teacher came out for a happy hour and popcorn (which she demonstrated how to make) and later some guys came out with the local liquor — 'tuba'. This is made from sprouting coconut, naturally fermented to the strength of wine. We laced it with the remains of a bottle of vodka which improved it a little.

Narlik wanted to spend the night on board, so we gave him a blanket and the saloon. At 3 in the morning, a southerly wind sprung up and was bouncing us against the quay and Narlik's canoe so we had to lay out another anchor. This always seems to happen when one is at one's lowest ebb, and at 3 a.m. after a bout drinking tuba, one is at a pretty low ebb. I was less than pleased when we were invaded again at 7 a.m. so I hurried a couple of lads off.

They were but the vanguard. Soon we were refusing requests for liquor; giving up most of my remaining sweets to one lovely little lad for another bag of shells. Eventually we managed to get the dinghy aboard, everyone off, two last letters were delivered to us from a passing canoe which we were to deliver to Kapinga and by 10.15 we had weighed anchor. It was dead low water, so the pass was quiet. It is shallow at one end, 26 feet, so the big supply ship won't come inside the lagoon, but lays off and supplies the island with its boats. They are planning to blast away a deeper channel.

Narlik was on the reef at the edge of the surf as we motored out. He suddenly leapt into the surf then climbed back on the reef and held up for us to see a fair sized fish he had just grabbed.

We found the wind was a nice force 3 and a reach for us with a course set due south for Kapinga, 160 miles away. A good sailing day with sun and clouds, so not too hot, and with such a wind, not too rough either. But we are missing our genoa, for we should be doing 4½–5 knots. As it is, we are struggling to do 4. Mind you, our bottom is getting whiskery again, so if we can find it, we will scrub off at Kapinga atoll. Pip's ulcerated leg is mending well, so he will be able to swim again.

17th Feb.   Darkness fell when we were about 20 miles to the north of the atoll so we hove-to for the night. At dawn, I got a dubious set of star and planet sights, with a hazy sky and poor horizon. As the sun rose, I took frequent position lines and these showed we should pass very close to the outer reef. After 15 miles there was no sign, nor after 20, by which time I was quite bothered. ¾ hour before noon, I hove-to again and took a longitude sight; waited for noon, and took a latitude one. The cross showed we were 16 miles to the SW. I had not allowed sufficient for the west going current which speeded up near the island. Also, as we went west about the atoll, that side there are no islands with waving palms, only coral reef which is only visible from a distance of two miles.

Using both engines, although the starboard one is not working very efficiently as it needs new piston rings, we thumped up against wind and sea back towards where the island should be. After 2½ hours I was about to give up as we had still not raised the atoll, when Pip shinned up to the cross trees. From there he could see a group of small, low islets. We reached the gap in the reef just after sunset. There were two canoes that had been tuna fishing returning at the same time, so again we had a pilot through. The tide was ebbing out strongly, and we only just had enough power — at times, our speed over the ground was less than ½ knot. Once into the lagoon there was hardly any current, and we motored through the gathering dusk to the lee of an island and dropped two anchors. It was setting into an evil night, with heavy rain squalls, but we were sheltered from the wind by the island which was apparently full of squealing pigs but no people.

It is best to have an anchor cable, on the bower anchor at least, entirely of chain. Like on most multihulls, in order to save weight, mine is made up with 4 fathoms of chain and the rest ¾ inch diameter (16 mm) nylon warp. You have chain from the anchor, as the weight of it makes the anchor drag in horizontally. If the nylon rope snags a rock or coral head, it may well chafe through. As it was dark when we arrived, and I could not see how clean the bottom was, I laid two anchors just in case one did chafe through, for if we went adrift in the night we would fetch up on the reef encircling the lagoon.

It was a beautiful morning, and after a visit by some fishermen in an outrigger canoe, we hauled up the anchors and motored the few miles to the two islands where the people live at the NE of the lagoon. As we approached, we were boarded by the law, his uniform a pair of tatty shorts, his transport a dugout canoe that had washed up on the reef. (It looked to me like a Central American river canoe). The main village was a hive of activity. Canoes being launched out of their boat houses, a large party of axe-men making two canoe hulls on the shore and ladies in the lagoon with their washing floating in plastic bowls in front of them. One swam up to the boat to look at us, her blouse on the scrubbing board she pushed ahead of herself. The jetty was lined with curious onlookers of all ages.

It was beautifully calm when we arrived. By evening a southerly wind was steadily increasing, causing foot or more waves. We warped around the side of the jetty for protection and lay over a sandy bottom. This was a mistake, as the wind veered to the west during the night, which left us exposed to a fetch of 10 miles, the full length of the lagoon. The seas sweeping in built up to a good 2 feet. At low water, about 2 a.m., we were bouncing on the bottom in the wave troughs. Our keels dug channels in the coarse coral sand, which wore away the front of the timber shoe on the starboard keel. How glad I was that I fitted fibreglass shoes with wood soles bonded on the keels to give protection when drying out. Without them, we would very likely have worn a hole through the fibreglass because this coral sand is incredibly abrasive.

Shortly after 4 a.m. we had dragged the holding off anchor and were banging against the quay. It was blowing a full gale, fortunately the tide had made up, so were only bouncing on the bottom in the very deep troughs. We transferred the holding off anchor warp to the big sheet winch, and slowly hauled her off the quay. We later found that the anchor had now fouled a coral head and was holding well. It was a wild, wild night. Soon after dawn it fell quiet, and the lagoon became like a millpond again. But we had had enough of this position, so hauled out into deeper water off the head of the quay, laid out three anchors in a fan shape ahead, and lines from our stern quarters to the quay.

The people here, Polynesians, are virtually self-supporting as they can grow and catch their food, and using wood grown on the atoll, build pole houses, tied together with coconut string and covered with either palm or pandanus thatch. They wear bright lengths of cloth as lava lavas, often printed in fluorescent colours. The older ladies, with big sagging breasts, go about topless, but to Pip's and my disappointment, all the young nubile maids wear bras and blouses. Not that it is so frowned upon for them to show their breasts, this inhibition is very recent, what is terribly erotic is for the girls to show their thighs. They never wear shorts or even jeans let alone bikini bottoms — that would excite their men beyond all reason. To bathe, they walk into the lagoon in their lava lavas. Sometimes they bring their babies, bathe them, then nurse them while in the lagoon. The water temperature is around 84°F.

The canoes they build here are no longer the traditional Kapamaringi model. For the last 40 years they have gradually changed to the Nuku'oro version as this is easier to build and takes but one breadfruit tree, while their original model took two. The Nuko'oro canoe is symmetrical while the Kapinga canoe was asymmetrical with built up topsides and high stem and stern posts. The Kapinga canoe was supposed to be the better sailing boat, though much more difficult to build. The present ones still sail very well indeed. We were motoring across the lagoon when one was tacking up. It lay close to the wind with surprisingly little lee-way sailing at a good 5 knots. Off the wind, they really fly, making 15 knots or more. But what surprised me was how close winded they were with just a lateen sail. The steering board is held against the leeward side of the hull and this is used more for lateral resistance than steering. They alter the sail balance to give steerage, much like a modern sailing surf-board.

Most canoes that go fishing outside the reef now dispense with sail in favour of an outboard, usually a Yamaha. This makes negotiating the pass through the reef much easier, and when they find a school of

173

tuna, they can keep circling it, whereas under sail they have to keep tacking back up to it, so their catches were much smaller. They go well offshore with their outrigger canoes, but they tell me that so far, no one has been lost, though several have had very close calls. Just as well, the nearest land to leeward is several hundred miles away, and that is a long way to drift with a broken down outboard. The verbal tradition strongly suggest that this was how the islands were originally settled, by a family blown off from their island hundreds of miles to the east. Neither this atoll or Nuku'oro are anywhere near the old Polynesian sailing routes.

The radio on the island was not working and we were asked to look at it. I delegated the job to Pip. Luckily they had an 'avo meter' obtained from a wrecked Jap fishing boat which drove up on the reef in broad daylight last year (this was manna from heaven, supplying much useful gear and lots of fishing line). With the 'avo', Pip discovered that it had been connected to the batteries with reversed polarity, thus blowing both fuses. The instructions were ambiguous, but Pip managed to sort it out, so for the first time for many months, they were once again in contact with the outside world and their administrators in Ponape. This is a very remote atoll.

Since doing this small job, we have been given much local food, fish, taro and breadfruit and coconuts. Taro and breadfruit are the staples, but neither Pip nor I find them tasty. The flavours are different from any I had previously experienced and I much prefer our staples of rice, potatoes or pasta. The taro and breadfruit are cooked over hot stones; the breadfruit may well be wrapped in taro leaves. Judging by the waistlines of all over 30, it is a fattening diet. The favourite protein is tuna, of which they catch an abundance if the weather is fit enough for them to fish outside the reef. Sometimes they go out at night for flying fish, using lights to attract them. The canoes come back laden to the gunwhales.

We liked this atoll so much, we decided we would change the piston rings on the starboard engine. (We had had a set flown out from England to Hawaii). Pip managed to do the job but found that two of the three engine mounts had fractured their rubber so the engine still is of limited use as our gluing up job can only be temporary.

24th Feb.   On Sunday we motored to the end of the south island where there are few people so there is more marine life. Pip saw a lion fish, with its long venomous spines. There were several clams, the largest about a foot across, just on the sand. The best eating variety are the ones embedded in the coral. These are very difficult to prise out. We took a few back for the locals as without the technique, or the special curved knife, we saw no way of getting them out of their shells.

25th Feb.　　As we were about to leave, the model canoes we had asked about arrived. These were of the traditional Kapinga canoe and beautifully made complete with little bailers and pandanas woven sails. We bought 4, so when we get home we can have races with them. Another craftsman, whose speciality was leopard sharks with real shark's teeth badly wanted some swimming fins, so traded 3 carvings for Pip's fins.

The quay was lined with well wishers as we left. I had to dive overboard to free an anchor warp from under a coral head. This was refreshing but in the sultry heat of a windless day, refreshment did not last long. The current was with us at the pass, so we went out considerably quicker than we came in. It was a flat calm. The Autohelm was used to steer, and the turbine streamed to charge the service batteries as we were just using the port engine. With a bucketful of fresh water, saved from the overnight rain, we both had the luxury of a hair wash and flannel bath. I fear we are right on the north edge of the doldrums. Sweat is just running off us, we are having to drink enormous amounts of water.

We had to motor the whole 300 miles to Kavieng, New Ireland (the NE island of Papua New Guinea). We were relieved to have an engine as otherwise we would have been lucky to make 25 miles a day under sail. The engine pushed us along at a constant 4½ knots and with the help of the current made good 110 miles a day. We used 24 gallons of diesel.

28th Feb.　　As Kavieng channel has no lights, we lay a-hull from 2 a.m. waiting for dawn. The loom of the town lights could be seen reflecting off low clouds, 7 miles to the south. We anchored off the wharf, and here, for the first time since Peru, the customs rummaged us. The guys here are trained by the Australians, and they always search you. The search took the two officers two hours. They were very good, not making the place much more untidy, it was a bit of a shambles anyway. To do a proper job would have taken two days. As it was, one of them spent most of the time down in Pip's berth reading a *Playboy*. Quite legitimately of course; he had to assess whether or not it was porno-

175

graphy.

Papau New Guinea seems an expensive country. Beer is a terrible price, diesel is half as much again as any price I have paid so far, and three hours alongside the quay to load the diesel cost 9 dollars. We managed to clear in and organise the chores and more necessary stores in a day and were away by the following midday for a pleasant motor sail through islands and channels and down the Albatross channel where we should have stayed the night. Instead we pushed on across the Strait to Bendemann harbour, Dyaul Island, which we reached just at sunset.

This harbour proved too deep for us, at 15—20 fathoms almost to the very edge. It had a shallow shelf of coral and rock, and after hauling our two anchors up and down like bloody yo yos, and finding ourselves dangerously near a coral head, we said 'sod it' and motored out into the gathering darkness.

It was a non-stop motor sail to Rabaul, New Britain, which we reached soon after dark the following evening. Rabaul is an easy harbour, and with its range lights and a full moon we even managed to find the correct yacht anchorage. The noise coming from the shore sounded as if someone was having his toe nails ripped out and his objections amplified. An outdoor disco I presumed. I went to sleep with tissue paper stuffed in my ears.

During the war, the Japanese planned to use Rabaul as their launching site for the invasion of Australia. The Aussies did not much fancy this, so, with the aid of the Yanks, bombed the place flat. The Japs went underground, digging huge tunnels in which can still be seen landing craft rotting away. Monuments to man's cock of the dunghill struggle.

Our next stop down the coast was at Put Put, a beautiful land locked bay with narrow entrance through two low necks of land. Here there was a Catholic mission, logging port and Seventh Day Adventist high school in the middle of a cocoa and coconut plantation. Cocoa and coconuts go well together, as the tall coconuts give the necessary shade to the small cocoa tree. Also if the cocoa crop fails, they still have a steady bread and butter income from the copra, though, at the moment, cocoa is the big money earner.

7th March. We left this delightful anchorage at midday with a fair wind and had a super sail for just 1½ hours. Then the heavens opened and it rained seemingly solid water. We were passing close to a ship going the other way at the time it started. The rain was so heavy

176

everything was blotted out, we could only see a few feet beyond the boat. After this rain storm passed, the wind dropped and freshened several times, coming at us from all points of the compass. Not ideal sailing weather. It was a very black night. The chart we were using was the U.S. one. The land by Cape Orford was hatched indicating that the U.S. cartographers were uncertain of its actual whereabouts — British and Australian charts of this area are much better.

From the south of New Britain, it was 170 miles across the strait to the Trobriand Islands. This being the time of the doldrums is also the time the currents change around these islands so they are unpredictable. The Trobriands are in an area of shallow sea with lots of unsurveyed coral reefs, so before entering the one charted channel, it is very necessary to make sure of your position. Fortunately I managed a dawn sight using four very bright stars which were strong enough to pierce the thin cloud cover. (Rigel Kent, Spica, Arcturus and Vega). The position showed we had a north setting current which had put us back 15 miles.

10th March.   After the calm night, the wind picked up to a pleasant force 3. Pip caught two good tuna, which we immediately cleaned and then swilled the blood and muck off the deck. We had just done this when the wind freshened from the SW to a force 6. We hardened the sails in, and *Ocean Winds* was sailing well when bang, the jib clew tore out leaving a madly flapping sail. It was time to reduce the headsail anyway, but I would have preferred to have done so in a more leisurely fashion.

In the channel between the two main islands of the Trobriands, birds were swooping on shoals of fish being chased by tuna leaping clear of the water. Satiated dolphins were leaping off our bow wave — even the sun was shining. We anchored off a village on the west of the channel and were immediately visited and boarded by natives wanting to trade shells and carvings or sell them at high prices. Here they trade for just about anything, clothing, thongs, food, fish hooks, we even traded our two tuna for some rather nice shells. But above all the natives were curious and it looked as if they were there for a long while, watching our every move. But before things got too embarrassing, we were saved by a heavy rain shower. I said a definite NO to thirty or forty natives all men and boys, coming inside the boat, so they reluctantly sought shelter ashore. In the evening, the girls were allowed the canoes, and they, dressed just in grass skirts, were a sight

177

for our celibate eyes. They looked gorgeous. Having my son aboard as crew was a definite inhibiting influence.

We motored across to the main island of the group, Kiriwina, to the anchorage of the town of Losuia. Our chart, 12 years old, showed a buoyed and spar marked channel. The buoy had vanished, and so had some of the spars so we crept in over the shoals at only 1 knot, and once anchored to give me time to climb to the cross trees to look for the deepest water through the shoals. We had planned it to come in at high water, but still only had 5 feet at one place, though I am told that if you are exactly in the channel, you can get through with 6 feet draught.

The town here is in two parts. By the shore is a slum village, very ethnic, with many of the girls wearing grass skirts and a traditional yam store in the centre, and a posh end of town built up of suburban type bungalows and well kept gardens. There was a hotel here where we managed to get a cold beer and hamburgers for dinner. The native village was one of the few places I have been where some of the children had stick like arms and legs and pot bellies indicating bad malnutrition.

12th March.   Now, more or less knowing the channel, we motored out at four knots into a freshening nor-wester. An ideal wind, or so we thought. We were sailing south at 6–7 knots when a thunder squall came over. The wind swung to the west and rapidly increased to force 9. Heavy rain in such a wind, hits you like hailstones. I was on the helm just wearing cotton knickers — God it hurt! I screamed for Pip who was below making a sandwich to come and hand the main. Visibility was reduced to no more than 50 yards. I was on the east side of the channel, so knew the reef was not far away to leeward, if anything went wrong we would be wrecked on it in an instant. We started both motors and tried to haul off into deeper water, with just the storm jib set to give us some help. We were in a very nasty position, with no land to shelter us, but no sea room either. The coral sea to windward is just a mass of coral heads and shoals and uncharted for hundreds of square miles. Had we not had the engines but been forced to sail off, we would have had very little time to bend in a deep reef and change the headsail. I am sure we could have done it providing we did not have a foul up or a sail blow out, which would have been very likely in that wind, and if that had happened, we would have been on the reef and the boat lost. The squall lasted about half an hour, but that was one hell of a long half hour.

178

Afterwards, I considered returning to our first anchorage off Kaileana Island, but the wind veered back to NW so it was now easier to sail south to Yaga Islet, a tiny, uninhabited tree clad island with fringing reef. It was only one third of a mile long but killed most of the sea and much of the fresh wind that was now blowing. We laid two anchors ahead and one astern to prevent us swinging onto the coral if the wind changed completely round in the night. It was not the best anchorage in the world, but in the circumstances we were pleased with it. With such black, heavy squalls passing every half hour or so, I did not want to carry on as the charted channel through numerous shoal patches was very narrow in places with several dog legs. So I usefully spent the daylight hours left, sewing up the clew of the No. 1 jib.

13th March. (Thursday) We were up as dawn cracked to heave in our horribly heavy anchors; with three of them down, a job that took us an hour. We were no sooner under way than the squalls started again. 1½ hours later the wind died completely as a bank of black rain shadow crossed our bows. Then the wind hit, from dead ahead. It had made a swing of 160°. So it was on with the engines and motor sail into it. This gave us 1¼ hours of wet misery but as Pip observed, a thousand times better than slogging into a squall at home where it is cold to boot. Midday, and the wind dropped completely away. This must be what the met men mean when they say "weather changeable".

I checked the port engine mounts on a routine check. One of them had sheered. This was a blow, as it means that engine was now temporarily out of use. The starboard engine has a mount held together with a hose clip. The exhaust is also awful black, which is giving me concern. We are using the engines a lot. Indeed, we have hardly had any sailing since we first hit the doldrums at Kapingamarangi. It is asking a lot to push this big heavy boat with one single cylinder 7½ horse power engine but it is so much more economical in fuel to use just the one engine.

We were approaching the Amphletts group of islands when it decided to rain. This time there was little wind, but the rain made up for it. In 20 minutes, we collected five buckets of water off the drip at the gooseneck.

The Amphletts (as in most of New Guinea except the Trobriands) are steep volcanic islands which rise abruptly from 30 or more fathoms. We motored around for 10 miles before deciding on dropping the hook between Wawiwa and Yabwaia Islands, the only place we could find shallow enough. It was exposed to the north and to the south and so a northerly swell set through, but it was not too bad and certainly preferable to being hove-to offshore all night which was the only other alternative. There was another anchorage we were told 10 miles to the east.

The evening was spent sorting out the engine mount, boiling it to clean off the oil, and gluing the split in the rubber with 'super glue'. We then bound it with a hose clip. As well we did too, for on leaving in the morning, the starboard engine overheated. We were motoring against a light head wind and sea. Once clear of the islands we took off the water pump cover; the impeller was a mangled mess. I suspect that the amount of debris in the water here keeps causing the water pumps to fail, as later that day, the other one also gave up and had to be replaced.

We reached Goodenough Island at midday, dropped anchor and put a stern line to the quay. The locals were a villainous looking lot, so Pip stayed on board while I went to look for the diesel supplier. Communication was a bit difficult, but at the store, I was told to go to the plantation manager who lived a short walk out of the village. Well, putting a brave English face on it, I staggered out in the noonday sun. After a sweaty half mile, I met two lads and asked them in my best pidgin.

"House im bilong plantation bossman?"

But no response apart from giggles, so I left the track to ask at a house set off the road on the hill.

Pounding on the door I shouted, "Anyone at home?"

A voice asking "Who is there?" came fittingly out of the top storey. It was the home of 'Father John', the local priest. He gave me a run down on the local situation, a lovely cup of tea, then, hearing an exhaustless truck roar past, leapt on his Honda, chased and caught it and arranged for me to get diesel at the plantation jetty 3 miles away.

Father John and the plantation manager, Fritz Maas, joined us at dusk for the 'happy hour' (or as Father J. accidentally renamed it, 'the holy hour') for a glass or two of whisky and a talk of various things. Fritz had made enormous strides developing the plantation and bringing money into the island. Father John, with love, kindness and advice was an outstanding missionary. He was a lovely person.

After the 'holy hour', we rode in Fritz's hot-rod pick-up to Father J's for a T bone steak dinner too liberally washed down with sacramental wine (remorse came next day) but it was Pip's 22nd birthday, and a jolly good party it was.

15th March.   We left in a flat calm under both engines. There were two possible anchorages, one 30 and the other 60 miles away. We were both somewhat fragile; however, a bottle of Guinness for elevenses greatly improved my outlook on life. A 'hair of the dog' is better than Alka Seltzers which only get up your nose and give you the runs.

Rounding the point, we found a light southerly wind. With its aid, I realised we could probably make the distant anchorage before nightfall, so pressed on to Sewa Inlet, on Normandy Island. This is a deep, land locked harbour but in the first bay on the starboard side we found an isolated small rise which suddenly shoaled from 15 fathoms to 15 foot deep. It had several coral heads and lots of beautiful fish so we dropped two anchors in the middle of it.

16th March.   As we came to lift the hooks, we found both anchor warps had fouled coral heads. Pip had to don mask and flippers to dive and free them. I quite envied him the morning swim. The wind was SSW so it was tight motor/sail across Goshen Strait to East Cape, the eastern extremity of the main island of Papua. This is a tricky corner with masses of reefs and off lying islands, and beset by strong tidal currents. There is a good small boat channel close to the Papua shore with markers along the reef. We had a strong foul tide with a nasty tidal chop creating spray and white caps. With both engines pushing us through at 5½ knots we found our speed over the ground was only 2½ knots. It was a good job we had a neap and not a spring tide against us.

Then life became painful. It was only 20 miles to the China Strait, but the southerly wind was freshening and we could not lay it even with the help of the motors. We were half way across when the tide changed and was now running against the force 6–7 wind. It was purgatory, so we hauled round and headed for shelter of some islands 10 miles away on the north shore of Milne Bay. The channel between the islands and shore was narrow so we lay an anchor ahead and one astern to prevent us swinging into the shore. We were glad to get in shelter and listen to the wind whining in the rigging.

17th March.   The wind was moderate and on our beam for the sail across Milne Bay in contrast with yesterday. At the China Strait the wind fell right away but the tide was sluicing north. The only way we could make progress south was to creep along the edge of the reef bordering the shore through some terrific tide rips. Pip stood on the bows, periodically shouting at me to move out into the stream when the shore reef bulged out. We skirted the edge of one magnificent whirlpool, about 30 feet in diameter with its vortex about 3 feet lower than its outer edges. Our speed over the ground must, at times, have been less than a knot, but once around the point and into the bay, the current lessened.

At the head of the bay we could see a yacht moored. As we approached a dory under outboard sped out. We were told to pick up a mooring. It was Peter, manager of the Belesana boatyard, welcoming us. Our neighbouring yacht was *Caravela of Exe* with Ted and Mary Lyne doing a leisurely cruise around the world. They were fellow members of the Ocean Cruising Club and also on their way to Port Moresby but were waiting here while a cyclone blew itself out off the N. Australian Coast.

Peter ran a cheap ferry across to Samarai Island, which used to be the capital of this province. We took our diesel drums across and had them filled. It was a windy day, and I was glad to be moored at Belasana. Samarai is an entry port for Papua, but in westerly winds like these, badly exposed and landing at the jetty, somewhat fraught. I would never have taken *Ocean Winds* alongside in such a lop.

19th March. Along with *Caravela of Exe*, we left at dawn twilight. Such an early start was necessary to beat the tide through the China Strait. The inevitable head wind was not, at first, very strong, so we motor sailed while I sewed away finishing repairing the clew of the No. 2. This job done, we slowly beat west. We were trying to make Baxter Harbour, as there there is a passage through the reef. Ted reached the Bay ahead of us, and found the gap through. There was not a lot of room inside, but Ted dropped his bower and we dropped a stern anchor and then rafted together. Soon we were visited by crowds of natives who looked over both boats and tut tutted in amazement.

20th March. A foul morning with heavy rain. At the first sign of it lessening, we weighed and moved out. Beyond the lee of the headland it was evil. A nasty sea, heavy rain and general misery. So I turned round and went back in. Ted carried on to the bay around the corner. It rained most of the day with occasional strong gusts of winds even penetrating our sheltered anchorage. I read Tim Severin's book,

'The Brendan Voyage' of when he sailed in a leather boat from Ireland to Newfoundland. By comparison we are travelling in the lap of luxury. Of course, we should be sailing this voyage in an engineless *Golden Hind*.

A story heard on the local radio news: "Four government people are missing in the Sepik River. They were travelling in an outboard motor."

21st March. The morning dawned drizzly, but, where we were, calm, with a trace of northerly wind. So, full of enthusiasm, we donned oilies and motored out through the very narrow gap in the coral reef. Once outside the lee of the headland it was horrible. Blowing a constant force five between the black, land blotting out, squalls of gale force. Using the lee engine, we motor sailed up to Lawes Bay. Ten miles made good in two days! Our chart of this area is a poor one and not to be trusted so approaching the reef, Pip stood on the foredeck yelling directions if he saw green water ahead of a black rock patch. Once in the lee of the headland it was again pleasantly calm, another world, and as we motored up, Ted and Mary were just preparing to sail. On our vivid description of the horror outside, they decided to stay another day, so we all had a drink that evening.

22nd March. At last a quiet day. How I prefer motoring through a calm to beating against a head wind. A sailing purist I am not. Progress was at last, good. We managed to motor right across Orangerie Bay, a large bay that has no bolt holes for shelter and like Ted and Mary, decided to carry on through the night while conditions were favourable. Next morning the inevitable head wind came back. This blasted westerly monsoon was hanging on late this year. On our inshore tack, the land marks did not add up with out ded reckoning. We knew from the chart and the pilot, that the currents along this coast of Papua may run strongly, but the strength and direction are unpredictable at the change of the monsoon.

As we closed the reef, we realised we did not know, to within 20 miles, where we were. (We later realised the current had, during the night, set us back 15 miles). We saw an entrance through the reef with a marking beacon, and thought it might be Rodney — which it later proved to be. The wind was rapidly increasing and was soon gusting force 7.

Being uncertain of our position, we guessed on two possible places, and marked both on the chart. (Later, one proved right). It was eyeball

183

navigation anyway; a note in the pilot mentioned that the shoals inside the reef were incorrectly charted. There was a channel going between many shoal patches and coral heads which was protected by a long coral reef. Behind it, we thought that it would act like a breakwater, which it did to an extent. But the fetch was still so great that the waves were often as much as 3 feet and very short. Even so, the water was so clear, you could easily see where it shoaled up to a coral patch.

By 3 p.m. I was getting worried. Each headland we beat past, the wind curled round, not giving us a lee. Behind one coral patch which broke the surface, there was a calm patch of water but no shelter from the screaming wind. It was a possibility, but not good and would have meant an anchor watch. Sailing through the night was out of the question as there were too many coral heads on which we could come to grief. We could see some islands inshore so, hoping there was enough water, made for them. This turned out to be Cheshunt Bay with a constant 25 foot of water almost up to the islands. We anchored in their lee, on gooey mud in 16 feet of water. We laid two anchors 50 foot apart and let out lots of scope. The seas were curving around the islands and making us bounce a little, but we were sheltered from the worst of the wind. It was a tremendous relief to find this lee — celebrated with a glass of Glenfiddich malt whisky from my last bottle. We were both wind and sun burnt, and very tired — but safe.

24th March.   The wind had dropped right away to a light breeze. I tried to call up Ted on the VHF but we were either not in range, or Ted did not have his set switched on. (I later learnt he was about 25 miles astern behind Dedele Point.) Some distinctive marks and islands proved that one of yesterday's position guesses was correct, so once more I knew where I was on the chart even if the chart was wrong. The only good chart of this area is an Australian one.

We left the inside passage via the Toeveli entrance and as the midday wind only picked up to, at worst, force 5 and moderated towards evening, we decided to bash on and beat overnight around Hood Point. As it turned out, this was not necessary, for it fell calm and so we motored through a peaceful sea with the phosphorescent trails of dolphins playing off our bows.

Port Moresby is well lit with leading or range lights, but the actual light on the NE side of the reef entrance, supposedly bright enough to be seen at 8 miles distance, is a pusillanimous thing, and had me worried until we found it two miles away. It is one of the great pleasures of sailing, coming in to port at dawn. We were surprised not to see Ted and Mary as we had convinced ourselves that they must have made a better passage, but wisely, they had spent an extra night at anchor and came in 16 hours later.

Port Moresby proved, in many ways, a good stop. The boss of the marine store, Ron White, was particularly helpful, getting our sails repaired and solving the gas bottle filling problem by obtaining a conversion nipple specially machined for us. Unfortunately the stay was marred as one night, some bastard stole our dinghy from behind our boat. None were surprised, Port Moresby has the reputation of 'nail it down or it will walk'. This gave me a day's extra work repairing a clapped out dinghy bought in extremis for £24 plus £10 for oars. Even after I had finished fibreglassing together the split joints, it still leaked like a colander.

The yacht club here is well worthy of mention as the members proved both helpful and interesting to yarn with. Of course having hot showers was a great facility, but the convenience of the club bar did rather inhibit the boat maintenance schedule.

One night the dreaded 'guba' blew. Ted dragged, so did a French 'Solaris' cat. Pip and I were just working out how to get *Carvela* off the rubber tyre breakwater which shelters the yacht club moorings, when Ted and Mary came rushing up in their dinghy. They had been wining and dining with the British High Commissioner. Apart from a broken tiller which was already cracked, he took no damage. We tied the Solaris on astern of us, as we had two anchors down, and then held a survival party aboard *Ocean Winds*.

The Solaris cat was being delivered back to Corsica, its home in the Med. The crew were pissed off. The Skipper had his lady on board, an attractive totty, but unfortunately not a great deal of use except for the Captain. The crew claimed the navigation was a bit haphazard; not using GMT only latitudes could be worked out. They even arrived at one island which was in a different country from the one intended. Coral heads they knew all about, having bounced off several. Only one of the two engines was working and no electrics, and this was one of the poshest production cats built. The crew were revolting. One of them, Henri, moved on board with us to go to Darwin — the others were also jumping ship here.

30th March.   After lunch at the yacht club, we motored out with a gentle southerly into a calm sea with the sun burning down and making

185

the decks painfully hot to our bare feet. Now with the crew of three, we arranged the watches 4 on 8 off once more. Henri never realised sailing could be so easy. The starboard engine, aided by the sails, was giving us 4½ knots as we sailed into a beautiful sunset ' 'cross the owl-light of the bay'.

Alas, the autopilot developed a hysteria. It would work out but not in. After stripping her a couple of times I had to admit technological defeat (to illustrate my skills and qualifications, I point out that many times, I have been known to knock in 6 inch nails without bending them so I had good qualifications for tackling the job). It was back to hand steering as there was insufficient wind for Quantock Pete. It was a good job we had Henri with us.

From P. Moresby, we sailed across the big bight for 200 miles. The Fly river debouches into the head of this bay, and deposits bloody great trees, many still with branches and even some with green foliage. How near we came to hitting one or more in the night, I do not know, but we had to alter course 3 times during daylight to avoid them. As it was, I heard hard clunks as small chunks of wood bashed their way past the hulls in the dark.

Bligh, prior to his crew's disaffection, kept telling them how difficult was this passage through the Torres Strait. We entered at Bligh entrance, leaving Bramble Cay 3 miles to starboard. It was then careful navigation through shoals, reefs and islets. As these were adequately lit for most of the way, we sailed through the night at 2—3 knots with the start of the SE trades coming in very lightly. I decided we would anchor for part of the next night, so motor sailed at 5 knots to reach Poll Islet in daylight (this is just south of the Vigillant reef). Anchored in its lee, we had a swim and explored the deserted island. These desert islands are not, as a rule, all that interesting except to the specialist botanist or biologist, and this one was no exception. The surrounding coral was, for the most part, dead too, with fewer fish than usual.

We left at 2 a.m. to carry the tide. The wind was much fresher, and for the last 50 miles to Thursday Island had a great sail. We sailed in shortly after 10 a.m. past a fine looking pearling lugger flying the red ensign and, I think, the burgee of the Royal Dorset Y.C. Geoff, the owner, shouted at us to moor well inshore of him, as it turned out, right over a coral head. We no sooner had the pick down than we had to weigh again and move to a clearer spot. Geoff, with his outboard powered dinghy, took us to the pier so that we could go to the customs house at its head to clear.

That, though normal procedure for yachts in most countries of the world, is the wrong thing to do in Australia. I had also, in the rush forgotten to hoist our yellow 'Q' flag. The customs were not amused. In fact they made a hell of a fuss, 'phoning their head office in Brisbane and considering fining me — but finally satisfying themselves with sitting me in a chair and bollocking me for ¼ hour. It would appear that they expect you to be smuggling booze and drugs and to bring ashore lots of prohibited food, such as mung beans. I filled in enough forms for half a dozen countries, had them out to seal the liquor locker and confiscate 2 kilos of mung beans and a tin of U.S. chicken and lots of old egg boxes. Then we were allowed to land, but apart from changing some money and buying a few victuals, I could see little point for while T.I. may be the metropolis of the Torres Straits, it hardly scintillates.

We had a pleasant evening on board *Cornelias* and next day dug into the many jobs on board. It was 'Good Friday' and for us a good work day. Ted and Mary arrived in the evening after a 2½ day passage from P. Moresby. (We took 3½). They had been bombing along with a good fresh trade the whole way, making 6—7 knots. They were even lucky on arrival, the food confiscating man was off duty until Tuesday, but the customs came out very quickly and efficiently and sealed up his booze and the 20 odd forms filled in. Of course Australia has a big desert where the forms can be filed.

5th April.   Pip and Henri rowed ashore for ice for beer cooling and also brought back 10 gallons of murky fresh water, which I left in the plastic containers as we had 25 gallons still in the main tank. With only 700 miles to Darwin, that should prove sufficient, but I like to have some reserve. We sailed at 10.30 with wind and tide. Outside the islands we found the trade wind was only force 3, giving a gentle sea with the odd white cap. It was, unfortunately, dead astern; without the genoa, we are sadly undercanvassed. Q.P. more or less coped, though he really needed more wind, and you could not take your eyes off the compass for too long. Our bottom is getting weedy too, so we are gently lolloping along at 3½—4 knots which is a bit of a disappointment as I was hoping for a force 4—5 with the wind on the quarter and a good fast passage.

7th April.   After much thought, discussed with Pip how to set the genoa. We finally decided to set it flying like a spinnaker. As the wind was now on the port quarter, we boomed it out to port. It set well, pulling us like a trojan. The increase in speed and improved sail balance meant that Q.P. also kept us on course better, leaving the watchman free to do nothing.

8th April. On Pip's watch, he recognised a Mobil tanker a mile or so to the north. He called her up on the VHF and asked for his job back as soon as we get to Darwin. They can radio or telex London for him. He is hoping they will fly him to a ship in the Far East, thus saving him having to spend out on air fares. *Mobil Producer* also gave me a radar check. Evidently we give a good echo at 5 miles, but at 8 miles are only just visible.

During the early night we had a major calamity. The bolts on the bottom pintle of the self-steering rudder sheared, and the rudder twisted up and broke. We finally recovered the rudder, but it is one more job to put on the list to be done at Darwin. Back to hand steering.

9th April. With the wind veering SSE, we had to hand our genny/spinnaker. This was a bit tricky, that heavy canvas flailing madly away trying to tear finger nails out by their roots. It was now a broad reach with the No. 2 set on the forestay and full main and inner jib. We are cracking on, pushing the average up to well over 100 miles a day.

We lost the generator turbine line. This sheared off at the delrin connector at the generator shaft. This is a major loss, but perhaps I can rig up an outboard prop as a turbine in Darwin for the long Indian Ocean crossing.

At dusk we sighted New Year Island light just where it should be — the first land sighted since leaving Thursday Island. Henri was most impressed, as the navigation on the Solaris was rather more haphazard.

10th April. To pass Cape Don, we had a favourable tide and zoomed along until almost past the light. Then as we turned the corner hard onto the wind, it was wind against a strong current which created short, steep seas — bloody uncomfortable. Pip, on the helm, took a wave splash down his neck. The language was frightful.

At midday I shot the sun for a latitude. The land is so low and the tides so strong, position fixing is a bit difficult. We reached Cape Hother by sunset, crept into 15 feet (judging from the shore tide line it was low water) and dropped the pick. Egrets flew over as we had a quiet sundowner in the cockpit prior to one of my excellent spaghetti dinners.

11th April.   At dawn's early light, Pip woke me with a cup of tea. There was little wind, so it was a motor/sailing day. I wanted to do this next leg in daylight as my chart is less than adequate for this passage with a scale of about a millimetre to the mile. We found our course taking us over the corner of the reefs NE of Vernon Isle. Standing on the cabin top, I could see the extent of the reef and directed Henri on the helm.

For breakfast, I made up, with grated cheese, onion, flour, salt and two eggs some rather tasty flapjacks. Henri, with his delicate French palate, refused a fourth, to Pip's and my gluttonous delight.

They have big tides with a 30 ft rise and fall, and strong tidal currents all along the NW coast of Australia. Coupled with a low lying, featureless landscape, this makes navigation difficult, especially as there are a lot of shoals too. The echo sounder first showed much greater depths than shown on our chart — then less. There was very little from which to fix our position and we were uncertain where the port was. Then we saw a lot of yachts in a bay, and guessed that might be the Darwin Sailing Club. We headed in and found a sandy beach, off which two huge manta rays were shrimping, and a friendly club with cold beer and showers.

Darwin proved a good place to refit except for the rather too many distractions. Pip vanished to a shore berth with the beautiful blonde yacht club barmaid, much to the chagrin of many male members who kept asking me when he was leaving. Henri disappeared in the direction of Alice Springs. Apart from the work I even found a few distractions and accidentally appeared on the local television perched on top of the mast re-fitting the cap. I got a smashing 'homers' with Stella Kirk and her daughter, both ex-long distance cruising yachties though now running a real estate office. They introduced me to a very good Australian champagne, 'Kaiser Stuhl'. It is a boozy place Darwin, despite which, I got a lot done.

Pip left me here and I got a new crew from the Youth Hostel: Tom, an American geologist, and Brenda his girl, a teacher from Canada. They worked hard for the last five days after joining me, helping to get the ship anti-fouled, cleaned and de-roached. We have killed hundreds of the perishers, and now our trap is only catching one or

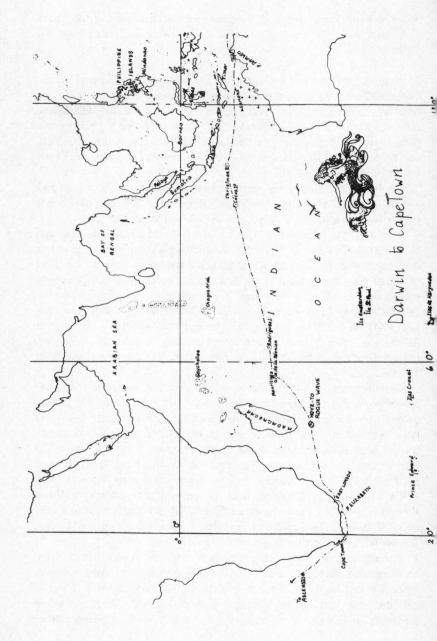

PHILIPPINE ISLANDS

Mindanao

Borneo

Malaya

Sumatra

Timor

DARWIN

Christmas I.

Cocos I.

BAY OF BENGAL

ARABIAN SEA

Chagos Arch.

INDIAN

OCEAN

Rodriguez

Mauritius · Ile de la Réunion

Seychelles

MADAGASCAR

HOVE-TO ROGUE WAVE

Ile Amsterdam
Ile St Paul

Iles de Kerguelen

· Iles Crozet

Prince Edward Is.

EAST LONDON

P. ELIZABETH

Cape Town

To ASCENSION

Darwin to CapeTown

130°

60°

0°

20°

two a night. The first time down it caught over 90.

On Friday, 2nd May we motored around to the docks to re-fuel. With a strong wind blowing this is a terrible berth to reach as there is very little room and hazards to drift onto at the first and only error. Tom, a bright lad, despite being new to boating, smartly moored us up alongside a fishing boat while I played with the engine controls. Even getting the fuel was a hassle. Had to walk several miles to the depot, get the key, hitch back to the boat, fuel up (323 litres) then go all the way back, tell them how much I had had and pay for it. A whole day's job. Meanwhile Brenda watered the boat and Tom went out for the bacon. He came back with two big slabs of smoked middle cut. This was a little moister and not as salty as I usually get, so we rubbed vinegar and salt over them and hung them up in the hot sun. It is beautiful bacon though, of smoked ham quality, and we have, to start with, scoffed slices of it raw.

We were also given by the banana grower in Darwin, two stalks of green bananas — 100 kilos. This was to do a practical test of banana preservation devised by the C.S.I.R.O., the Australian food research organisation. The bananas had to be sealed in polythene tubes with potassium permanganate absorbent blocks. This should so inhibit the ripening, we will be able to take off a hand of green bananas whenever desired and ripen them.

4th May. At 8.10 a.m. weighed anchor and sailed quietly out through the moored yachts only 3 days later than originally intended. We have cleared for Rodriguez, but perhaps will stop over at Christmas and Keeling Cocos Islands. Another yacht, the 30 foot *White Foam*, left yesterday for Christmas Isle.

The SE trade was much lighter today, but we have ambled along at 4 knots. The generator had to be stripped and greased (I think the bearings are now square) as the outboard prop we were now using as a turbine, was knotting up the tow line rather than turning the alternator shaft. Halfway through the day, Tom succumbed to the dreaded seasickness but Brenda, with the aid of a 'Kwell' kept bright and cheerful and sussed out how to strip the alternator.

It is grand to get to sea again. Away from the heat of the land I find I am eating much more — Tom and Brenda not yet likewise. Lounging in the cockpit with a cold beer and a slice of raw bacon, what a life.

The first day out was idyllic sailing. Quantock Pete doing the steering, the breeze keeping the heat of the day reasonable and the seas from astern pushing us bravely on. What a voyage this was going to be, 5000 miles of this trade. Oh well, it lasted for one whole day before falling calm.

On the second day we made only 70 miles, so from then on, if the wind drops to force 1–2, we start the port engine. Even so, these first few days were halcyon ones. Tom felt a touch fragile, but Brenda soon got her sea legs. We played music and sang folk songs — Tom on the guitar, I, on either the recorder or melodica. Brenda has a sweet voice and knows lots of songs and funny ditties — some we say line by line:

"I eat my peas with honey, I've done it all my life.

It makes them taste quite funny, But it keeps them on the knife."

The happy hour from 6 to 7 each evening has, so far, been a great success. Then the day is just cooling down, we maybe read a little poetry or prose excerpt, usually with a fittingly nautical bent, and also listen to a tape of maybe classical or folk music.

We have had a problem with the water generator. The bearings now being square, the resistance proved too much for my new turbine, the rope knotted up and it all parted, prop and all our fishing weights. This is a nuisance as, from now on, to keep the battery adequately charged, it means running the starboard engine for a couple of hours every second day. But still, if we run a black ship at night (no navigation lights) and for those off watch, go to bed as soon as it is dark, we will use up very little electricity.

8th May. The 4 a.m. log entry reads (written by Brenda) 'Moon rose orange — can see the stars' reflection on a flat sea.'

This afternoon we had a delightful dolphin show. They seemed to like me playing the recorder for great numbers were attracted and they were jumping so close to the boat that, sat on the bows, we were getting splashed by them. Tom and Brenda had never experienced these lovely animals so natural and close so we were particularly thrilled.

By 8 p.m. we were once more sailing. Close hauled with a gentle force 2 pushing, or rather pulling us along at 3 knots. I went off watch to a blissful innocent sleep. Two hours later was awakened by a God awful bang. I came leaping out to find Tom struggling with the genoa in the water over the starboard side.

"The sail just fell down." he said, in a most surprised and hurt voice, as if he did not think that this sort of thing happened on a well run

192

ship. (It probably does not.)

The cast stainless steel toggle I got in Australia had parted. Brenda momentarily woke with the bang (it was over her berth), but then immediately fell back asleep. Tom and I quietly worked at getting the sail off the luff spar and stowed. Fortunately I had had a good star fix at twilight, so decided to alter course for the Ashmore reef, and see if we could tuck inside it and anchor for a day to fix the whole lot back up again. This reef was only 70 miles away. With the help of the main, and using the port engine, we could make a comfortable 4½ knots.

I got another twilight fix at dawn so when Tom came on, I was able to tell him that he should sight the reef after a further 10 miles. Actually it was 11 miles before he did. The islands behind the reef are just sandbanks on which sea birds nest and are only visible for a yachtsman's height of eye, at the best, 8 miles, so accurate navigation is essential.

As we approached the reef, we could see a couple of boats anchored behind it. In the heat haze they were standing up above the horizon. We were still a mile from the reef when Brenda asked if that was the bottom. Tom stopped the boat for the bottom could be clearly seen. I checked with the echo sounder, 80 feet.

We had 10 miles to motor to the western point, past some Indonesians fishing from canoes; their mother ship anchored on the inside of the reef. From the point, we had to motor 8 miles back east. As I ran off my chart at the point, it meant 'Guess and by God' navigation and good use of the eyeball. We crept through the first gap in the reef then over shoal patches towards middle islet. Though the water was no longer so clear, we lost the bottom at 45 feet, we could see turtles swimming up for air, sea snakes galore and around the coral heads many brilliantly coloured fish. It was Brenda's first visit to a reef and she was entranced; taking photos looking straight down at the beautiful coral shapes.

We were still 2 miles from the islet when it became very shallow, about 4 feet, so we turned round, and after the second attempt, found a sandy strip with 30 feet of water in which to anchor fore and aft. I do not like fore and aft anchoring, but we needed to keep the anchor lines straight along the sandy strip to avoid them snagging around the coral. 30 feet is too deep for me if they do foul a coral head, as I am a poor diver. This was where Pip was good, he found 30 feet no problem.

It was hot, very hot. So, sea snakes not withstanding, we all stripped off starkers and dived overboard. The water was beautiful. The sea snakes greatly inhibited our swimming. There were a lot of them. I

I

understand that they are not aggressive but their bite is deadly. We all knew so little about them that we did not like to test any theories. After the swim, we soaped off our last five days of grot using washing-up liquid as with this you can get a lather in sea water.

It was lovely and quiet here so climbing the mast was no problem. By dusk I had done ¾ of the job, 2 more hours work in the morning should see it done. Meanwhile Tom and Brenda were busy trying to stop up the many leaks in the dinghy.

10th May.   By midday we had finished all the jobs so, with the swimming gear, in the dinghy rowed the 2 miles to the islet. In 15 feet of water we could see shoals of large clown butterfly fish and other brilliantly coloured fish. As we got into the shallower water, I went over the stern and dived for shells. Tom gently rowed the dinghy on ahead. I was on the bottom around a coral head, when, through my mask, I saw a black snake come swimming towards me. I discovered man can not only be a very fast swimmer, he can also launch himself out of the sea like a Polaris missile. I landed back in the dinghy, hardly touching the transom, to the surprise and hilarity of Tom and Brenda. The snake surfaced just astern.

At the island, myriad birds were wheeling overhead. The coarse green cover, a form of succulent, over the sand was thick with black and white terns, screaming their heads off, and mobbing us as we walked towards their nests. To the side was a smaller colony of charcoal grey terns which, while resenting our intrusion, were not as vociferous or as aggressive as the black and white ones. On the other side of the islet a small group of frigate birds were nesting. They were the magnificent species, as they had the brilliant red breasts. Littered around their site were the remains of many small terns that they had fed upon for frigates prefer to raid other birds than fish themselves.

On the islet were the graves of two fishermen. The reef lies 90 miles south of Roti Island in Indonesia, and although Australian claims sovereignty, the Indonesians traditionally fish them, drying their catch. They spend weeks here until they get a full cargo, and if a crewman falls sick, well that is tough. But apart from the sea snakes, it looked to us a pretty healthy place.

11th May.   It is 1040 miles to Christmas Island and no wind. After putting back our clocks an hour, at 7.00 a.m. we weighed both anchors and slowly motored out between the coral heads, some of which were all but breaking the surface. The sun was already burning hot. For clothes, Tom and I have taken to wearing sarongs, as they are more comfortable and cooler than shorts. It is not modesty that prevents us going naked, but the arse burning sun.

12th May. There was a little wind towards the close of yesterday, dead astern, so we hoisted the second genny boomed out to port to sail wing and wing. This entails taking out the usual genny sheet lead from the port side and reeving through the blocks a separate sheet for the port genny. I told Brenda to do this without instructing her to coil and tuck away the loose sheet. Being new to sailing, she could not be expected to do this automatically.

At about 6 in the morning, motoring through a calm, the port engine went clunk and stopped. I knew immediately there was a rope around the prop, and later, with the dawn light, found out which one and why. A light breeze was just starting. At full daylight, Tom and I tried diving and cutting the rope free, but a short piece was firmly jammed in between the boss and the shaft, that after an hours struggle we gave up and hoisted the twins to get the boat sailing. This meant that the port engine was inoperable. The breeze had firmed up to give us a good three knots. Was this the start of the trades?

13th May. At last the trades have set in — a good force 4, sometimes 5. Quantock Pete is doing all the steering and life is easy. Tom is still feeling a little queasy on occasion, particularly down in the galley. Towards evening it freshened so we handed the main, and are running before the wind with twin headsails only, boomed out to port and starboard. Each sail is about 350 sq. ft.

14th May. The noon to noon run was just over 150 miles by log. We also have a fair current pushing us another 20 miles a day. We have a canopy over the boom and cockpit to give us shade, and with the breeze taking off the heat of the day, it is very comfortable, wearing the minimum of clothes. (The minimum is none.) The 1600 hr log entry reads:

"Crew lazing around like a bunch of out of work Folie Bergere musicians."

We were trying to play our various instruments in unison.

17th May.   We have been hurtling along. My dawn sight showed we were 525 miles further on than the dawn sight 3 days ago. That is an average of 175 miles a day. With the twin gennies boomed out, we would pick up a wave and surf, often 8 or 9 knots, occasionally as fast as 11. If the boat took a sheer, Q.P. could not cope, try as he would, so the boat might broach (swing beam on) if the watchkeeper was not quick enough to unpin the wheel and correct up. This would usually happen once or twice a watch. My berth window was open, a breaking wave caught us badly and we broached. My bedding got soaked. But even worse, it happened during happy hour. Quick as a flash my hand went out for my whisky and I caught the newly filled glass in mid-air. Alas, ¾ of it had spilt. After swigging my glass, I then unbroached the boat.

This was yesterday evening. The twilight fix showed Christmas Isle 190 miles away. At this rate, we would reach it at midnight 17th/18th, but a dawn arrival is to be preferred. We rolled up half the starboard genny which slowed her down so that she rarely exceeded 6 knots and averaged 5½. Since doing this she has not broached once and Q.P. has coped admirably. What is more, it has been a lot more comfortable for sleeping.

18th May.   Brenda shook me awake for the 4 a.m. watch. I staggered out, glanced around and asked;

"Are those ships' lights fine to port or is that the island?"

"What lights?" Brenda looked startled and hurt for they had only just popped up and were only visible when we were lifted by the larger wave crests. They were the lights of some of the Phosphate workings on Christmas Island.

Dawn saw us 6 miles of the NE corner. We handed the twins and reached in just under one jib to anchor in the corner of Flying Fish cove. There was a sandy patch a few yards off the jetty into which we dropped the C.Q.R. The rope we buoyed to lift it above the many coral heads and dropped a second anchor for added safety.

We started attacking the fouled port prop. This proved to be a hell of a job. In order to stay under water for a lengthy while, I extended a snorkel with 3 feet of tube, and then one of us held this clear of the water while the other sawed away at the snarled rope. We must have spent about 2 hours on the job. Even working at just two feet depth and sucking the air down from the surface it is surprising how the pressure affects you. My chest ached.

We were called to go ashore to clear immigration and health. The police sergeant who was doubling as immigration officer was off duty so welcomed us ashore dressed in a most fetching bikini with a rose embroidered on the arse. Ah that all immigration officers were so comely and pleasant.

The British Phosphate Commission run the island with mostly Australian technical and administration staff and Malay and Chinese workers. There are some 500 whites and 2,000 Malay and Chinese. When you realise that a lot of the Chinese are clerks you can see that the ratio of pen pushers to producers is in full compliance with Parkinson's law.

The people here, of all nationalities, were very friendly and seemed pleased to have someone new to yarn with. The Chinese restaurants were good and reasonably priced and the trade store was good for victualling — their prices being on a par with or possibly slightly lower than those in Darwin.

While there, a ship came in to load phosphate, but they had to hang about offshore for a day as a one day strike happened. Nowadays they get paid Australian minimum wages, no taxes, subsidised housing and free films about 5 times a week. All in all pretty good conditions but the young men miss, very badly, female company.

With costs rising and the phosphate lodes becoming more difficult to extract, several people we met thought the island would not be viable much longer, but then, presumably phosphate prices will rise to compensate for the increased costs. They must be feeling the pinch; they have this year started charging yachties 5 dollars per person for the use of the facilities. We each had two showers and one free filmshow.

There was a pleasant easy atmosphere on the island and we enjoyed our three day stay. Another yacht came in. The Skipper and girl crew were very unhappy with one another. The crew was going to leave here and fly on to Singapore. The Skipper demanded a larger contribution than originally asked, and would not allow the girl to take her gear ashore. She swam to *Ocean Winds*, borrowed a sarong from Brenda and hitch-hiked to the police station to sergeant Eileen, who trundled down and sorted it all out.

21st May. After the usual tedious nonsense getting a clearance, some final shopping, mostly for fresh fruit and vegetables, and watering ship, we weighed both anchors and were sailing by 2 p.m. Just before leaving, we found one of our banana stalks expanding obscenely and

197

smelling like a sewerage works so, while we still have a lot of firm unripe ones, one third of our stock had to be jettisoned.

I was expecting a vigorous passage as the wind was quite fresh at the anchorage, but as soon as we were out of the lee of Christmas Isle, we found it had moderated to force 3. It was a nice broad reach.

22nd May.   The crew unanimous in praise of my cauliflower cheese. The wind dropping light so our speed down to 3 knots.

23rd May.   Becalmed. Picked up a hitch-hiker. A dark grey tern with a whitish pate landed on Brenda and then on the deck and stayed with us for the night. The wind picked up again in the evening, which was a relief as it was once again strong enough to work the self-steering.

24th May.   This morning's sights indicated a strong current had set us 20 miles to the SSW. I corrected the course and made allowance for this. This current coming down from Sumatra is indicated on the pilot chart so I should have anticipated it. During the day a lot of frigate birds attacked the red knob on the end of the VHF aerial at the mast-head. They gave up before destroying it. We finished the day with a musical happy hour and a super pork stew.

25th & 26th May.   The current was not now setting us so strongly south. I kept the boat sailing inefficiently as otherwise we would arrive at Keeling Cocos soon after midnight. Brenda picked up the loom of the light at 2.30 a.m. and gave me a shout, but as it was fine off the port bow, and still only the loom, I said 'OK' and turned over for another hour's kip.

Dawn saw the islands of the atoll just where they should have been. We just had to motor the last half mile over some coral shallows to where three other yachts, one French, 2 Aussies, were moored in 15 feet (sand) behind Direction Isle. The holding for a patent anchor is excellent so, for once, we hung on just the C.Q.R.

Direction is a delightful Isle, with a tent and barbecue set up for the Aussies when they come across at week-ends from West Isle. There they have an air strip and are setting up an animal quarantine station for Australia. Home Island, to the south of Direction I., used to be 'King' Clunes Ross' stronghold and where only Malays and their descendants live. Clunes Ross sold out to the Australian Government and now the Malays run the copra business as a co-operative. Visitors are not welcome there.

We got the impression that yachties are not welcome anywhere at Keeling, but as about 90 yachts pass this way each year, they just tolerate them. On West Island there is a well stocked store, but yachties have a 150% surcharge on all marked prices, which is obviously a rip-off designed to so piss off yachties that they will not stay long.

As an atoll, we naturally compared it with Kapingamarangi and I am afraid it came out second best. Both atolls are isolated but Kapinga has the two advantages of not being on a yacht route, so might get one to three visit it each year, nor has it an aerodrome and administration centre so does not have a large influx of aliens. I suspect that we yachties, in the past, have proved a bit of a pain to the bureaucrats here. Our apparent freedom and casual way of life and obvious dislike of regimentation would not endear us to them and if any misbehave (and in a way we all do by their standards) we all gain approbrium.

One of our neighbouring yachts could not understand why, after a long passage, we did not immediately launch the dinghy to rush ashore to feel land once more beneath our feet. There were 6 of them aboard a 36 ft sloop, *Sea Honey of Freemantle*. They must have been on top of one another while we had a lot of room for three. Besides we had to work on the starboard engine which had an injector blowing. This had carboned up and so was a hell of a job to extract, took Tom and me hours. Out of copper sheet we made an extra washer and, after cleaning it out, tightened down another injector. So this engine was now working once more. But this small job took us almost all day.

29th May. We motored across to West Island to post some letters. The anchorage here is not so comfortable as it is rather exposed. It was some job weighing the big fisherman out of the hard clayey bottom. The boat was pitching a bit as there was a nasty short lop. When aboard, the three of us stumbled aft with it, 56 lbs of anchor and as much weight again of chain and 200 foot of warp. Its ocean stowage is beneath the cockpit sole.

The wind was SSE force 5. We zoomed out of the entrance just under genoa, and once on course, were sailing at better than 5 knots under this sail alone; the self-steering was working well, so we left the main stowed. It was a heavily overcast day and I kept a beady eye on the barometer, but this only altered by the usual diurnal amount.

We have set our ship's time back two hours and our bodies are not yet in tune to the new time, but we can hold this time now all the way to Rodrigues. On passage I do not like altering the clocks as that means, unless you change the watch times, someone has to do the extra hours on his watch.

30th May. It was a black night with occasional rain and sheet lightning. I took in the genny with six rolls which slowed us about ½ a knot. This made life a lot more comfortable. The seas coming up from the south were very big, estimated at 20 feet. With the morning, the wind moderated, and after clearing all the little flying fish off the deck and out of the cockpit (none were big enough to eat), we tried putting up the main. This, however, spoilt the set of the genny as the wind had backed to the SE. But still, putting it up and down was a good and needed exercise. We then set the port genoa and boomed them both out. This was successful, but even so our speed was down to 3—4 knots. We were suffering a light drizzle and overcast sky — not trade wind sailing.

Brenda was pleased to see a ship. I tried calling it up on the VHF but could get no answer. I would have liked to have heard a weather synopsis. Towards evening the wind veered, so we handed the port twin and reached along under main and genny.

31st May. Shortly after midnight I came leaping up to assist Brenda in reefing. The wind quickly freshened so we rolled up most of the jib and deep reefed the main. There was rain and lightning. I leapt out in such a rush, not staying to don oilskins. The bath certainly freshened me up; besides, one's skin is waterproof.

When the rain squall left us, so did the wind. We slatted in an uncomfortable calm. With the first streaks of dawn came a light south-easter, and then it started to rain steadily. It was developing into one of those days. By 10 p.m. on Tom's watch, we again had to roll up most of the genny and deep reef the main. By midnight, if it was not blowing a gale, it was giving a passing imitation. We were cutter rigged with about 90 sq. ft on the jib, and 100 sq. ft on the inner jib and on the main. The wind was SSE which meant we were reaching. The seas were getting uncomfortably big.

1st June 1980. Little change, except the seas have got bigger. Every time a wave catches us broadside, it squirts in my window so half my berth is damp. With the lurches, the boat has become a shambles — cleaning up can wait. Cooking, in such conditions, is the worst job.

Things spill and slop over so the galley gets horrible. The ventilator above the galley leaks so there is a constant drip onto the galley floor. By log, our midnight to midnight run was 150 miles.

2nd June. The glass is rising and there is some blue sky and occasional sunshine. It still picks up to force 8 (full gale) when a rain squall passes, with the tops of the seas being whipped off the breaking crests and blown to looard but in between, in the brighter spells, the wind is rarely more than force 6. We are still under our reduced rig of 2 days ago, and still making 6 knots. The really big seas of maybe 30 feet, trough to crest, are now less frequent. I tried to shoot the sun but gave up in disgust. As the sun has to be shot on a wave crest which is when the boat jerks most violently, and one needs both hands to operate the sextant, I was frightened of crashing over and damaging the precious instrument. There is no land to hit so we can well wait another day or two for a fix. I have only managed one position line since leaving Keeling Cocos so do not know if we are experiencing a favourable or cross current.

On the stove, I have boiling away, a cup of rice, lots of chopped up bacon and an onion with a dash of soy and hot sauce. It smells super. It was also easy one pot food that needs little preparation or attention. It is all done in the pressure cooker which, with its compressed lid, cannot spill.

On my watch, the self-steering had been coping admirably. I sat by the wheel feeling dozy; shut my eyes and nodded off. 5 seconds later awoke in a crumpled heap along with the bucket and mainsheet on the cockpit sole.

3rd June. After a moonlit night with the wind moderating to force 5, we greeted a vastly improved scene. There were still a few extra big seas which slapped the weather side (still squirting into my window), but generally they were down to no more than 14 feet. I managed a couple of sun sights and Tom and Brenda managed salt water baths. In the evening I made a sweet and sour pork meal which brought words of praise from the whole crew. Altogether a good day.

This was our first starlit night since leaving Keeling Cocos. What a joy to see them again. But there is no chance of fixing our position from them until the seas go down a little more. Using the sun is much easier as you can see the seas approaching so can plan the moment when you roll the sun on the horizon. With the limited light at twilight, this is much more difficult, so, from a yacht at any rate, when shooting stars, the conditions do not have to be too vigorous.

5th, 6th, 7th & 8th June.   The seas gradually moderated. Quantock Pete has done all the steering. Daily it is getting colder. Now a sea-water bath is a bit of a shock to the system. We are all becoming very lazy for, with the twins and main set, there is little to do but read a book or have the occasional yarn. We have managed to pick out that wonderfully named star of Libra, Zubenelgenubi. At Saturday happy hour we each rendered a limerick or two and Brenda gave:

i)   At navigation our Captain is tops,
     We were spot on at each of our stops.
He sights the stars first
Then attends to his thirst
     Choosing rum, whisky, brandy or hops.

ii)   Our Captain's pet star is a doozy.
    It sounds like the name of a floozy.
     Zenelgenobie as such
     Doesn't mean much
Unless you are a Libra or boozy.

9th June.   Since the first of June we have made 130 miles a day or better. The last few have been over 140. Unfortunately the Equatorial current has not shown itself, but even without its help we are making a terrific passage — so far. Having said this, the mast may fall down in an hour's time, putting a new face on it. Our D.R. position this morning (the sky was too overcast for star sights) puts us 325 miles from Rodrigues. We have a force 5 SE wind with seas 8 to 10 feet high and vigorously breaking crests. As I was writing this, we surfed ahead of a sea at 8+ knots sheering off too far to starboard. The main gybed and the leech of the sail snagged the end of the cross trees. I managed to jerk it free before it ripped, and gybed her back on course. Poor old Quantock Pete is having to work like mad. If the seas get any worse I will have to put a reef in the main. I am trying to push on as fast as possible hoping to reach Rodrigues by Thursday the 12th. The following day, Friday 13th, one should be securely anchored.

10th June.   Deep reefed the main and she was much better and not much slower. Then we rolled up some of the genny and we were still averaging a comfortable 5½ knots. Sailing 140 miles a day is getting the crossing of this huge ocean done nicely. We are having to check the eggs as the odd one is now bad. We are on our last dozen anyway so it is no great loss. We bought them in Darwin and coated them in lard to seal out the air.

12th June.   At dawn I managed three star sights. I worked them out and plotted the fix which showed we were 25 miles due east of Rodrigues. By the time this was done it was virtually daylight, so I looked out over the bows; there sure enough, was a smudge of land on the horizon.

Port Mathurin is on the north of the island. There is an outer submerged reef then an inner reef through which a channel is cut. As we arrived, this was being made deeper by a Dutch dredging company to a minimum depth of 20 ft. A tug came out of the port to show us the channel. Then our starboard engine control siezed — it was the old problem I had had in Costa Rica — so we had only the port engine to thrust us against a fresh breeze. It proved just powerful enough, though at one stage I thought I was going to have to ask our pilots for a pluck. A new quay has just been built and this proved a very convenient berth, tied up right in the town.

AhKhee, the immigration officer, came on board and invited us to his home after work to take a shower. He also showed us the bank and the market. Incredibly obliging chap, but then we were to find that the Rodriguans generally are. They speak creole, or a bastard French, as before 1810 this was a French colony. The British captured it along with Mauritius. Since then the administrative language has been English, even so, English is still not widely spoken. Now, in conjunction with Mauritius, it is independent.

As it is winter time, the sun is actually nearer Britain at midday than here, so the climate is very pleasant. During the day, the temperature gets up to 80°F and at night it is cool enough for a blanket.

The people are spread out over the island working small subsistence farms. But it is an easy life with few pressures and with a population of 30,000, not too crowded. The population has been doubling itself every 20 years. In 1810 there were basically two French families each with a handful of slaves. A few Chinese and Indians have immigrated but the vast majority are descended from the 40 or 50 original slaves. There does not seem to be any racial prejudice here, in fact, there is a lovely easy going attitude.

We were ashore for a meal at 6.30 p.m. and found all the restaurants shut. Two cheery locals, seeing our predicament, pounded on the closed door of one of the hostelries, which reluctantly agreed to sell us food and drink. Alex and James, our guides, turned out to be policemen. In my limited experience, policemen the world over are great boozers, so we had an enjoyable boozy evening.

The following night Alex was holding a party in a night club and invited us. The most popular dance is the local one, the 'sega'. It is incredibly sexy. You jerk your hips and thrust your pelvis in a manner most suggestive. It has, I was told, been toned down somewhat on the insistence of the church, as in days of yore it so inflamed the passions, an orgy could well result. It was still the sexiest dance I have seen — the mind boggles at what it must have been.

15th June.　　Sunday, and sailing time was 8.00 a.m. We were all a touch fragile so somehow sailing time got delayed until 10.30. We motored out past the Dutchmen engaged in their national pastime of digging canals who waved and clowned from the deck of their dredger.

It was a double reef in the main and several rolls in the genny day. After this exercise Brenda flaked out in the saloon while Tom looked aghast at me downing a couple of beers.

"You can keep your aspirins and Alka Seltzers," I told him "for me it is the hair of the dog that bit you."

The wind soon moderated and as we dropped the island astern, the genny was unfurled and we settled down to a comfortable passage with little to do but read a book a day.

17th June.　　With the wind falling light — we were under twins — I expected, after a good evening fix, to arrive off the north end of Mauritius in the early hours of the morning. There was a 29 mile light on one of the islands which I could use for a running fix. I showed Brenda how to take a bearing, and told her to take one as soon as she saw the light, note the time and log reading, then call me after we had sailed a further 15 miles. Fortunately we were almost becalmed, making only 2 knots.

When I got up for my watch, Brenda pointed out the light.

"That's not it, that is a fixed white on the mainland. The one we want should be further north and flashing."

"I thought it funny it wasn't flashing." Brenda replied.

The D.R. by log showed we were 14 miles from Flat Isle light

204

and that it should be clearly visible, but there was nothing showing. I let the boat jog gently on until dawn. Then everything fell into place – we were where our D.R. said we should be. I later learnt that a cyclone last February which had done a lot of damage had also bust Flat Island light.

Using both engines, we motored through the channel to the north of Mauritius and south of all the islands, leaving the startling island of Gunnar's Quoin starboard. Through this channel the tide runs fiercely, often with overfalls, and requires careful navigation, which it got, but there are lots of easily distinguished landmarks from which to take bearings.

We passed 'Grand Bay', the yacht stop for the island as you must clear in at Port Louis, 15 miles to the south. It took 2½ hours to clear us in and then they advised us, if we stayed overnight in Port Louis, never to leave the boat unattended or it would be stripped. The alternative was to drive back to Grand Bay, which we did, arriving in the last of the light. Actually the yacht club do have leading lights of a white over red which makes the entrance easy and, if you know about the lights, possible at night. We motored right up to the village and moored close to the beach among several other boats and two French yachts.

Mauritius is quite an island. 950,000 people of which 65% are of Indian stock, their ancestors brought over to work the sugar cane as, after being given their freedom, the African slaves who had had enough of grafting growing sugar cane, became subsistence farmers. It is a curious amalgam of East and West and the market is a real Eastern Bazaar. Vendors sidle up with watches, gold bangles, and dope of various kinds while store holders call out to you to come and inspect their wares. It was a superb market for vegetables which were mostly of good quality and cheap. Not much had been available in Rodrigues, and we needed to restock on potatoes, onions and cabbage.

The yacht *Delphine* with Henri, a Frenchman and his New Zealand girl, Megan, had been sailing around the now deserted atolls in the Chagos group. His stories made me long to go there, as the swimming must be superb. When the military took over Diego Garcia they moved the local fishermen away, so, while you are allowed to visit Diego Garcia for a 24 hour stop over and re-victual, the other atolls in the group are deserted.

22nd June.   After watering at the yacht club jetty on Saturday evening,

I retired with an upset stomach leaving Tom and Brenda to have a last romantic night ashore. We sailed out on the Sunday with a good SE wind — the weather men saying we had a stable air flow over Mauritius. As soon as we cleared the island, this became unstable, and it was a damned uncomfortable night, with 2 reefs in the main, the storm jib and the genny rolled up to a pocket handkerchief. We were close reaching at 5 knots; I managed only a little sleep. Fortunately, soon after daylight, it moderated.

I was surprised not to see Reunion, but we had been working up to weather and I had a 10° allowance on for current and leeway so, while our D.R. said we were 20 miles off, I guess we must have been nearer 30.

Once past Reunion we altered course to pass 60 miles south of Madagascar. Then sun was shining, the crew naked on the deck, a school of fish could be seen in the waves and the wind was almost astern. So it was down with the mainsail and inner jib and hoist the port genny. Once more we were running under twins — the most comfortable way to sail. (I have long since forgotten how uncomfortable this can be in a mono-hull when you roll like a pig.)

23rd June.   Last night, at about 1.30 a.m., the boat was bouncing excessively and the sails flapping, so I struggled out to find Brenda swearing at our faithful helmsman, Quantock Pete.

"The bloody thing's stuck."

No way to talk about Q.P. whom I hold in considerable affection. I corrected the helm and got her to steer. A control line had jumped its drum and was quickly replaced. Back in the cockpit, I noticed over Brenda's head, a white arch, like a huge rainbow. I guessed it must have been thin cloud lit up by the moon, but below and above it the sky was clear and starlit. I tickled Brenda's fancy by describing it as "the dreaded white arch" and gave her a lurid description of what ills were about to befall us.

24th June.   It has been a calm day with only enough wind to push us at 3 knots and not really enough for Q.P. The watchkeeper has had to keep a careful eye on the course, frequently correcting the boat. But it has been a sunny day and the lunch time cole-slaw was delicious. With the evening, a light SE set in, which gave us a close reach at 4 knots and Q.P. could then manage after careful adjustment of the sails. When the wind blows from the south it has a decided nip, at least, to our now tropicalised skins. Me? I'm back to long trews, socks and carpet slippers. I opine that all self-respecting Skippers on sensible cruising yachts wear carpet slippers, particularly during the night watches.

25th & 26th June.   Two delightful yachting days, running before an easterly 3/4 under twins, with little to do but enjoy the winter sunshine — at midday just warm enough to strip off — and read a book or two. At each twilight I have managed to get good fixes. We have been making a steady 120—130 miles a day.

On the afternoon of the 26th the barometer started to fall. The wind backed and cloud covered the sky. As the wind freshened towards evening, I went to bend a reef in the main. The topping lift broke and the boom fetched me a right bang. The seas were getting lumpy and as I did not fancy gyrating at the masthead reeving a new topping lift, I called for Tom to take the weight of the boom on his shoulder while I, at the mast, bent in the double reef.

On the starboard tack, the furling genoa which is rigged to starboard of the centre of the boat, chafes on the port side forestay, especially when off the wind. For this reason, we had the old genny hanked to port in the traditional way and the other furled. So we changed this down to the No. 2 jib. I no sooner had it up than the patent snap shackle on the end of the sheet opened, and left the sail snapping and flapping like a machine gun. So it was lower away again, Brenda on the halliard; me, with finger nails flying, gathering the mad thing onto the foredeck without letting it droop into the sea. I took off the patent shackle and tied the sheet on with a bowline.

At 10 p.m. I was awakened by the motion. Tom, on watch, said the wind was freshening. He lowered the inner jib, reducing sail by 100 sq. ft which made her much quieter. However by midnight I was up again. She was banging madly through the waves and the wind was howling.

"We took the wrong sail down, Tom." I told him.

He rehoisted the inner jib, then lowered the No. 2, just bundling it into the forward sail locker. The wind, in the gusts, was up around gale force. Even with so little sail set, we were still averaging five knots. The wind soon moderated to force 5—6.

It was a lovely dawn, clouds breaking up; big seas with white foaming tops. I hoisted the No. 3 to make us once more cutter rigged and sailing at 6+ knots. By 11 a.m. there was not a cloud in the sky though the wind was howling again. The seas were heaping up with the foam tops being blown as spume to looard. Occasionally the boat would cream off a breaking sea at 10 knots. Tom handed the inner jib and this reduction slowed her down so that she rarely exceeded 7, and mostly maintaining 6. High speed sailing is very thrilling but a terrible strain on the crew. I must say, a gale never seems quite as bad though, if the sun is shining.

During the afternoon, the wind gradually moderated to a fair breeze and in the night dropped to no more than force 3. The barometer steadied, but then began again a slow fall and the wind to back so that by morning we were close hauled. Close hauled of course, the motion was uncomfortable and we could scarcely lay the course. Tom's midday log entry read "A real pain in the ass!"

Half an hour later, the wind suddenly backed more so that it was from dead ahead. One tack pointed us to the South Pole, the other, right into the residual seas. So I hove-to with the genny partly rolled, held aback. As it looked so black up ahead, as a precautionary measure, also bent a double reef in the mainsail. No sooner than this was done, the wind piped up to 6—7. To relieve our lot, Brenda heated up a can of apricot self-saucing pudding, which was very tasty.

30th June. After a rough night, the morning was little better — in fact worse. The winds would pick up to force 8; the tops of the waves blown off in spume. The seas were getting big, sometimes well over 20 feet, and occasionally catch us awkwardly and we would get thrown around and thumped heavily. The crew is getting fed up with nothing to do but read and nowhere to go but bed, and that is damp from spray forcing itself in the sliding windows.

At the end of Brenda's watch, I noticed a piece of sail flapping. The clew of the reefed main was torn for about 4 feet. So we had to tie in the 'Cape Horn' reef, which had hardly been used since departing that stormy area. And then reduced the jib to very very small. No sooner was this done, than the wind howled in stronger than ever, whining, as if with vicious, evil intent, through the rigging. I did not want to lose ground by running before the gale; the seas were not shock-like and we were riding them well though yawing taking them sometimes on the beam and at others, almost on the bows. In an attempt to stop this yawing and persuade the boat to lie at a constant angle of about 45° I let out a rubber tyre on 300 ft of warp off the weather bow. This technique once worked well for me hove-to in a gale off the NW tip of Ireland in a Heavenly Twins cat, but this time, seemed to make little difference. However, it certainly was not making it any worse, so we left it. I think the problem was not enough resistance as this is so much bigger than Heavenly Twins. We should have used two or possibly three tyres.

There was a lull, with the wind moderating to about force 6. I was standing in the cockpit, looking out at the magnificent sight of these huge rolling seas coming up from the Southern Ocean. Tom was yarning with me through the open companionway door. Then I saw this enormous sea bearing down upon us. It was a towering great wave, much bigger than all the others and the top of it a mass of frothing, turbulent white. It was a magnificent sea, an awesome sea, and filled me full of dread. I thought, "Is this IT?"

Up, up we went, with that huge long crest thundering above us. We were lying at an angle of about 60° to it when wham! — The bows were knocked off and we were broadside on (theoretically the worst position). Spume and breaking water fell over the decks. The whole boat was carried surfing sideways with terrific acceleration down the wave.

"It has got to capsize, it has to capsize." I said to myself, not believing that any multihull could survive such a wave. And then, after what seemed an age, with a lurch, we were over the crest.

It is difficult, if not impossible, to give accurately the height of big seas from a small yacht. I reckon it was a conservative guess to say the general run of seas was between 20 and 30 feet. This one towered over them, as if a wave had caught up with the one in front and climbed on its back. Being so much bigger but the same distance between waves, it had to be a lot steeper. The top third of the wave was one continuous break. Normally a wave builds up and then topples, forming a white-cap, which lasts for maybe half a minute, and then subsides, the venom gone out of it. For as long as we saw it, the break of this one never stopped. Indeed, it was so steep, it had to keep breaking.

I reckon that the most dangerous wave of the voyage so far, and one of those is one too many for any sailor. Good old *Ocean Winds* showed no sign of coming unstuck, let alone capsizing; but only, I am sure, because she could be carried along sideways in the top fast moving water like a beach ball. If we had had a deep keel like a monohull which would have had a grip in the denser water under the break, then we would have been knocked flat at least, and I think, most likely capsized. Of course a monohull would probably have righted itself if all the hatches were shut, and not like us, with the companionway open.

Ocean Winds may have survived that one, but even so I never want to see another rogue wave like it.

We had just finished a rough meal at 8 p.m. when, looking around the horizon, I saw some ship's lights. So on the VHF called up:

"Calling any ship, any ship in radio contact. This is Ocean Winds, Ocean Winds, yacht Ocean Winds, requesting weather information. If you read me, please come in, over."

We got an immediate response. It was *Mangan*. The radio officer gave us our position and a recent weather forecast and synopsis. She was a Liberian ship with German officers (fluent English) on a voyage from Brazil to Jakarta. It cheered us all up to have a yarn with them — somehow made us feel less isolated, hove-to in the storm.

1st July.   The radio officer of *Mangan* very decently called me on 2400 kcys. (I could listen, but not transmit). He meticulously went twice through the new forecast and synopsis, despite the fact his transmitter was overheating and giving him problems. He had no way of knowing that we heard it okay, but this was a great boost, for from it we knew we only had to wait another day before we could once again get sailing.

The day was spent hove-to just under small jib, beam onto the wind and sea, mending the mainsail. We glued on a patch then laboriously sewed with good length 'homeward bounders' around it and along the tear. Fortunately the wind had moderated to 5—6 but the swell was still huge, many waves over 30 ft from trough to crest. At the end of the day the radio antenna had had enough of jerking about at the top of the mast. It fell into the cockpit norrowly missing impaling Brenda on the cockpit sole. Now we can no longer contact other vessels.

2nd July.   A dawn fix showed we had been carried about 100 miles west during the gale. There must have been quite a current helping us on. The wind was now SW x S so in the early light, I bent on the main and hoisted it so by the time Tom got up for his watch, we were under way and making 5 knots towards Africa.

3rd July.   It often seems to me that sailing is a bit like farming — either a harvest glut or a crop failure. In our case, either too much wind or not enough. By midnight we were becalmed.

4th July.   Tom drew the Stars & Stripes in the log, drawing our attention to the great day. It was a great day too – for a power craft. Our little port plonker pushed us along at 4½ knots. At noon we spotted a large school of big whales. At first I thought they were razorbacks, but then saw their dorsals were rounded, and we could not identify them. Our whale book is one by Cousteau and is not very good for identification use. Brenda was particularly pleased; for a long while she has been asking if we were likely to sight any whales.

We celebrated the close of Independence Day with a delicious sweet and sour meal and a bottle of Australian Champagne.

Brenda, in a panic, called me out at 2.30 a.m. The whales had reappeared, surfaced, and blown right alongside. As we were virtually becalmed, I started the engine, assuring Brenda that the engine vibration and exhaust noise would dissuade any self-respecting whale from ramming us.

Despite there being no wind, the swell was still very big. Tom likened it to the prairies. In the troughs, there was just the long sea rolling towards us; as we rose over the crest, one's horizon suddenly extended, seemingly enormous distances across those majestic seas. Sooty albatrosses came gliding past and also the small chubby cape pigeons, with their strongly contrasting black and white speckled wings.

6th July.   Despite a falling barometer, we still had no wind except for one brief spell in the morning. At eventide, dolphins joined us for happy hour, sporting off the bows. Durban radio weather forecast is for SW winds, 5–15 knots. This will mean a head wind.

7th July.   And sure enough, the wind with the dawn was from the WSW. Fortunately it soon pulled round to the SSW at force 2 to 3. We are only 150 miles from Durban so can pick up their radio programmes clearly. It is the same idiot beat noise the world over. They do have a neat twist to the weather forecast – each pronouncement is followed by a burst of urgent jingle, thus making the forecast doubly difficult to remember.

I do S.A. Broadcasting an injustice. As we have got closer and been able to pick up the FM broadcasts, we have found good variety and excellent music programmes.

For a few hours the wind freshened against the strong south going current. The bloody seas were almost vertical, their nastiness out of

211

all proportion to the strength of the wind. We had to pay off to 65° off the wind and still hit and bounced horribly. By midnight, it had once again fallen light. We were some 60 miles from Durban and could see the glow of the city on the horizon. We motor sailed SW, a course which gradually closed with the coast.

8th July.   A light NE wind started in the morning so we once again sailed under twin genoas and mainsail. The wind gradually freshened throughout the day until it was blowing about 30 knots (force 7). We were surging off the waves in great style, often doing 10/11 knots, several times 13, and for one wild wild surge, just touched 15 knots. We were carrying far too much sail, so after that last splendid surf, handed the port genny, rolled up part of the starboard one and deep reefed the main. Even so, over a four hour period (half of which reefed) we still averaged 7 knots, and with an added help from the current, were making great progress south.

9th July.   By daylight, the wind fell right away so it was back on with the engines. We closed the shore to confirm our position — we had been using radio fixes for the last 100 miles. There is a lot of traffic along this coast, frequently dirty great super tankers going to or from the Gulf. I tried several times to call passing ships up on the VHF, but none answered, making me think that my aerial repair was not successful, but nearing East London, their radio came through loud and clear.

The weather prophets were promising a cold front with westerly winds, fresh to strong. It was a beautiful warm calm day. I was undecided whether or not to press on or use East London as a bolt hole. I did not want to be caught in the Agulhas current with a strong wind blowing against it. A tap on the barometer showed it still steadily falling. I decided on discretion, and we motored in to tie up at the head of the harbour. I had no chart of the entrance, but it was easy to enter and a good refuge port.

After the usual nonsense with forms — mind you, the officials were all kind and helpful — we showered and were ready for a night on the town. The restaurant we decided on, 'Paul's', seemed to us, cheap. They apologised that with increasing meat prices they had had to decrease steak sizes; the steaks were monsters, and half British or U.S. prices. The wine was also half British prices but then we drank twice as much. Clearing out next day, the Customs told me we had been to one of their 'expensive' restaurants.

It was a fine passage south. At first with little wind, so we motored, then a good quartering wind pushed us along at 6 knots. By gum! Are the nights getting cold.

We reached Port Elizabeth after a 23 hour passage (150 miles), berthing astern of three S.A. yachts down from Durban. The Yacht Club here is very good, but does not yet have a licence, so of an evening time you take a bottle along.

This was a mail drop for me. How much one looks forward to reading gossip from home. I tried to call England from a pay 'phone, and found this cannot be done in South Africa. 'Phoning abroad, even if a transfer charge, has to be from a private 'phone which is damn difficult for us. I had the good fortune to meet Pierre and Dolly who took me to their home to 'phone when they found me frustrated with the S.A. telephone system.

Sunday 13th July.   After laying over a day of strong westerlies, we sailed out with clearances for all ports to Cape Town. I forgot to file a 'flight plan' and got called up on the VHF by the harbour authorities shortly after leaving, but as I had a clearance, all was okay. 2 miles from the harbour entrance, a group of seals lay in the water, seemingly all tangled together. A seal orgy? As we passed, the odd head looked up as if to say 'shove off'.

Once around Cape Recife, the South East Cape of Africa, it was a head wind. We close hauled offshore. By carefully adjusting the sails I found I could get the boat to steer herself better without using the wind vane. We had to bend in a reef and roll up some jib as the wind increased to force 6. This southern ocean is cool.

14th July.   During the night, the wind fell light, the sea was horribly lumpy and I could not find a course she would comfortably steer. So I hove her to and waited. Two hours later, the wind changed round to a NE. Not strong, but enough to push us in the right direction at 4 knots. What a relief to lose that strong head wind and that bitterly cold spray being blown back into the cockpit. Our course was set for Cape Agulhas, 250 miles away.

The evening forecast promised west winds, 15–20 knots, which, against the strong Agulhas current, would be nasty. We therefore altered course for Mossel Bay in the hope of reaching there before the wind changed. But the head wind set in so rather than beat on, we headed due north for Nysna Harbour, reputed to be the prettiest

213

on the coast.

We arrived off the magnificent entrance at dawn and hove-to until it got lighter. When we made the approach we could see the swell breaking right across the entrance in a surf line. The tide, I thought, must be ebbing, so we turned around and hove-to crabbing back out to sea. 4 hours later, at midday, we went back for a second look; it was still breaking right across. Perhaps we would be able to get in near high water, 5 p.m. But if the wind, as the forecaster had just prognosticated, went fresh southerly, would we be able to get out? I doubted it, and south winds would allow us to lay our course. So we gave up trying to get into Nysna, deep reefed the main and close hauled to the SSW.

The mutton, bought four days ago in P.E., was getting a touch ripe. I dissuaded Tom and Brenda from giving it a burial at sea. Instead, we made a damn fine mutton curry. Always a good saw 'The riper the meat, the better the curry.'

And a jolly good job we carried on sailing. Four hours later the wind backed to the south. We tacked to head west. At first we were bashing straight into the old set of the sea so had to keep the speed down to no more than 3 knots. Any faster we would have been hitting hard into one wall of water after another. However, the set of the sea soon changed to follow the new wind direction and then we were bowling along at a comfortable 5½ knots towards Cape Agulhas, the southern tip of Africa.

We spoke a Swedish ship who gave us the weather forecast and our exact position via satellite navigator. This was to within hundreths of a degree.

As the wind freshened up to force 7, we reduced sail, rolling the genny up a little, and booming it out. We had rather too much sail up, the self-steering could not cope so we were hand steering, but I wanted to make up time and get out of this cold southern ocean.

We passed Agulhas as nightfall — 160 miles to Cape Town. A fishing boat, *Benguela Pride* called us up to find out who would be lunatic enough to sail around the South of Africa in mid winter with a gale threatening. We gathered, that in contrast to Europe, where the fishing has been disastrous, this year the fishing here has been good.

As we cleared the Cape, Tom and I handed the boom off the genny. It is bad enough doing this in a calm, now it was best part of a full gale. Each time we have to do it in such conditions I fear a bad accident, for if we lost control, it would have us overboard in a flash, and as like as not beating us unconscious at the same time. We took off all sail except for the No. 2 jib. With the wind broad on our starboard side, the seas now only had a short fetch with the wind coming over the land; we were sailing at 7 knots much of the time. As there was so much shipping, I scarcely slept all night, but with a lot happening and such a fresh wind, the night soon passed.

17th July.   As morning dawned, we were changing down from the No. 2 to No. 3 with gusts of force 9, a lot of spray flying, and the sun rising over Cape Point, Cape of Good Hope —

'The fairest Cape in the whole circumference of the earth.' to quote my precircumnavigator of 400 years ago. In the last 48 hours we have sailed over 300 miles.

2 hours later, under the lee of the Cape, the wind disappeared. Soon we were under full sail and looking for more wind. The weather forecast still gave gale force wind south of the point. It was as if there was a line across the ocean with force 3 to the north and force 8–9 south of it. What a glorious feeling to struggle out of multiple layers of clothes and let some actual air once again attack our fetid bodies.

As we got up to off 'Lion's Kop' we were virtually becalmed so called our trusty Volvos back into service to motor into Cape Town and berth right outside the bar of the Royal Cape Yacht Club. What could be more convenient?

Cape Town proved a good stop. People as helpful and hospitable as anywhere I have been. We met a pretty wide cross-section of the white English speaking locals, but not, I am afraid, the coloureds, as this is not easy as the only ones we saw were shop assistants and servants apart from the time we went out 10 miles to David Jordan's farm. Then he gave lifts to anyone walking, so at times we made up a very mixed crowd hanging on for dear life in the back of his Land Rover.

I met David on the quay at Puntas Arenas a year last Christmas, and he rashly gave me the address of his farm and an invitation. We spent a delightful Sunday there, and Tom and Brenda plan to stay a few days after leaving the boat.

Tom and Brenda were leaving me here. I was sorry to see them go. They plan to hitch-hike and otherwise travel up through South Africa to Kenya and thence across to India. They have been a jolly, happy crew. I had to promote them on entering the first port in South Africa; Brenda to first mate, Tom, to second. Mere crew-members are not allowed a liquor allowance but officers are allowed a duty free litre every 3 days. Not that we drunk that much, but it meant that we could have plenty around for entertaining.

A letter left on the cabin table:

"Dear Captain Pat:
        We, the former crew
        Of the Ocean Winds II
        Wishing you the very best
        Good winds, smooth seas, and all the rest.
        Think of us walking o'er the land
        Being beheaded by some Zulu band.
        We'll think of you on the raging seas,
        Cold, and tired, and weak in the knees.
                Have fun, take care
                Look for the best
                Laugh lots

                Brenda and Tom

My new crew are both South Africans, Tim Chilwell, a 6 ft 2 in. blond he-man, and a cable wireless technician, Allan Daly. Beth, Allan's wife, took me to the supermarket to victual. We only just managed to get the three trolley loads of food into her mini, I spent £100 at the supermarket; similar loads cost a lot more in Australia and the States. Fortunately Tom and Brenda were still aboard to help me stow it all. Somehow we found room for it all and for a side of bacon and 7 kilos of rump steak to be pickled in brine in the dustbin.

25th July 1980.   What a pantomime to go foreign from South Africa:

1) Letter from Yacht Club saying I had paid my debts.
   (Very good here, full marina facilities for £1.5 a day)

2) To passport control to fill in a form telling how much money I had spent here and other personal details.

3) To Port Captain's office to fill in form describing boat and give addresses of next of kin in case we sink.

4) To Custom's office to fill in 2 forms and obtain clearance.

5) By radio, call Port Control and request permission to leave harbour.

While all this nonsense was being done, Brenda and Tom topped up the water tanks and washed the grime of the port off the decks.

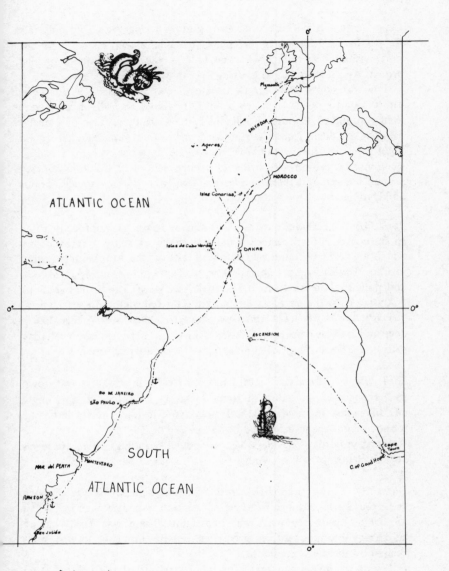

ATLANTIC OCEAN

SOUTH

ATLANTIC OCEAN

Plymouth

SALVADOR

v. Açores

MOROCCO

Islas Canarias

Islas de Cabo Verde

DAKAR

ASCENSION

Rio de Janeiro

São Paulo

Mar del Plata

Montevideo

Rawson

Cape Town

C. of Good Hope

San Julián

0°

0°

0°

0°

Outward bound :-
Plymouth to Port St. Julian

Homeward bound :-
Cape Town to Plymouth

217

J

Cape Town air, if there is no gale to blow it clear, is highly polluted. As we handle the ropes our hands become black. As we leave the port, visibility is reduced to one mile — the fog is not damp, just brown. And it stretches to halfway up Table Mountain.

I do not know how far to the north the SE trades are this year, but I aim to reach them as soon as possible, so both motors were kept running all through the daylight hours, pushing us on at a steady 5 knots. At dusk, I cut the starboard one so that Tim could get a good night's rest in his berth. With the engine under my berth, I had to sleep in the saloon. At twilight, a large school of dolphins sported around us; amongst them were several seals who were obviously curious and leaping out of the water alongside.

26th July.   Tim woke me at 3.30 a.m. as a ship was approaching fine to starboard. A light easterly wind was setting in, so by the start of my watch at 4.00, we found we could sail, take off the Autohelm (repaired in Cape Town), and set Quantock Pete. The wind soon freshened to ¾ and pulled to the north east. This meant we were close hauled at about 5 knots. With the increase in motion, Tim fell victim to seasickness, but Allan was fine. The sun rose through a haze over Africa, like a deep red button mushroom. There is always something new. Yesterday seals in a school of porpoises and today the peculiar sunrise.

28th July.   Just after 5 a.m. I heard a fog horn (visibility was down to a few yards), sounding at times far away, at others, frighteningly near. I called up on the VHF. It was a tug heading north and as he sounded from ahead, I realised he had passed us.

Since yesterday the glass has been steadily falling. There are wisps of high cirrus but still no wind.

29th July.   At midnight, a fresh nor-easter quickly set in allowing us to sail. I was out again at 3.45 as the motion had awoken me. Allan too came up to see what was happening. There was Tim, shaking his shaggy blond beard. A wave had caught him and he was quite excited by the new experience.

I bent in the second reef. The wind was out of the north, so we rolled up a lot more of the jib, then backed it, and lay hove-to for the rest of the night.

I was feeling rotten with a sore throat and, I suspect, a bit of a temperature. In the medicine box, I found some tablets given to me in Chile. I could not fully understand the Spanish instructions, but as they were not only for sore throats but, as far as I could grasp, also for haemorrhoids, I suspected they might be suppositories. Allan thought not. Anyway, I sucked them and they tasted just like I imagine suppositories do.

This is being written while hove-to in the gale. A bloody great wave has just caught us badly; much of it splashed over the top and squirted in the companionway door.

By 14.00 hours, I thought the main under too much strain for it is now ageing cloth, and remembering off Madagascar and the day spent repairing it, decided to reef it to the Cape Horn reef. A gust of strong gale hit us while I was struggling at the mast — Sod it, I thought, I will hand it completely otherwise it is bound to tear.

We also rolled up the jib, except for the last 20 sq. ft which, because it was all so tightly wound would not go as there was no more winding wire left on the drum. This was quite an improvement. Less motion and the seas, coming on the starboard beam, not hitting us as hard. Even so, I would still rather be home in bed with the missus.

Tim asked "How long do we keep the sails down?"

I replied "Until your Captain is no longer frightened."

At dusk it had moderated to 5/6 and the seas were no longer so vicious. Allan asked about making progress, perhaps with an engine, but I explained that in such seas and against a head wind, the engines were virtually useless; all we would be doing would be, metaphorically, pouring fuel into the sea. It was far better to wait until things quietened down.

The reverse happened. By midnight the wind was screeching straight out of Hell. It came up quickly, and so far the seas were not dangerous, but I knew they soon would be if the wind continued at that strength.

"We'll tow rubber tyres and run off before it." I told the crew.

"But you can't go out in that," said Allan, "you'll be blown off the deck."

"Oh, we'll wear safety harnesses — but we have to do all we can to help the boat survive when the seas really get up as they soon will."

A quarter of an hour was spent donning warm clothing and oil skins. Allan then took the wheel, heading SW with the wind on the starboard quarter. Tim looked out of the dog-house window and prayed. I crawled along the deck with my harness clipped on the starboard safety line to the forward locker. Out came the rubber tyre and warp, and pushing them in front of me, I belly crawled back to the

219

cockpit. It really was blowing great guns.

I middled the warp and tied on both my tyres, then led the warps around everything and onto the two stern cleats. Despite my care, I still managed to loop the wrong way round the mainsheet, so one side had to be re-led. All the time I was being buffeted by driven spray. Allan was doing a good job on the helm. The tyres went over; I adjusted them up to as even a pull as I could. They gave a strong tug astern and we slowed to 2 knots. Since we were headed for the Antarctic, the slower the better.

I told Allan we would do hour watches at the helm. Unfortunately Tim had not yet really got the hang of steering. All went well right up to the end of my watch. I was standing in the cockpit steering when I heard this roar astern. As the stern picked up I automatically corrected the slew with the wheel. To no avail. A bloody great wave engulfed me, filling the cockpit. God then sent a follow up immediately behind it which joined the first. I was up to my knees in water — my boots were full — how I hate wet feet. I groped around the drains making sure they were clear — they were. Even so, 4—1½ inch drains are slow to clear even such a small cockpit as *Ocean Winds*. She has a stern cockpit too, but deep sea I always stow the dinghy over that thus protecting her from just this eventuality.

I was surprised that she was pooped; it must have been quite a sea as she rose all the rest superbly. I suspect she would not have been had we not been towing rubber tyres which conceivably held the stern down, tugging aft as we tried to lift and surf forward. We are also very heavily laden with more weight than at any other time of the voyage. Even so, I do not think we were in any immediate danger, but how glad I was not to be in one of those cats with enormous cockpits. Actually I reckon big cockpits on any boat are a menace at sea, not only for the amount and weight of water they hold, but even more for the danger, in rough weather, of being thrown across them and breaking one's bones.

Allan then relieved me, saying he hoped he did not get any sea like that. I am glad to say he did not. He did give me a shout after half an hour. A ship was approaching our stern — it passed but a cable or so away. I called it on the VHF as I would have liked to know the weather synopsis and our position, but I guess they did not speak English as I got no reply.

The glass was starting to rise and the wind to back north westerly. On my next spell I found I had to head due south, then could gybe her onto south east and gradually pull her round to east. The wind too moderated, much to everyone's relief. So much so, that by 5 a.m. I decided we could once more peg the helm and safely leave her to ride it out while we awaited the dawn.

At first light Allan made a welcome cup of tea, then we all hauled in the warps and tyres, Tim doing the muscle bit on the quarter, Allan stowing in the forward locker while I directed and photographed the operation.

We let out a little more jib, (great, our Cooney jib reefer) and then hoisted the deep reefed main. The wind was no more than 5, but we were sailing due north into a confused sea so I limited the sail area to keep the speed down to 3 knots. I really have had my fill of gales around this bottom end of Africa. I note Slocum too had a pasting here, saying they were as bad as around the Horn.

Just after midday I looked out to see an enormous container ship approaching which somehow, Tim, on watch, had not seen. I called her up on the VHF; the *City of Durban*. She confirmed that the gale and depression was now to the south of us and also gave us our position, 28°31' S 13°36' E. I had a noon sight but with such seas running, a good fix was going to be impossible, so I was pleased to be given one.

The night was a bore. The wind fell away until we were only making 1–2 knots. The sea was so lumpy and confused I felt it would be a waste to use the engines, so the crew had to struggle with hand steering.

31st July. By the early hours I decided that the sea had at last quietened sufficiently to run the port engine and use the Autohelm. Despite there being no wind all day, the sea has remained quite choppy. It must be because there is a swell crossing the Benguela current which is helping us along at ½ to ¾ knot.

We had an exceptionally good nosh this evening; 'Boeuf Patanough', with sweet and sour red cabbage and potatoes. The B.P. is rump steak (from the brine pickle) cut into strips. 2 sections of garlic, 3 onions fried in oil and ½ a green pepper. When all was cooked in the deep frying pan, I added a gravy mix of 'Bisto' and soy sauce and a little water. A little more cooking, and what a super dish it turned out to be.

1st August. By the end of my watch the engine was switched off (after 27½ hours running), the twin genoas boomed out and the main boom held with a retaining line, to starboard. Quantock Pete, albeit reluctantly, as the wind was scarcely strong enough, was given the job of steering. The sun was warming the day up and drying the dew off the decks; we were all looking forward to a pleasant day's yachting. Even the birds came around to add interest — the large black topped Albatross, Cape pigeons, sooty albatrosses and stormy petrels kept flitting across our wake.

It turned into a great day's sail. Alas, that is all it was. We went bounding along before what appeared to be the start of a good SE trade, making 6 knots under twin genoas when the port one burst into two. We handed the tattered remains and hoisted the No. 2 in its place. Morning dawned with dolphins off the bows and a falling wind. By early afternoon we were struggling to make 2 knots and by evening I reluctantly gave up and went back to motoring.

4th August.   For two days now, each time I have come up from below, I would look around the horizon for signs of clouds building; tap the barometer which remained steady at 1014 mb. There was nothing. How good it was to have the engines and enough fuel for a few more hundred miles of motoring, otherwise it would, for days and days, have been the Ancient Mariner touch: "As idle as a painted ship upon a painted ocean."

5th August.   A thousand miles from Cape Town. 11 days out, and only for 3½ of them have the engines been silent. This is expensive and frustrating, but better than rotting on the sea. Without the motors we would, I guess, be no more than 400 miles from Cape Town. Mid-afternoon; we have stopped the engine, switched from Autohelm to Quantock Pete and are sailing at 3½ to 4 knots with a f.2 wind just rippling the sea. It seems odd — so quiet. I have to keep looking over the side or at the odometer to confirm that we are moving. The glass has also risen a whole millibar to 1015. The course is set for Ascenscion as I need to refuel if possible. Ascenscion is 1500 miles.

11th August.   It was the start of the trades, and good progress of 120 to 130 miles a day has since been made. It has been cool and overcast so generally no star sights except for one morning when the sky just cleared at dawn. Otherwise we have had to use the sun faintly piercing the clouds. The breeze has not been at all constant, down to force 3 and up to force 6. With the varying strength of the wind, the wheel has to be altered to give the rudders a bias, otherwise the waves try to broach her and one of the genny's will set aback. Allan caught on immediately but it has been a bit of a struggle with Tim. However I did not have to get out once last night to bring her back on course so I think he may at last be getting the hang of which way to turn the wheel.

Today saw some flying fish which means the water is warming up. The air temperature at midday reached 76°F. Soon it will be warm enough to strip off and have a wash!

In the rigging we have hung the remaining 5 kilos of our steak to dry in the breeze. It has been in pickle (salt, sugar and salt petre) for 14 days. It has been jolly tasty up until now and has shown no indication of going off. This is the first time I have tried drying a chunk after pickling and wonder if it is best left as a chunk or if it should be cut up into strips and dried.

16th August. I managed some morning sights which showed we were 60 miles SE of Ascenscion. If there was a reasonable current, I reckoned we could just make it before dark with the aid of one motor. In the late afternoon, we saw a small cargo ship with smoke billowing out of the aft hatch and enveloping half the ship. They got the fire under control and made way again only for it to all flame up once more. Their second attempt at putting it out was successful and they set a course south of Ascenscion headed as if for South America.

We, meanwhile, reached the south east corner of the island at dusk. I reckoned it was too late to reach up the coast in the dark so hove-to off the SW corner for the night. The boat jogged away just under the mainsail making about ½ knot.

17th August. I got her sailing 2 hours before dawn to arrive off George Town at first light. I was surprised to see a cat from Durban 'Scott's Ark' and a French steel ketch that had been down to the Antarctic, anchored off.

The police sergeant, a pleasant chubby St. Helenan came down to his office to clear us in.

"Welcome to Ascenscion" he told us "This is a closed port, but you are welcome ashore during daylight hours only, unless a resident sponsors you with special permission each time, then you can remain ashore until 11 p.m. Anyone ashore illegally is liable to a fine of up to £200. No free enterprise. No trading and do behave yourselves. You can stay 72 hours."

O – ho, I thought, bloody police state with a vengeance here. And

223

the English and St. Helenan clubs practised apartheid. The American one, the Volcano Club, did not, and was the most popular; showing how ridiculous the other club's policy was.

There was a lot of surf running but we managed to land without getting very wet. It was as bad as anywhere I have been except when we rescued the guy in Mauii. As Allan had worked on the island and was due here again in a few months (he works for the South Africa Cable Co.) we were able to be sponsored for an evening ashore. The police inspector said, on being asked if yachties gave trouble.

"You name it, they have done it."

I thought this was stretching it a bit, but just before we arrived, a South African yachty had tried, while in his cups, to get into a punch up with a St. Helenan at the Volcano Club. Also, a long while ago, another molested a St. Helenan girl.

Tommy, the boss of the S.A. Cable Co. office here, took us on a quick tour of the island. It is an almost barren volcanic pile but usefully situated in the middle of the ocean to act as a booster station for two cable companies. The Americans run the airfield and a satellite tracking station and the BBC, with their usual efficiency, run the power station and the local radio.

Tommy went to considerable trouble to help us get fuel and victual the boat. In a short visit we met many interesting and friendly people so, despite my first impressions, I would have liked to have spent more time on the island, and certainly the full three days allowed.

On Monday the swell had lessened considerably, which was an enormous relief as we had to load 67 gallons of fuel, 20 gallons of water and 3 boxes of food and a plateful of grouper fish fillets (given us by a St. Helenan fisherman filleting them on the quay).

I had a swim to inspect the bottom. It is beginning to get foul in patches, but if you scrub the latest anti-foul just comes off in a cloud. It is not at the moment too bad.

18th August.   We left at 2 p.m. after stowing stores, vinegaring 6 loaves, and doing a book exchange with the other yachts. It was a broad reach with a course set for the NNW. If the doldrums are wide, I plan to refuel in the Cape Verdes and try and make as fast a passage as possible north to the Azores and then NE for home.

23rd August.   For the first 24 hours we had a good breeze but then once more the wind fell frustratingly light with our speed dropping down to less than 3 knots at times. The average went from 113 miles; 92 miles; 87 miles; 88 miles and then once more a better wind came and again our hopes soared with the average jumping to 103 miles.

The warmth of the sun is tempered by the breeze and today, as we sailed across the line just before midday we were all relaxed and getting nicely suntanned. Accompanying us across the Equator was a large school of bottle nosed dolphins sporting around us until a school of flying fish were frightened from under our bows. Evidently, as they took off after them, the dolphins too decided this was lunch time.

26th August. After 2 days of gentle 2/3 trade it freshened again to force 4 and we were once more bowling along just under the boomed out twin headsails. But this was a funny trade this year, for by midnight the wind had gentled to force 3 again and our speed slowed to 4 knots. It was black up ahead. Within 20 minutes, we were becalmed with rain. Allan called me; a northerly had set in. So we handed both jibs, swore, got wet doing it, and lay broadside to an evil sea; the northerly against the set, shortening it and throwing us around something horrible.

What to do? Well it seems a pretty good adage — 'When in doubt, do nowt'. So I went back to bed and Allan read a book in the saloon. This proved the right decision, for by 3.30 a.m. the southerly was back and Allan, commendable fellow, got us sailing north under the twins without my help.

Gradually the day improved and our noon sight showed we were only 15 miles south of tying the knot which we did 4 hours later, at 1700 hours GMT on 26th August 1980 in position 6°08' N 19°00' W.

By log, *Ocean Winds* had sailed 34,825 miles, to which must be added a few hundred as I have had considerably more favourable current than foul. It was 2 years less 2½ days ago when she cut her twin furrows through this particular bit of ocean, and I must say, it has not changed much. I wonder how much I have?

From the log book, I see she logged 3,200 miles to here from Plymouth on the way out.

27th August. The bottom is getting depressingly bad. The anti-fouling put on in Darwin at the beginning of May is no longer working and some evil stalks are growing below the water line. I have not seen this particular growth before, but as a velocity retardant, they work exceedingly well. If we sail at 4½ knots I know we should be doing 6, but the real trouble is when we should be doing 4—5 knots, most of the time we are lucky to be doing 3.

28th August. Heavy rain, but not with as much wind as I expected. Tim collected lots of water, some of which went into the tanks and several gallons put aside for bathing. After the rain came a brief spell of calm, but not enough for the seas to go down sufficiently for us to swim and try to clean the bottom.

29th August. Soon after dawn, the wind, force 3, veered WNW. We have to be on a reach or run to make an even passable passage as our bottom is so foul. Hard on the wind we can make little progress. With this wind shift, we would be close-hauled if we continued to try for the Cape Verde Islands. So we paid off for Dakar, Senegal which lies under Cape Verde as this was a reach and 40 miles nearer.

A large school of dolphins jumped around us. This was a sporting bunch, many jumping clear of the water as if putting on a show in Miami Marineland.

30th August. By midday we were approximately 200 miles from Dakar, still with the wind on the beam and another school (or perhaps the same ones back again) of dolphins sporting off the bows. Off to starboard it was as black as the inside of a cow and rumbling thunder. This was to leeward, but life being perverse, instead of going away it spread up to windward. It did not reach us until 5 p.m. and then, fortunately, only the NW corner of the enormous black area. And it rained. A torrential downpour which lasted well over an hour. Sometimes with a strong wind which varied in strength and boxed the compass and had me constantly tending the sheets. I find such awful black rain storms frightening. In this case the wind never got over force 6; the lightning not too near and the rain was so heavy it flattened the sea with visibility reduced to yards.

1st Sept. With both engines going since yesterday, we reached Dakar by midday. Ile Gorey, which shelters the harbour on its south side, is an interesting looking place; well fortified in days of yore with some attractive buildings of colonial days nesting at the cliff base. It was an important slave shipping port and on the island can still be seen the slave pens.

We motored into the large commercial harbour. Despite a call to harbour control, nobody cared where we went. Eventually we found the 'Club Sportive de Peche' which allowed us to tie up at their jetty. We were too wide for their slip but while there took the opportunity to fill up with diesel and do all the police clearance nonsense. Not that anyone seemed to care; it was all as casual as it is in France.

In the evening the sport fishing boats returned. They were holding a big international sport fishing competition with competitors from Texas, Mexico, France, Spain and Germany as well as Senegal. Each boat brought in a good haul of 10 foot sailfish. An American told me it was the best game fishing he had known.

We learnt there was a marina with slipping facilities 3 miles away tucked right up in the corner of the hook of land on which Dakar is built. We motored round and entered the roughly breakwatered area, the echo sounder indicating a six foot deep channel. We beached *Ocean Winds* in the SW corner which was not really ideal, as the stern was over the deeper channel but it had the advantage of enabling us to gaze, with considerable pleasure, at the lady in the adjacent boat who wore the minimum of clothing. (See earlier definition of minimum). She appeared to be alone and Tim suggested she might be lonely, but I pointed out to him, a girl is never alone with a figure like that, as was proved next morning when a man left for work.

The scrubbing off took considerable labour. The 2 inch bladders of growth were very firmly stuck. While we were scraping off a heavy squall came over. Lightning flashed, thunder roared and it rained a virtual solid sheet of water. We had to continue working.

Allan and I got up at 3 a.m. to let the boat off into deeper water. It was still raining, though not so heavily. By morning the rain was intermittent but with strong squalls. A large power boat was sunk at its moorings, the heavy rain having filled it through the large cockpit. The wind had swung southerly which was fair for us once we got around the point. There was the problem. The squalls were still heavy but time was pressing. We got in the shore lines, Tim having to swim across to untie them, the anchor up, and a wave to our pretty neighbour. The entrance to this marina is very narrow and tricky but the boat handled better and was much faster with a clean bottom.

Once out of the marina, we hoisted a deep reefed main and storm jib. Beyond the shelter of the Navy Breakwater, a gale of wind hit us. It took me but a few minutes to decide to turn back to shelter, and near some fishing canoes, we dropped anchor. All morning, heavy gale squalls would pass across. At each clearance, full of hope I would look out but over the breakwater waves were crashing with undiminished force and heavy black clouds hung ominously to windward all prepared to smash down on us. As I sit, penning these lines and fuming with frustration, I can see all hope of reaching Plymouth by 26th Sept. fading away.

By 1500 hrs., I decided that the moderate spells were now more prolonged than the nasty ones so once again we weighed anchor. Beyond the breakwater it was rough. Gale force squalls were hitting us straight from the unprotected south. In the shoal water, the seas were particularly vicious; the green tops of the waves curling over and dropping vertically. Periodically the heavy rain would blot out the vast fleet of Eastern Bloc factory fishing ships at anchor. We had but 5 miles to go to clear the headland, but because of the wind direction, this meant a leg of 5 miles to the SE and then one to the SW. We motor sailed using both engines, deep reefed main and storm jib. *Ocean Winds* did very well, and 2 hours after leaving, we could bear away, set more sail, switch engines off and sail clear of the headland by the comfortable margin of 2 miles.

4th Sept.　By 4 a.m. we no longer had enough wind as, under full sail with a force 2 wind, we were just making 3½ knots. But oh what a difference a clean bottom makes. By mid morning we were motoring.

To the north of Cape Vert (Verde) my sights showed that instead of the contrary Canary current, we were experiencing a favourable one which was helping us north at 12 miles a day. This lasted from 15°N to 20°N, 60 miles south of Cape Blanc. I presume it is a back eddy caused by the projection of Cape Vert.

6th Sept.　A northerly wind gradually hardened in so we close hauled on the starboard tack to the NW. We had to go NW anyway to clear the shoals of Banc d'Arguin just south of Cape Blanc and Port Etienne of North Mauritania. As we were sailing by the edge of these shoals we had an ominous black dorsal and tail fin cruising alongside. Not a moment to fall overboard.

At sunset I noticed that the clew of the No. 2 jib had almost pulled out. So much for my repair job done in Papua New Guinea. We handed this jib and put up the No. 3. (I had the genny fully rolled as the furling gear is at last showing signs of irremediable senility so do not want to use it in the reefed mode.)

The wind was up around force 5 and the boat was steering herself nicely cutter rigged. I was kept on my toes until midnight as we were passing diagonally across the busy shipping lane. Just before Allan came on watch, I bent in the first reef of the main. This made only a little difference to our speed but a great deal to our comfort.

I should have bent in the deep reef for at 8 a.m. the main split above the clew. I bent her down to the deep reef. It looks a big repair job so will have to wait for calmer conditions.

Allan has spent the day patiently sewing the clew of the No. 2. Tim has spent it on his berth. Poor lad is completely (no pun intended) out of his depth. He still does not know which way to turn the wheel when she needs correcting and I dare not let him up on deck as he cannot remember from one day to the next which rope belongs to which sail. Apart from this, if it is at all rough, he is terrified at the idea of leaving the cockpit. But on his watch he seems to keep a good eye open for other shipping so he is not absolutely useless.

8th Sept.   The wind, from the NE, had moderated to 3—4 and we needed the full mainsail. Allan and I unbent it; spread the area needing repair over the saloon table, cut out a fine overlapping patch in bright red sailcloth (I had no white piece large enough) and, using all our remaining contact adhesive, glued the patch in place. We reinforced the gluing by sewing around all edges. This was so much sewing we quickly decided on ½ inch long 'homeward bounders'. The contrasting red patch looks very pretty. Hope the poor old main holds up for the rest of the way as all this fine needlework is getting a bit trying.

12th Sept.   Very little change in four days. We have been close hauled on the starboard tack; sails set and the helm pegged and she has steered herself without the aid of watchkeeper, Quantock Pete or Autohelm. Our course made good has been NNW and about 90 miles a day. There has been little to do other than eat, read and sleep.

13th Sept.   The wind was gradually backing north and by 4 p.m. we tacked and at last had the bows of the ship pointing towards Plymouth. The breeze is very light and so we needed the help of the engine and Autohelm. We have about 1,600 miles to Plymouth and, if we were to arrive back on the anniversary of Drake's arrival, 13 days to do it.

The starboard engine overheats if she is run for a long period. I suspect that one of the waterways in the cylinder head is clogged — probably with pieces of broken down water pump impeller. I have checked all the easily get-at-able pipes and junctions but to no avail. So this means that the engine can only be used for short periods to charge the battery. To thrust through the calms we will have to rely on the port one. What a joy it is to have two engines on a sailboat.

15th & 16th Sept. Into the area of the Azores high pressure; the sea a glassy calm. We bravely motor onwards at a steady 4 knots using ·306 imperial gallons of diesel an hour.

18th Sept. We are sailing at 5 knots with the wind on the port beam, Quantock Pete on the helm; all sail set. What is more, the sun is shining. (According to the radio it is peeing down and blowing like hell at home.) The nights are getting cool. The early morning temperature in the cabin was 76°F. Almost long john weather.

Alas that lovely sailing did not last the day. The wind veered to make us close hauled, and piped up at times making us reef the genny. To do this, Allan or I have to go onto the foredeck and revolve it by hand while the other winds in the wire control line at the cockpit winch.

19th Sept. At times today the wind has freshened to force 7 from the NNW which is giving us a bumpy ride. Fortunately I baked a loaf yesterday, so simple fish paste sandwiches have been looked upon as a treat. It was too rough for a dawn sight, but while we were reefing the genny at midday, out of the murk to weather appeared the *Marco Placibo* carrying coal from Norfolk, U.S.A. to Algiers. This Italian ship had an English radio operator who gave us our position, 38°10'N 18°00'W and the weather forecast, which included a warning about Hurricane Francis 400 miles SE of Newfoundland and moving north. This is due to re-curve east so we will probably cop it when it turns into a mid-latitude depression. Let us hope it passes well to the north of Britain because if it does not, it is going to make life decidedly uncomfortable.

The seas coming at us from the NW are enormous considering the strength of the wind. Obviously they are gale generated. At the moment there is a gale attacking West England and Ireland. I feel I have already had my ration of gales and with my sails getting tired really need quiet weather to complete the trip.

20th Sept. A depression 600 miles west of Ushant is moving towards the NE corner of Spain and slowly filling. It is throwing a lot of rubbish at us from the NW. We have two reefs in the main, the inner or storm jib set and the genny rolled to a similar size. Quantock Pete is steering us on a close reach at 4—5 knots. Some of the seas must be well over 20 feet, trough to crest; it is quite impressive, heaving up them, over the top, then sliding down the back. Generally the wind seems about force 6 but all too often picks up to a full gale. Fortunately, with it on the beam, life is not too uncomfortable, but bad enough. The irritating thing is that, with this wind direction, if it was force 4 we would be averaging 6 knots. With such big seas, it would be stupid to carry the sail now, and bash into them. They are giving us quite enough punishment as it is, and in the gusts, the strain on the sails and cordage is terrific.

21st Sept.   Just after dawn, the steering went haywire. Looking aft I saw the self-steering rudder over at a crazy angle. The bottom bracket of 1½ inch by 3/16 inch stanless steel had fractured. I had to call Allan to help me get the rudder inboard. There is no way I can repair the bracket at sea — certainly not in this mountainous swell — and as it is pretty rough for the Autohelm, we have to hand steer.

Because Tim has so much trouble on the helm, I have shortened the watches to only 2 hours. By gum, Tim is stubborn at learning the feel of the helm. During the day, conditions did improve but during his night watch he 3 times managed to get us 180° off course. And you cannot get much wronger than that.

22nd Sept.   Morning forecast for sea area Finisterre: westerly winds force 4—5 increasing 6—8, rain.

By midday, with the main boomed to port and the full genny to starboard, the speedo was waving between 5 and 7 knots. It looks like it is going to be a vigorous sail across that bay of ill repute, Biscay.

23rd Sept.   After a good 12 hour run the wind gradually swung 180° and by 2 a.m. had dropped right away so we were under engine once more. Later, we got a fair wind again and were running under twins and main. Heavy rain and a lot of wind persuaded me to hand the main. No sooner was this done than the wind swung onto our port beam so we had to hand the port twin and re-hoist the main. 15 minutes later, the rain cleared and the wind swung back so had to re-set the port twin.

24th Sept.   400 miles to Plymouth, but the Gods have decided on a fight. A bitterly cold north wind set in making us pay off for NW

231

France. What a nasty shock to our tropicalised bodies a north wind is.

By dawn I decided we should motor sail so getting as close to the wind as fast as possible. I have a warm bath and bed waiting for me in Plymouth and do not feel like spending a week yachting in the Bay of Biscay.

The loaf came out very well today. I made it with grainy flour and a little fat and honey. We had it warm with sausages.

25th Sept.   Hardly a breath of wind all day so we have been motoring directly for Plymouth, 300 miles away. With it being such a quiet day but a bad forecast, we have had a modicum of a clean-up. Tim has tidied the saloon and brushed the carpet while Allan and I have emptied all the bilges. The stanchions mostly need re-seating on new mastic so have been leaking a little. As this is only the second time we have pumped out since leaving Cape Town, quite a lot had seeped in. We took out about 15 gallons which is 150 lbs in weight. We are 400 lbs lighter on drinking water and 400 lbs less fuel. Add to this the food, gas and other consumables used we must now be half a ton lighter so should be faster. It is a pity but the hull is starting to foul up again. She is not too bad as yet, but daily the buggers grow, so daily it gets worse.

Just before midnight the engine stopped with a clunk. It was full moon and very light. Trailing astern I could see something in the water. Hooking it up, we found a bloody great length of old courlene net. For the rest of the night had to ghost along. Gradually a light SE wind set in giving us a speed of 2—3 knots by morning.

26th Sept 1980.   400 years ago today Drake reached Plymouth. We are some 180 miles away. First job was to find the various items of my wet suit, then de-corrode the zip. After furling the sails I went overboard to see if the prop could be freed. The increasing wind was causing waves which made the boat pitch. The best I could do was to cut the net clear which got rid of a lot of drag, but the prop was still solid. I came up gasping, having swallowed too much sea-water.

That job half done, we hoisted main and twins, and were soon running at 5 knots. The weather prophets promise a front moving through with winds of force 5/6, in which case we will not need the engine. This is the first time on the circumnavigation I have not had one engine in working order.

27th Sept.   At first light, 7 a.m., the Lizard (England!) was sighted with an echo at 47 fathoms. For me, this was quite a thrill after such a time and voyage. I felt a very personal sense of achievement. But frustration soon set in. Instead of the wind remaining fair, it veered to the north so once more we were close hauled. By 10 a.m. we were only 12 miles off but the wind dropped right away leaving us slatting around. Allan bravely donned the wet suit and jumped overboard to try and cut the prop free. As there was little sea, he was not thumped too badly by the boat's movement. Tim jumped up and down in excitement and fear for Allan when I pointed out the black tips of a shark's dorsal and tail, cruising a few feet off. I assured Allan, when he popped up to the surface, that sharks never attacked in British waters. It is easy to be brave, standing 4 feet above the sea looking down on your mate and a friendly shark keeping him company. Allan, a natural hero, buried his head once more beneath the sea and carried on sawing at the tough courlene.

After struggling away for half an hour, he could at last turn the prop, though it was still stiff. I helped him back on board with hands and feet blue with cold. I started the engine, and let it warm up for several minutes before putting it into gear. It hiccuped a bit, but struggled on; gradually the revs built up as the courlene remaining worked thinner. Within a couple of hours it was working as good as ever and just as well too; a light, bitterly cold wind was setting in from dead ahead.

A NE wind is uncommon in this area. What rotten luck. To make life even less comfortable, a fine rain accompanied it, and visibility closed right down. Soon, with less than ½ mile visibility, we were threading our way between big mid water trawlers cleaning out the mackerel shoals.

After dark, the Eddystone light was picked up, fine to port, which confirmed our position. Visibility was improving nicely but it was getting even colder and despite 2 sweaters, 2 pairs of socks and an exposure suit, I was freezing. Tim was shivering in his berth; Allan, sterling man, let me get below for frequent thaw outs.

These last few miles proved a most uncomfortable reminder of how bloody awful sailing in British waters can be. There are so many lovely warm places we have been with no yachts, it makes you wonder why the sport is so popular in Britain.

28th Sept 1980.   We handed the sails off the Breakwater light and motored the last 2 miles into Millbay Docks, Plymouth, tying up at 2.15 a.m. after 2¼ years and 41,000 sea miles.

Despite the weather, it is great to be home.

OCEAN WINDS

Designed by Pat Patterson

OCEAN WINDS

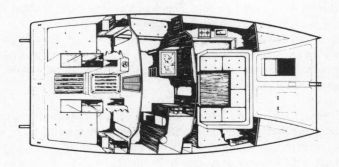

OCEAN WINDS

Length over all	33 ft	10 m
Beam	16 ft	4.88 m
Draught	3 ft 3 ins.	1 m
Sail area	594 sq. ft	55.18 sq. m

Construction: One piece glass fibre hull and bridge-deck with balsa core sandwich in bridge-deck.
Deck one piece moulding with balsa core sandwich in all top surfaces.
4 plywood athwartship bulkheads.

Spars: Aluminium alloy mast, boom and jib booming out poles.

Sails: 8 ounce terylene (dacron) with slab reefing on main, genoa reefing & inner storm jib.

Engines: Twin Volvo MD5A 7½ h.p. single cylinder diesels with Sailboat drive & folding propellors. Electric start and alternator charging.

Fuel tank: 45 imperial galls. (54 U.S. galls.) (205 ltrs.)
+ 30 galls. in portable containers.

Water: Same amount as fuel.

Gas: 2 x 15 kilo calor gas bottles.

Anchors: 35 lb C.Q.R., 56 lb Fisherman, 44 lb Holdfast.
all with 4 fathoms chain and nylon warp.

Design copyright owned by: P.T. Yachts Ltd., Foss Quay, Millbrook, nr. Plymouth, Devon, England PL10 1EN.
Tel. (0752) 822303

Self-steering Gear

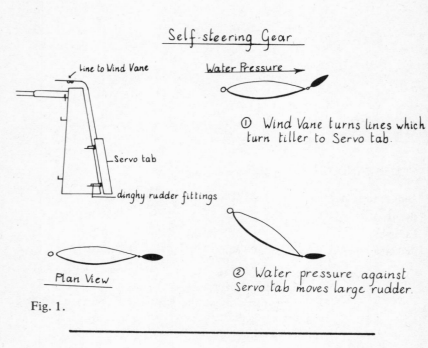

line to Wind Vane

Water Pressure →

① Wind Vane turns lines which turn tiller to Servo tab.

Servo tab

dinghy rudder fittings

Plan View

② Water pressure against Servo tab moves large rudder.

Fig. 1.

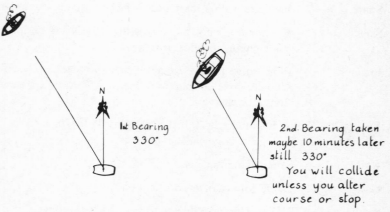

N

1st Bearing 330°

N

2nd. Bearing taken maybe 10 minutes later still 330°

You will collide unless you alter course or stop.

Safest procedure would be to alter course to **starboard** and thus pass around its stern.

Theoretically sail has right of way over power.

Fig. 2.

Choice of Boat and Conclusions.

A question often asked was 'Why choose a catamaran for the voyage?' The reasons were several. I designed the boat as a catamaran capable of ocean voyaging. I obviously had to have faith in my own designing. A successful test voyage ought to help sales. I could afford to build one (from a hull and deck moulded by South Coast Marine) and still have enough money left for the voyage if done cheaply.

Not many multihulls are, in my opinion, suited for ocean cruising. If you design and build for speed, you must have light weight and large sail area. Light weight may mean questionable constructional strength with low safety margin and certainly means very limited weight carrying. Some multihull designs have capsized. Much depends upon the design and not whether it is a catamaran or trimaran.

Ocean Winds is very strong. It was designed to be of medium displacement with a very high stability factor. An ocean cruiser has got to be a good load carrier. Such a multihull, even though it has not got the heavy ballast keel of a monohull, still cannot bounce away from a breaking sea in as lively a way as a very light one. Therefore it has to be enormously strong. This is why the lightly built racing variety, when heavily laden for ocean cruising, receive structural damage or break up. I was pleased to see, on my return home, that *Ocean Winds* was still structurally sound and could have set off on another circumnavigation.

I designed her with a low rig. I think the light weather performance should be improved by adding 6 feet to the mast height, thus enabling more sail to be set. This would necessitate earlier reefing.

Shallow draught, ability to take the ground level on her keels and fantastic manoeuvreability under her twin engines make her a superb coastal cruiser. A lot of the voyage was along the coasts of different countries. Also the fact that I never had to pay for slipping or craning out in order to anti-foul, was a great money saver.

The engines were just adequate. It would have been better to have had slightly larger ones (minimum of 10 h.p. each). But it was certainly better to have two small ones than one big one.

Running down wind under twins is very good in a cat as the twin hulls prevent the rolling such as you get in a monohull. Reaching (wind on the beam) is also more comfortable than in a monohull. Close hauled against ocean seas is very disagreeable, I think probably more so in a cat as you get quite a lot of slam under the bridge-deck. (Not so in a Wharram type cat but then in these conditions the crew is too exposed). The best type of yacht for beating to windward in the ocean is a heavy displacement keel boat, preferably over 45 feet long.

It is difficult to imagine a roomier boat for its size with a comparable performance. Overall performance I would compare to a good cruising monohull of about 35 ft long and accommodation to one of 45 ft.

At no time did I feel I could have been in a more sea-worthy boat of similar size.

The boat was easy to handle. Perhaps too easy for, as must be obvious from the account, most of the voyage was spent reading. It might have been psychologically better for the crew to have had more work to do.

The twin headsails were a success but I was frightened of the booming out poles which were, at times, difficult and dangerous to handle. Two different sized cruising spinnakers might have been better for down-wind sailing, but I have had no actual experience of them. The slab reefing on the mainsail was excellent.

The self-steering gear *(see fig. 1)* was a slightly modified Q.M.E. and functioned well as it was used to turn a small servo tab on a larger rudder. It is of paramount importance to have an adequate self-steering gear. The best I have heard of have either been the Aries gear or the Hasler. A Q.M.E. is good when taken to a servo tab and NOT direct to the wheel or tiller, and has the great merit of being cheap, simple and sturdy. If you have not got a good self-steering gear, do not consider an ocean voyage.

An electronic pilot is excellent and so easy to use. If you intend to use it continuously in all weathers, you need one built for commercial use. Such are very expensive and still go wrong. I believe it best to use a vane gear when sailing and an electronic one when motoring.

APPENDIX III

SEAMANSHIP

It is not necessary for all the crew to have sailing experience. It is necessary that at least one person on board should be experienced, preferably the skipper. This need not be obtained through ocean voyaging, and only so much general seamanship can be learnt from books, the rest has to be learnt by the 'seat of the pants' method. Go out and sail every week-end in anything from canoes and dinghies to large crewed yachts.

Everyone on board depends upon the skipper's seamanship and the decisions he takes. The standing orders should be that if the watch-keeper is in any doubt or if on a possible collision course with another vessel, he should call the skipper in plenty of time. This means that the skipper will sometimes be called unnecessarily, but must never show annoyance for then the crew might fail to call him early enough on another occasion.

To the uninitiated, ship's lights are confusing. From them, you can tell the classified type of ship (power, sail, tug etc.) and its approximate course. If the bearing of another vessel remains constant you will collide *(see fig. 2)*.

If you think that the wind is getting strong and wonder whether or not to reef — reef.

Ocean voyagers must nurse their gear or they will have heavy repair bills. When conditions are lively, those off watch sleep badly. If possible, crew fatigue is to be avoided. Having said this, you should not so slow the boat that you suffer extended passages. You have to strike a compromise between good passage making and being kind to gear and crew. I have often noticed that after reefing, the average speed may only be reduced by half a knot or so, but the strains very much reduced. Only to a racing boat is that half a knot essential.

The good seaman takes great pains over anchoring. The holding

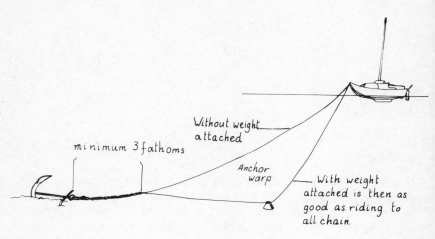

minimum 3 fathoms

Without weight
attached

Anchor
warp

With weight
attached is then as
good as riding to
all chain.

Fig. 3.

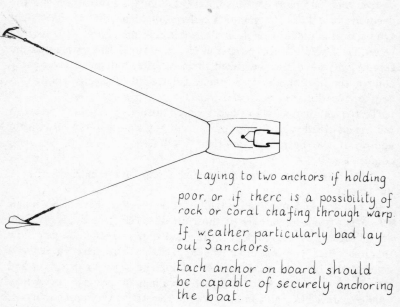

Laying to two anchors if holding
poor, or if there is a possibility of
rock or coral chafing through warp.

If weather particularly bad lay
out 3 anchors.

Each anchor on board should
be capable of securely anchoring
the boat.

Fig. 4.

power of an anchor depends upon the type of anchor, its bite into the sea bed and the direction and amount of pull. An anchor chain's catenary acts like a spring, lessening the strain on the anchor. If you ride to mostly nylon warp (always the first 3, and preferably 5 fathoms from the anchor MUST be chain) you can attach a weight (about 30 pounds) halfway down the warp *(see fig. 3)*. The longer the length of chain/warp, the better. The rule for the minimum amount is:

3 times depth at high water when riding to chain.

5 times depth at high water when riding to warp.

My crews were often fed up with me for the fuss I made over anchoring. If there was the least doubt, I would lay out two anchors, usually spaced out ahead. The anchor warps, taken from each bow, also helped to cut out shearing at anchor *(see fig. 4)*. Multihulls, as high windage boats, will tend to sheer about. This can be prevented by either mooring from one bow, or better still, from a bridle and not from over the centre of the bridge-deck.

The best type of anchor to use depends upon the sea bed. There are some new-fangled anchors advertised 'as shown on Tomorrow's World' which I dragged on in many anchorages when the tried and tested vintage ones all held. I believe the three best to carry are: *(see fig 5)*

1) Fisherman. It will hold in rocks and dig into hard clay and through weed. It will also hold in sand and mud though not so well as No. 2.

2) C.Q.R. This must be the genuine one and stamped as such on the shank and not sold as 'plough type'. The balance of this anchor is critical and many 'plough type' are not worth carrying. The C.Q.R. is one of the best high holding power anchors. It is less likely to be fouled than a fisherman, and if lowered carefully to the bottom will not foul.

3) Danforth or Meon. Holds as well as the C.Q.R. and may stow easier. I have known the shanks and the flukes of this anchor to bend. The Holdfast is similar to the Meon.

I give pride of place to the fisherman, as this is the most versatile of all small boat anchors.

A vessel should not go offshore with less than 2 anchors, both capable of safely mooring the boat, or ocean cruising with less than 3. Ocean cruisers should also carry at least one long warp with which they can extend the anchor chain or warp. This can also be used in heavy weather. If you use an anchor warp, this should be nylon. However, if there is a chance of snagging rocks or coral, it is better

241

K

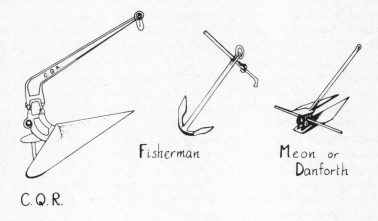

Fisherman

Meon or Danforth

C.Q.R.

Fig. 5.

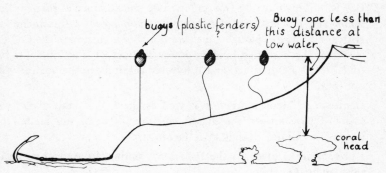

buoys (plastic fenders)

Buoy rope less than this distance at low water

coral head

When anchoring amongst coral heads — warp must be buoyed to always be suspended above them.

Fig. 6.

then to use a floating warp such as polypropelene. Alternatively buoy the nylon warp *(see fig. 6)*.

Heavy Weather Seamanship

Seas are very different depending upon fetch, depth, current, how long it has been blowing and strength of wind. My reaction to them depends upon whether they are coming from ahead or blowing towards my destination.

Winds from ahead. I would only bash to windward in a gale if land was too close under my lee. Generally I would lie hove-to *(see fig 7)* until the winds got stronger than force 8. Then I would lie a-hull *(see fig 8)* (no sail set) beam on to the seas. If land lies within 60 miles to leeward, a warp can be put out from the weather side bow to stern cleat in a bight and with rubber tyres or sea-anchor drogues to virtually eliminate drift. You have to batten down, as some waves will probably break over you. If seas get shock-like (force 10+), given sea room, I would run off before it with wind and seas on the quarter. It helps steerage if a very small jib is set. So as not to lose too much ground you can tow a warp (+ tyres) in a bight astern *(see fig. 9)*.

With a gale of wind from abeam or astern I would just carry on. If the seas got to a possible dangerous state, I would put them on the quarter. Usually I would sail with a small head sail and perhaps a deep reefed main. But each occasion is different so one cannot make a hard and fast rule as to what sail to carry. I found it best to keep the speed down to 6 knots or less which markedly reduced the tendency for the boat to run off and try to broach.

I think that cats like *Ocean Winds* are safer than similar sized monohulls in bad weather. The cats (tris too) have good directional stability so are less likely to broach when running before the wind, and the fact that they can surf before a sea also lessens the likelihood of broaching. They are very stable when lying a-hull. Although, at times, the motion is going to be bad, it would be much worse in a monohull. Crew fatigue in a cat is likely to be less. People suffering from fatigue may make poor decisions.

The rogue wave experienced south of Madagascar was particularly frightening. I believe it would have been less dangerous running before it as, being a cat, we would have surfed ahead and so absorbed its force gradually. This was the sort of wave that might well pitch-pole a monohull. Even hove-to as we were, I believe, contrary to traditional opinion, we were actually safer being in a cat like *Ocean Winds*. Many

243

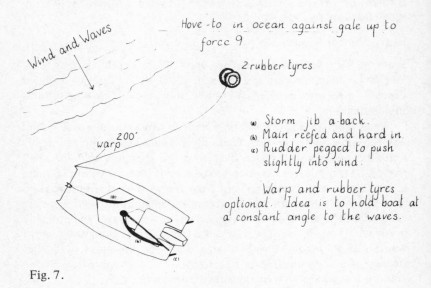

Hove-to in ocean against gale up to force 9

Wind and Waves

2 rubber tyres

warp 200'

(a) Storm jib a-back.
(b) Main reefed and hard in.
(c) Rudder pegged to push slightly into wind.

Warp and rubber tyres optional. Idea is to hold boat at a constant angle to the waves.

Fig. 7.

Lying A-hull – to maintain minimum drift

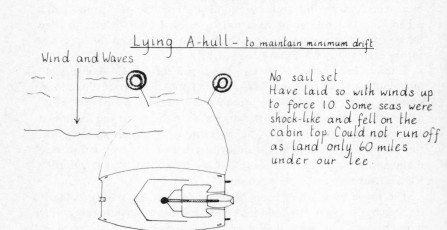

Wind and Waves

No sail set.
Have laid so with winds up to force 10. Some seas were shock-like and fell on the cabin top. Could not run off as land only 60 miles under our lee.

Fig. 8.

244

trimaran types with moderate to low lee hull buoyancy might, like a monohull, capsize when hit by such a wave if hove-to or lying a-hull. With luck, your monohull should self-right but would probably be dismasted in the process. We survived because of shallow draught (remaining in the moving surface water), an enormous amount of reserve buoyancy in our hulls, and a large righting moment. When hit by the break of the wave, we moved sideways so fast the wind in the sails was so reduced as to not greatly aid the capsizing forces.

Fortunately such 'rogue waves' are rare but must be allowed for when there is a great fetch, a gale of wind and a current running against the set of the sea.

Running before a storm

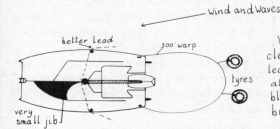

Wind and Waves

better lead

300' warp

tyres

very small jib

Warp attached to stern cleats – no chafe. Better lead, (to allow stern to lift), attached to mast and through block on gunwhale amid ships but may chafe.

When wind increases to force 10 and waves become shock-like best to run off before it. Rubber tyres and warp will help slow the boat but may hold the stern down.
   Probably better not towing warps, but speed should be kept low as boat must not surf off a wave into the back of preceding one.

Fig. 9.

APPENDIX IV

NAVIGATION

One occasionally reads of tiros setting off on a voyage and learning navigation en-route. I consider this unnecessarily foolhardy. Astro navigation is easy when using the pre-computed SIGHT REDUCTION tables. The Admiralty ones are marginally better than the Air ones but so much more expensive. I used the ones for air navigation (A.P. 3270 in U.K. or 249 U.S.). You can buy a small computer (calculator type) which is good, but being electronic, may malfunction so the book of tables has to be carried for emergency use. A satellite navigator is now available for small boats, and while it works, renders all other methods obsolete. It too is electronic so its reliability is suspect especially for use in the humid atmosphere of the tropics.

An ocean voyager has to be a good coastal navigator too, and able to use as many aids and techniques as possible. Indeed, it is more important to be certain of your position when near the coast than when in mid-ocean. One's position can be found by:

1) 2 or more compass or radio bearings or a combination of compass and radio bearings.

2) Distance off with a bearing using the sextant to measure the angle.

3) 2 horizontal sextant angles.

4) Lights seen dipping and a bearing.

5) A running fix when only one position line is available.

6) Reading the name off an adjacent buoy.

7) A useful indication can be obtained from an echo sounding particularly if a bearing line (visual or radio) can also be obtained.

8) A sample of the bottom from the hand lead.

I used all these methods except the last one. The hand lead was used when anchoring.

Navigation hardware used on the voyage in order of importance:

Compass   (Sestrel, grid steering)
Hand bearing compasses   (Sestrel, Radiant & Mini eye level type)
Sextant   (Sestrel 6 inch)
Chronometer/stop-watch   (Casio AQ 1000 or later model ML 90)
Log/speedometer   (Brookes & Gatehouse Harrier)
Hand lead   (Home made)
Radio direction finder   (B & G Homer/Heron. Also gave radio
                                 time signals)
Echo sounder   (Seafarer)

Plotting instruments were:

Vast numbers of 'B' pencils + 2 pencil sharpeners + 2 rubbers
Parallel rules
Patent plotter (more convenient to use for bearings than parallel rule)
Protractor (Portland 6 in. square type)
Dividers and Compasses.

Charts:

When planning the voyage, I bought, from the chart agents, a catalogue of Admiralty charts. (U.S. Hydrographic office publish one too.) This was of enormous help both in planning the voyage and learning which charts were available.

As a general rule, the best charts are published by the country. e.g. U.K. Coast by Admiralty, U.S. Coast by U.S. Hydrographic Office, Chilean Coast by Instituto Hydrografico de la Armada Chile. Otherwise I thought the best charts were the British Admiralty ones and printed on the best quality paper. The U.S. charts are about half British chart prices and are usually adequate.

For a circumnavigation, you require so many charts, to buy new the cost is astronomical. I spent about £100 ($200). I have been saving old ones for years and managed to buy many second hand ones. Many of the charts used were out of date — some by as much as 30 years. I was careful to use them in conjunction with a list of lights. Even 'up-to-date' charts are often wrong and inaccurate, with lights not marked or those marked not working, so using out of date charts is not the risk, at least for small vessels, the Hydrographic Office and chart purveyors will tell you it is. You know they are not to be relied upon (at first, you tend to have blind faith in the current ones) so you take care to use them along with a list of lights. The land configuration does not alter much although ports do sprout extra piers and breakwaters. These have lights – the positions of which are given in the relevant list, so can be plotted.

The more coastal cruising you do, the more charts you need. You can frequently swop charts or sell them (generally at ½ price) at places where yacht routes cross. e.g. Panama, Azores, Gibraltar. Another possibility is to advertise for them well in advance via yachting magazines and yacht clubs.

For astro work, you can use plotting charts. These are blank charts with compass roses and the correct Mercator relationship of latitude and longitude. Within 15° of the Equator, it makes little difference if you use graph paper. In higher latitudes, you can use graph paper and correct the longitude using a d. long., to departure table. Even better is to use as a plotting chart, a chart of anywhere of the same latitude.

e.g. When in the middle of the Atlantic, you can plot your sights on a large scale chart of the Philippines if the latitude is the same. Just alter the chart longitude to the one at your position. You can also use a northern latitude chart for plotting when in the southern hemisphere of the same degrees of latitude (e.g. 10°N for 10°S) by using the chart upside down. Again, just alter the longitude.

Navigation books:

All coasts of the world are described in various Admiralty pilots (U.S. ones also available and probably cheaper). These are written for big ships but have such a wealth of detailed description that they are also very useful for small yachts. I had no chart of Mar del Plata, so made one up from the description in the pilot. This made entry much easier.

I used 'Nories' nautical tables; others, such as Burton's are just as good. If you carry a 'Reed's', this too has all the necessary tables, and much other useful information besides.

Reed's Nautical Almanac is adequate for working sights. It is not so convenient to use as Brown's N.A. or the Admiralty Nautical Almanac. (The U.S. one is identical but lower in price.) Reed's is worth having for the other information it contains, so I used Reed's the first year, retained it for the other tables and information, and used Brown's the following year (1979) and bought a U.S. almanac for 1980. A current Nautical Almanac is required to obtain the Greenwich Hour

Angle (G.H.A.) and declination of the sun, moon and planets, and to obtain the G.H.A. of Aries for star sights.

In addition to the almanac you need Sight Reduction Tables A.P. 3270 (U.K.) H.O. 249 (U.S.) volume 1 for selected stars, volume 2 for latitude 0° to 40° and volume 3 for lats. 40° to 90°. You also need a sextant. Plastic ones may be adequate but even an old brass one will almost certainly be a lot more satisfactory. You also need to know Greenwich Mean Time to the nearest second. For this I would recommend a Casio stop-watch, watch and calculator ML—90. (It also plays Beethoven, but I feel this is an unnecessary sophistication.)

Using these books and instruments it is easy to work out a position line. Make a KISS card out of thin cardboard, cutting out boxes where shown. Place card over plain paper, fill in boxes, add and subtract where indicated, and you obtain an intercept which can be plotted to give a position line:

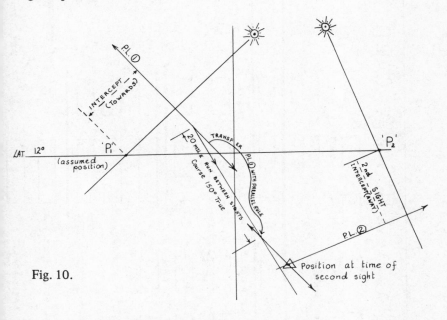

Fig. 10.

1) Start stop-watch on a whole minute.
2) Shoot sun with sextant & stop stop-watch at time of sight.
3) Note down in relevant box sextant reading.
4) Note down in box minutes and seconds on watch.

KISS ASTRO-NAV CARD © P.M. PATTERSON

1 (i) [ ] [ ] G.M.T. (ii) D.R. LAT DEGREES ONLY [ ]°
       MONTH   DAY   HOUR   MINUTE   SECONDS

4 STOP WATCH + [ ] [ ] [ ] LONG [ ]°
                  HOUR   MINUTE   SECONDS

5 TIME TOTAL [ ] [ ] [ ]   LOG. [ ]

6 & 7 G.H.A. FROM ALMANAC DAILY PAGES   SUN & PLANETS NOTE →
       [ ]° [ ]'   DECLINATION IN BOTTOM BOX
       DAY   HOUR

9 [ ]° [ ]'
   MIN.   SECS.

10 GHA [ ]° [ ]'   ☉ ♃ ♀ ✳
         ⊙♃♀✳   SUN JUPITER VENUS STAR

11 (iii) + 360° IF NECESSARY [ ]° [ ]'
                                +

    (iv) ASSUME LONGITUDE W−   [ ]° [ ]'   IF W. ASSUME SAME MINUTES AS GHA.
                           E+   E ASSUME MINS. TO MAKE 60' TOTAL

12 ⌐ LOCAL HOUR ANGLE H.A. [ ]° 00' −[ ]'
                                          POSITION ON CHART AT Hc
13 └ D.R. LATITUDE [ ]° −[ ]'   [ ]°
                                          DECLINATION

250

8

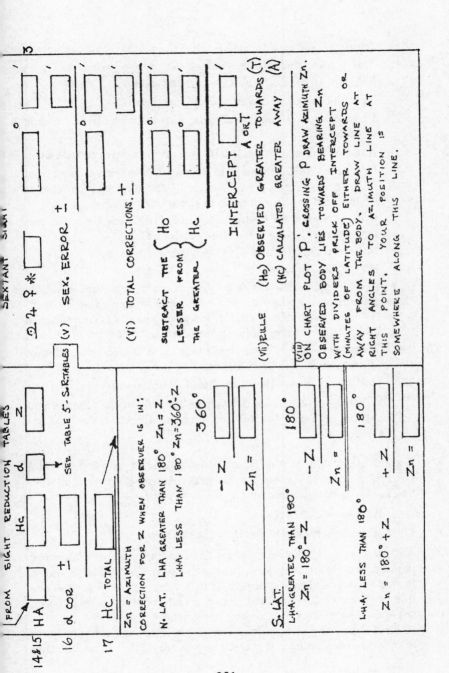

SEXTANT START

☾ ☉ ♃ ✱

SEX. ERROR ±   (v)

(vi) TOTAL CORRECTIONS. + —

SUBTRACT THE { Ho / Hc } LESSER FROM THE GREATER

INTERCEPT [ ] [ ]°
A or T

(vii) RULE   (Ho) OBSERVED GREATER TOWARDS (T)
(Hc) CALCULATED GREATER AWAY (A)

(viii) ON CHART PLOT 'P'. CROSSING P DRAW AZIMUTH Zn.
OBSERVED BODY LIES TOWARDS BEARING Zn
WITH DIVIDERS PRICK OFF INTERCEPT
(MINUTES OF LATITUDE) EITHER TOWARDS OR
AWAY FROM THE BODY, DRAW LINE AT
RIGHT ANGLES TO AZIMUTH LINE AT
THIS POINT. YOUR POSITION IS
SOMEWHERE ALONG THIS LINE.

FROM SIGHT REDUCTION TABLES
Hc   d   Z
SEE TABLE 5 - S.R.TABLES

14&15 HA
16 d cor ±
17 Hc TOTAL

Zn = AZIMUTH
CORRECTION FOR Z WHEN OBSERVER IS IN:
N. LAT. LHA GREATER THAN 180° Zn = Z
L.H.A. LESS THAN 180° Zn = 360° - Z

360°
- Z
Zn =

S. LAT.
L.H.A. GREATER THAN 180°
Zn = 180° - Z

180°
- Z
Zn =

L.H.A. LESS THAN 180°
Zn = 180° + Z

180°
+ Z
Zn =

251

5) Add mins. and secs. to G.M.T.

6) Transfer total time to left hand boxes.

7) Read out from almanac G.H.A. sun day and hour.

8) Same line, take out declination and note in box.

9) From correction tables in almanac note addition for minutes and seconds.

10) Add ° & ' column to give total G.H.A. of sun when you took sight.

11) Note your D.R. longitude in degrees & make same number of minutes as above if in west long. & if east long. enough minutes when added to above minutes to give whole degree.

12) If in the west long. subtract (11) from (10) & add them if in east long. Answer is your Local Hour Angle (L.H.A.).

13) Note your D.R. latitude — whole degrees only.

14) Note L.H.A. in lower box.

15) In sight reduction tables at your latitude, look up H.A. side column and declination top horizontal column. (lat. N Decl. N = same name. lat. N Decl. S = contrary names.) Write down in boxes figures from table. (Note whether 'd' is plus or minus.)

16) From loose card or inside cover look up 'd' correction & minutes of declination note down in box.

17) Hc $\pm$ d correction = Hc total. (Height calculated.)

Z is the bearing of the body from the pole of the observer and can be corrected to 360° notation by filling in the boxes as instructed.

Sextant sight. Fill in the boxes as instructed. I use Reed's Total Correction table. If you use the Admiralty Almanac, you need another box as they split the corrections up into two sums.

Ho = Height observed.

The difference between Ho and Hc is the Intercept.

An Intercept is the distance along a line (bearing) from your assumed position towards or away from the sun to a position line at right angles to this bearing. Unless you can cross this position line with another one from a different heavenly body or by a radio or land bearing you do not know where along this position line you lie.

Each sight will give a position line. 2 sun sights, taken several hours apart, will give a position if you run up your first P.L. to cross the later

252

one exactly as a running fix in coastal navigation.

After a little practise, such a sight working takes about 10 minutes.

A local noon sight (when the sun is due north or south) is even easier. It is called Latitude by Sun Meridian Altitude and clear instructions are given in Reed's.

Admiralty Star Finder N.P. 323 is very good for star identification.

APPENDIX V

FOOD

Victualling for a long passage is difficult. You need to be able to maintain variety and yet with only two burners and a grill, the meals have to be kept simple. An oven widens one's culinary repertoire, but does use a lot of gas. A pressure cooker is a great gas saver and being a sealed container, is excellent for use in bad weather. It is all too easy to live out of the frying pan.

Our staples were — potatoes, rice and pasta.

Onions were bought by the small sack full and lasted well. Other fresh vegetables would last at sea for the first 4 or 5 days. We then used tinned or quick freeze dried vegetables (peas are particularly good).

Fresh meat can be preserved by pickling in brine for two to four weeks and then drying. To make the brine, boil 2 lbs salt, 1 lb brown sugar, 2 level teaspoons of salt petre in 6 pints of water for 10 minutes. Allow to cool, and cover meat in a plastic bucket or bin. A pedal waste bin is just the right size.

In Britain, Brazil, Chile, Peru, Australia and S. Africa I bought sides of smoked bacon which lasted well. At the first sign of mould, I would wipe it down with vinegar and sprinkle on more salt. This bacon can be eaten thinly sliced raw, sliced as bacon or thicker slices as gammon and cooked with pineapple. (Pineapple is a natural tenderizer of meat.)

Salamis lasted well even through the tropics.

Whole loaves of bread can be preserved by wiping them over with vinegar and then sealing them with food wrapping plastic film (cling).

Eggs are preserved by keeping the air out. I wiped the shells over with lard. Others use Vaseline or other grease.

Bananas ripen quicker in the dark. If you buy a stalk, remove the hands, and seal them in clear plastic bags. Exclude as much air as possible and make air tight. Keep them in a light and preferably cool place until 3 or 4 days before required then put in a dark cupboard to ripen. I did not find a potassium permanganate inhibitor an advantage, as then they never ripened before swelling and suppurating. The cooking type of banana is best left to blacken before frying.

Green coconuts are excellent if you have a machete to slice off the top to get at the milk. This is a very refreshing drink.

The Itona dried soya bean 'meat' was very good. The hamburger style proved most popular. It kept well in its sealed plastic bags, the ones put by as emergency food were used after 2½ years storage. We would, at the cook's whim, liven it up with various herbs and peppers.

In heavy weather we used soups and stews cooked in the pressure cooker. If feeling fragile, Complan was eaten as the only meal. We also found it good as a mid morning or afternoon drink down in the cold Magellan Straits. An excellent emergency food/drink.

Oxo cubes (beef only) were popular as drinks during cold weather. Hot chocolate drink was the most popular evening drink and night watch drink.

We carried lots of dried herbs like oregano, thyme etc., curry powder and cloves of garlic and peppers.

Filling up our bottles of cooking gas was, at times, difficult. We had butane. Propane is easier to obtain particularly in the United States. The alternative would have been to take an adaptor with the opposite thread. Butane bottles have male threads, propane, female. Quite illegally, I filled the empty butane bottles with propane gas if that was the only type available. It made little difference even though it was run through the wrong regulator but did probably cause extra carbon to form in the burners.

While I had no sponsorship as such, the following products, by the case, were kindly donated by their manufacturers and were of great help towards keeping the overall cost of the voyage so low.

Plymouth Gin.

Guinness.

Tate & Lyle Golden Syrup.

Long John Whisky.

Whitbread pale ale.

Brooke Bond Tea.

Morning Glory Porridge oats in sealed containers — ideal for yachts.

Record Pasta from St. Albans.

Lockwood Foods — canned fruit and vegetables.

Itona Products of Wigan — dried soya bean meat substitute.

Dried yeast in cans from the Distillers Co. Ltd.

Complan and Glucodin from Glaxo Farley Foods of Plymouth.

Nivea cold cream and Atrixia hand cream.

Whitworth's dried fruit.

McDougall's Bread and Pastry mix.

If I have forgotten anyone (the original list of donations has been lost), please forgive me.